DELINQUENCY
ITS ROOTS, CAREERS
AND PROSPECTS

D. J. West

Harvard University Press
Cambridge, Massachusetts
1982

Library of Congress Cataloguing in Publication Data

West, D. J. (Donald James), 1924–
   Delinquency, its roots, careers, and prospects.

   Bibliography: p.
   Includes index.
   1. Juvenile delinquency—England—London.   I. Title.
HV 9146.L65W47   364. 3'6'09421   82–3124
ISBN 0 - 674 - 19565 - 5   AACR2

Contents

Acknowledgements

The survey on which this book is based took nearly twenty years and was directed throughout by the author. The project, known as the Cambridge Study in Delinquent Development, was carried out for the Cambridge University Institute of Criminology, supported by grants from the Home Office and, in the later stages, by a contract from a Joint Working Party of the Department of Health and Social Security and the Social Science Research Council. The Working Party was interested in evidence about the transmission of deprivation through families from one generation to the next, a topic on which delinquency research has considerable bearing. None of these authorities is responsible for our findings or interpretations.

Accounts of various aspects of the research by the present author and his collaborators, written at different stages of the work, have appeared in three books (*Present Conduct and Future Delinquency*, 1969; *Who Becomes Delinquent?* 1973; *The Delinquent Way of Life*, 1977), all published by Heinemann Educational Books, and in scattered contributions to specialist journals. A numbered list, set out in chronological order, appears in Appendix IV.

Many people have worked on the project at various times, some over many years. The names of some of them are given in Appendix I. They must collectively take credit for all the information that has been produced. My chief collaborator, Dr D. P. Farrington, devised and carried out most of the statistical analyses of the material and has been the guiding hand behind all the research in the latter half of the life of the project. In this book I have drawn freely upon his ideas, his expertise and his publications. In an effort to maintain factual accuracy he has given most generously of his time and his advice on the text, but the opinions, interpretations and speculations it contains are my own responsibility.

D.J.W.

CHAPTER I

Collecting Evidence on Disputed Issues

Aims of the study and of this book

The research was a systematic survey of a sample of some four hundred ordinary young males recruited, at age 8, from a working-class neighbourhood in London, and followed up to age 25, by which time a third of the group had acquired a criminal conviction record. The aim was to obtain a better understanding of the reasons why youngsters become delinquents. Although many of the results have been published in previous books and technical papers, there was an obvious need for an overview of the entire project, bringing together the essence of numerous scattered reports (especially those compiled since the last volume was published in 1977), and reflecting upon the implications of the findings for social policy: hence the present volume. As far as possible technical and statistical minutiae have been avoided, since full details can be found in the original reports (which are listed and numbered in chronological order in Appendix IV, and are cited in the present text by reference numbers in parentheses). A few of the figures quoted differ slightly from those previously given because they have been updated and one or two errors corrected.

Sensible discussion of delinquency is confused by two opposing stereotypes. The first portrays delinquents as perfectly normal. Self-report studies show that nearly everyone is at least an occasional law-breaker. Opportunity, temptation and the social tradition of one's peer group are the important causes, and these have nothing to do with individual weakness or wickedness. If convicted delinquents appear to deviate from the norm — for instance in being poorly educated and predominantly lower-class males — this is because the legal definition of what constitutes a crime, and the current methods of police surveillance and prosecution, catch such persons more readily than others. The different social classes may vary in their favourite forms of dishonesty, depending upon their particular circumstances and opportunities and the probable consequences of being found out, but in all classes it is a natural, human choice to disregard the law on occasion when the chance for quick personal gain with slight risk of detection presents itself.

Since the decision to break the law is neither unusual nor abnormal, offenders should be held fully responsible for any damage or distress their behaviour brings about. The correct reaction to all apprehended delinquents is to punish them in just proportion to the seriousness of their offences.

The second stereotype pictures delinquents as different from the rest of their age-group, a special category of persons lacking in restraint, primitive in their sense of right and wrong, unable or unwilling to conform to reasonable rules. They are seen as 'maladjusted' individuals who, by virtue of their 'damaged' personalities (due perhaps to hereditary flaws, perhaps to a deprived upbringing), fail to learn civilized standards of behaviour and are liable to persistent trouble with the law. Their deficiencies indicate a need for help, that is, for social training, attitudinal reorientation and psychological treatment for their emotional disturbances. As an instrument of social policy this second stereotype is something of a two-edged weapon. Although often used by those arguing for a humane and tolerant approach, it can also be used to justify extreme measures, on the grounds that dangerous social misfits need strict control in the interests of society at large, or, at the very least, rigorous, prolonged and compulsory institutional 'treatment'.

Partly as a result of the persistence of these exaggerated and contradictory stereotypes social policies for dealing with youthful delinquency remain in a state of flux and confusion. The aim of this research was to discover where, in between these two extremes, the reality lies. In retrospect, one can see that the need for such an enterprise was even greater than we imagined at the outset. The intervening years have seen the development and hardening of ideological interpretations, with conservatives calling for swift and more punitive reprisals against disruptive elements, and radicals demanding — in the name of civil liberty — that do-gooders should lay off the children and pay attention instead to the oppressive nature of capitalism. Meantime liberals are fighting a losing battle to preserve the notion of helping delinquents to cope better with the society in which they live. A hard look at the character and circumstances of actual delinquents, the nature of the offences they commit, their declared motives, and their prospects of reform should do something to moderate the blinkered, one-track approaches, unreal stereotypes and simplistic solutions generated by too close an adherence to one or other of the rival ideologies.

We wanted to study the personalities, the social backgrounds and the family histories of young offenders in order to discover differences between them and their non-delinquent social peers that might help to explain the offenders' deviant conduct. Some radical criminologists would challenge the validity of an enterprise concentrating upon the individuals involved instead of upon the social conditions that make individuals behave in the way that they do (Parker and Giller, 1981).

Some would doubt that there are any real differences between delinquents and their social peers — except for those produced by the misfortune of happening to be detected in misbehaviour, labelled a delinquent and dealt with accordingly. In the event we found our delinquents really were different from their peers in background, in life history, in social behaviour and attitude as well as in their propensity for illegal exploits. There is therefore no need to apologize for having carried out the investigation on a false assumption.

Research with established delinquents can be misleading. Once it is known that one is dealing with a delinquent, recollections and interpretations of his upbringing and previous behaviour may be biased towards a preconceived stereotype. Moreover, deviant attitudes may be the result rather than the cause of being convicted for an offence. In spite of the length of time involved we decided to embark upon a prospective study, collecting and assessing the sample while they were still below the legal age for finding of guilt by a juvenile court. Those who subsequently became official delinquents could then be compared with their non-delinquent peers, using unbiased assessments made before it was known to which group any individual belonged.

Our plans were inspired by previous American surveys, notably the work of Glueck and Glueck (1950) and McCord et al. (1959), which pointed to the strong and continuing influence of early upbringing and family circumstances in determining who became delinquent. We wanted to assess the relative importance of social pressures (such as low income), individual style of upbringing (manifest in parental attitude and discipline), personal attributes (such as intelligence, physique and aggressiveness) and extraneous events (such as the mischance of being found out). As a by-product, we hoped to identify criteria, present at the early age of 9 or 10, that could be used to predict which individuals would be likely to become delinquent. The Gluecks had claimed that this was possible, but no similar prospective data were available on the predictability of delinquency in an English setting.

Theorists, both sociological and psychological, have sometimes tended to place enormous emphasis on one particular event or circumstance. A broken home, lack of parental affection, insufficient discipline, poverty and neighbourhood culture have each in turn been credited with being the main cause of delinquency. Our study, because it encompassed a wide range of items, was able to show that delinquency most often arises from an accumulation of different pressures rather than from any single salient cause.

Because the study went on so long, we were able to observe which of the delinquents continued their criminal careers into adult life and to investigate the predictability, not just of juvenile delinquency, but of the rarer and more important phenomenon of persisting recidivism.

Our findings suggest that, for better or worse, it is possible, and indeed relatively easy, to identify at an early age a small group of vulnerable boys who are at great risk of becoming persisting recidivists. These findings are particularly controversial, not because the observations themselves are in much dispute, but because they could so easily be used in misguided forms of intervention or in the implementation of suppressive policies that might prove, in the long term, more damaging to society than the delinquents.

It has to be admitted that our study began as a basic, fact-finding venture without strong theoretical preconceptions and without much clear notion of where it might lead. As time went on, however, and more and more data accumulated, it became evident that the exercise was yielding information of relevance to many of the practical and theoretical issues of current concern to criminologists or to the general public. A normal sample, surveyed over a substantial period of time, provides information on the entire range of criminality from the trivial and temporary to the serious and persistent. We could see how many males among an ordinary working-class population become involved in officially recorded crimes, we could assess the prospects of juvenile criminality persisting into adult life, and we could test the belief that most youthful crime is attributable to a hard core of extremely troublesome incorrigibles. With access to the criminal records of other family members, we could check the claim that relatively few families are responsible for the bulk of recorded crime and we could gauge the strength of the tendency for criminal parents to produce criminal offspring.

The notion of a criminal character or criminal predisposition implies the existence of some underlying tendency to antisocial nonconformity, likely to manifest in different ways according to age and circumstance. It follows that young delinquents would be expected to be versatile rather than specialized in their misbehaviour, committing truancies, thefts or aggressive offences on different occasions. They might also be expected to differ from their social peers in displaying a variety of deviant characteristics in addition to the behaviour defined as criminal. Examination of the pattern of offences by the same individuals over time provided good data on the issue of versatility versus specialization. We could see, for example, whether those destined to become involved in muggings, robberies or other more serious crimes as adults had been, in their younger days, thieves, vandals and truants.

According to the theory of the delinquent of 'sociopathic' or anti-social personality (as it has been variously named), one might expect to find a hard core of chronically maladapted individuals with a variety of antisocial habits. In an extensive survey at age 18 we were able to show how many young recidivists, at that stage, were disruptive and anti-social in their behaviour, attitudes and general life-style, in addition to their involvement in criminal exploits. Later, at age 24, we compared recidivists who had apparently reformed with others who were persisting in crime. We wanted to find out how many persisting delinquents conform to the stereotypical sociopathic personality and how many former delinquents lose their other antisocial characteristics as their conviction careers come to an end. It may be that the delinquent personality is not so fixed and unchangeable as is often supposed.

As the study progressed many other questions attracted attention. Since we had the benefit of individual interviews, including self-reports of involvement in delinquent acts, it was possible to judge the extent of the distortions that arise from studying only those delinquents who are detected and officially processed by the courts. Are the uncaught offenders merely occasional or minor delinquents, or are they perhaps equally serious offenders but more cunning in escaping detection? Are the background characteristics supposedly associated with delinquency – poverty, broken homes and the like – true of all delinquents or only of those selected for prosecution?

Criminologists have pointed out that schools may be amplifying the antisocial tendencies among some of their pupils. By denying status to the least attractive and less able children, and relegating them to inferior classes, schools tend to increase the frustrations and pressures experienced by those least fitted to cope (Polk and Schafer, 1972; Kelly, 1980). We were able to assess the extent to which some London schools influence delinquent careers, since members of the sample attended a variety of secondary schools with sharply contrasting delinquency rates.

Labelling theorists suggest that some of the alleged characteristics of delinquents may be exaggerated, if not actually generated, by the processes of trial and punishment and the consequential social stigma and loss of reputation to which those who happen to be caught are inevitably exposed. Using repeated self-report evaluations, we were able to study changes in attitude and behaviour following a first conviction and to determine whether, as labelling theory predicts, an individual's misbehaviour increases following conviction, or whether, as deterrence theory suggests, delinquency is nipped in the bud by timely official action.

Some theorists contend that neighbourhood influences, such as schools and housing estates with high concentrations of delinquents, the proximity of large shops, warehouses and street markets that make easy targets for theft, or easy access to a network of receivers facilitating the disposal of stolen goods, are more important as determinants of the likelihood of an individual becoming involved in crime than his personal attitudes, temperament or family circumstances. We were able to obtain data relevant to this issue by comparing the subsequent criminal career of delinquents who moved away from the area to places where the incidence of crime was generally lower with that of the delinquents who remained in the district.

At a late stage of the inquiry, when most of the sample were aged 24 or older, it became possible to test the popular notion that delinquents reform more quickly if they get married. Another interesting question is what happens to those who avoid becoming delinquents in spite of having been reared in circumstances similar to those of the worst delinquents. A group of this kind was identified and followed up by interview at age 23. Confronted by increasing evidence of crime in high places and of crimes committed by apparently respectable adults one is led to wonder to what extent the disturbed backgrounds and deviant attitudes and life-styles of the stereotypical young delinquent are shared by persons who take to crime later in life. One of the more interesting inquiries that became possible during the later stages of the study was a comparison between the early backgrounds of juvenile delinquents and of latecomers to crime.

Longitudinal studies, though in principle ideal as a research method (Janson, 1978), are exceedingly difficult to put into practice. The remainder of this chapter (which may be conveniently omitted by readers already familiar with our previous publications) explains some of the problems and describes how the project was set up and how the interviews were conducted.

Setting up the project

Important and interesting questions about delinquency are easily identified, but the practical difficulties in obtaining reliable and relevant evidence to resolve them are daunting. The prosaic problems of securing financial sponsorship, obtaining access to confidential sources of information (such as names and addresses of pupils, or criminal records of individuals), or recruiting suitable research workers are not much discussed in the published reports of social research. Such considerations may be of little interest to the general reader, but they are very important. They determine the scope and quality of research and set limits to the kinds of questions that can be investigated.

We were fortunate in having commenced the study in 1961, before the furore about confidentiality had reached its present level. We were able to obtain a larger measure of co-operation from official agencies than would be likely today, when so many potentially useful projects are blocked by real (or conveniently assumed) scruples about the release of confidential information, or about permitting researchers access to the persons they want to question. In reality, unlike official agencies, professional researchers do not have to make decisions affecting their subjects and have no reason to misuse information in ways that could adversely affect the individuals concerned. Nevertheless, negotiations to secure permission from the education authority to contact parents and interview children were so protracted that we nearly gave up, and would in fact have done so but for the last minute intervention of a friend in an influential position. The questions we were allowed to put to pupils and teachers were heavily censored. Had we known in advance how many difficulties of this kind would be encountered throughout the project we might have had second thoughts about embarking upon it.

Although we started with Home Office finance and approval and worked for the Cambridge University Institute of Criminology, under the Directorship of the prestigious Professor (later Sir Leon) Radzinowicz, it was by no means assured when we began that support would continue for the duration of the study. Grants were allocated from year to year, subject to satisfactory progress. We felt under pressure to produce results as quickly as possible, and this affected the quality of the work in the earlier stages. For example, there was inadequate pre-testing of the reliability of the interview methods used to obtain information from parents. The insecurity of tenure of research assistants, a problem common to most university research (see correspondence in the *Guardian*, 19–22 February 1979), was also a considerable hindrance.

We intended to carry out detailed interviews and case studies, as well as make statistical comparisons, so numbers had to be kept down. The study sample was made up of 411 boys and included all the males on the registers of six state primary schools who were of an age to be in fourth-year classes. They were 8 or 9 when first contacted. The six schools were all within a one-mile radius of our research office, which was located in a crowded urban area in London. The odd number of individuals arose because entire school classes were enlisted, until a sample of about four hundred was achieved. No boy of the correct age attending one of the schools in the sample was left out. Since relatively few girls become officially registered delinquents, to obtain enough of them would have necessitated a larger sample than we could manage, and thus they were excluded from our study.

The neighbourhood of the study was chosen because it had a reasonably high delinquency rate, because migration was low (in fact 85.7 per cent of 405 men in the sample in the UK at age 18 were living in London postal districts), and because there was a convenient office available in a local social centre which we were able to use throughout the research. The nearby primary schools were allocated by the education authority, after the headmasters had signified willingness to co-operate. They were typical of the generality of local schools.

As there were no private schools in the vicinity, we were confident that the sample was fairly representative of the schoolboy population of the neighbourhood, which was a typical working-class, residential area, where families were inclined to stay put for long periods, most of them housed in local-authority accommodation. The area was not prosperous, but not especially impoverished. At the time there were few immigrants and the boys were almost all of Caucasian appearance.

Only 12 boys were negroid, most of these having one or both parents of West Indian origin. The vast majority (371) were being brought up by parents who had themselves been reared in the United Kingdom or Eire. Judged on their fathers' occupations, 93.7 per cent were 'working class' (III, IV or V on the Registrar General's scale), compared with a national figure of 78.3 per cent at that time. In other words, it was an unremarkable and traditional white, British, urban, working-class sample. The findings are likely, therefore, to hold true of many similar places in southern England, but they tell us nothing about delinquency in the middle classes or about delinquency among girls or among immigrant groups.

In order to spread the work of intake-interviewing over a reasonable period, two consecutive classroom generations were included. A majority of the sample belonged to the first generation and were taken from all six schools. A smaller number, recruited from four of the six schools, were a year younger. In addition, one whole class from one of the schools, taken from the year previous to the main group, provided what was originally intended as a small pilot sample, but they were, in fact, incorporated into the study sample. Finally, a quota sample of 12 boys of appropriate age was taken from a neighbouring school for the educationally subnormal, in order to make the study sample more representative of the total school population. (These arrangements produced a final sample made up of 231 born 1 September 1952–31 August 1953, 157 born 1 September 1953–31 August 1954 and 23 born 1 September 1951–31 August 1952. The age-groups and classroom groups did not coincide exactly because one or two boys were not in the classes expected from their date of birth.) The sample included 14 pairs of brothers, so the actual number of families involved was 397.

Changes in social conditions produce changes in the patterns of officially recorded delinquency. Since the study sample was composed of males all born around the same time, the findings refer to a particular generation and might have been slightly different for an older or a younger population.

Interviewing the sample

The first task was to compile a list of names and birth dates of members of the sample from the school registers. Psychologists were employed to visit the schools, contact the boys and their teachers, and administer tests and questionnaires. All 411 were seen at age 8–9. Repeated visits to schools had to be made in order to catch some persistent absentees. Nearly all were seen a second time at age 10–11, in their last year at primary school, and again at their various secondary schools at age 14–15, shortly before the earliest permitted age for leaving. After that, the whole sample was re-interviewed twice more by young male graduates, at age 16–17 and, more extensively, at age 18–19.

The interviews at age 18, which usually took place in the research office, lasted on average some two hours and were tape recorded. As well as open-ended inquiries, which encouraged the youths to talk spontaneously, a large number of precise questions were put, the answers to which could be translated into numerical codes. At age 21, in the last systematic coverage, repeat interviews on similar lines to those at 18 were attempted with all of the delinquents and a quota sample of non-delinquents. Although at each stage the interviews were not all conducted at exactly the same age, the great majority took place at 14, 16, 18 and 21 years respectively, and for convenience will be so referred to from now on. Finally, at ages 23 and 24, some particular subgroups were re-interviewed. These included persisting recidivists, former recidivists who had been free from convictions for five years, men from deprived backgrounds who had not become delinquents and some randomly selected non-delinquents for comparison.

For the interviews at age 16 and later, the youths were offered a small fee and expenses for attending, but this was a less important inducement than the interviewers' friendly persistence. Few declined to co-operate. At age 16, 96.8 per cent of the original 411 and, at age 18, 94.7 per cent were traced and interviewed. Of the 22 not seen at 18, only 14 were refusers, 6 had gone abroad, 1 was dead and 1 untraceable. At age 21, from a target sample of 241, 218 men were successfully interviewed.

In preparation for the interviews at later ages an enormous amount of time and effort was expended on tracing the whereabouts of the elusive, calling repeatedly at various hours on individuals who were rarely at home, and persuading the more reluctant to co-operate. The task of locating men who had moved was carried out, for the most part, without the help of official agencies, such as the National Health Service or the Department of Employment, whose records would have greatly helped in the discovery of addresses had the rules of confidentiality permitted it. Instead, in the course of this study we found ourselves frequently in the curious position of using finance from one government department to secure, by expensive, inefficient and roundabout means, information kept from us by other departments. Of course, individuals need protection from unwanted intrusion into their lives, but the collection of information for research purposes, where anonymity is safely preserved and no action affecting the persons involved can be taken, meets with what seems excessive and often arbitrary restrictions that have little relevance to the public interest.

While the boys were still at school, experienced women social workers were employed to interview the parents, talking, wherever possible, to the father as well as the mother. These interviews, which were much less structured than the interviews with the sons, ranged over a large number of topics, including the boy's health and development, conduct and habits, and the parents' disciplinary methods, attitudes to the boy and their financial and marital situation. On the basis of a detailed case history, built up during three or four interviews each lasting on average an hour, the social worker recorded an assessment of the home in respect of over fifty items, such as family income, maternal attitude, maternal discipline, marital harmony, separations from parents, parental vigilance, parental inconsistency, and father's job record. Each item was categorized according to previously defined criteria. For instance, maternal attitude was categorized as cruel, passive, neglecting, loving, anxious or over-protective; the definitions of these descriptive groupings were taken from previous research by McCord *et al.* (1959). These assessments were all completed and recorded by the time the boys were 10. Thereafter, parents were re-interviewed approximately once a year until the boys were 14—15, when most of them were expecting to leave school shortly.

The interviews with parents also served for the collection of identifying particulars of family members, so that necessary record searches could be carried out. A large number of birth and marriage certificates were obtained in order to check and supplement this information. It was a very long time before we were confident about which of the matching names located in criminal records did in fact belong to the individuals in whom we were interested.

The social workers were persistent and persuasive in their efforts to secure co-operation. Parents were told that the research was being directed by a psychiatrist from Cambridge University and was a study of boys' upbringing and development. The Institute of Criminology was not mentioned, but the workers' particular concern with behaviour problems and delinquency may have become apparent as time went on. It was explained that the information would be kept anonymous, but that the results might prove helpful to children and parents in the future. Most parents co-operated readily, and indeed some mothers found their long discussions with a social worker rewarding; but the parents of 22 boys had to be written off as total refusers and in a further 21 cases parental co-operation was very reluctant and the information obtained, sometimes limited to what could be gleaned from 'doorstep' encounters, was correspondingly scanty or unreliable.

As time went on it became evident that we had been over-optimistic about the range and quality of information that could reasonably be expected to be elicited from parents. Allowing social workers to operate in their accustomed manner, that is to say providing a list of set topics with few rules about precisely how to put questions, gave too much scope for individualistic interpretation, especially as some of the assessments involved subjective judgements by the interviewers. The distribution of the more objective items, such as number of children in the family, did not differ from one worker's cases to another's, but from the different frequencies with which each social worker located such items as physical neglect of boys, or paternal discipline 'erratic', it was obvious that, in spite of their efforts to preserve comparable rating standards, they did not always succeed. More troublesome still was the pronounced 'negative halo' which exaggerated the unfavourable assessments made on certain families. Where one or two items were found to be unfavourable there was a strong tendency for most other items to be similarly assessed. For example, of the boys said to have been exposed to serious conflict between parents, well over half (compared with only about one in seven of the rest of the sample) were also rated positively on unsatisfactory paternal attitude and discipline (see Appendix IV, ref. 2, p. 59). For this reason it proved impracticable to use the social workers' ratings to discriminate very far between different kinds of parental unsatisfactoriness. Another difficulty was that boys with communicative mothers, keen to discuss all their troubles, were likely to be recorded as having a large number of family problems. In contrast, if the mother was assessed as of dull intelligence, and was presumably less expressive, marital disharmony and other problems were recorded much less often, although in reality they were probably at least as frequent. The difficulty of eliciting accurate information was also reflected in inconsistencies between the notes recorded at successive interviews. Sometimes the social workers' final ratings were, whether by mistake or change of view, startlingly at variance with their own descriptive accounts.

In the earlier stages of the study, these problems were the source of considerable friction between the research-trained members of the team, who valued numerical precision, and the clinically trained social workers, who had faith in the quality of their impressionistic judgements. In later interviews with parents, attempts were made to achieve greater objectivity by using set questionnaires. As a general rule, however, these methods of measuring family variables were less predictive of future criminal convictions than the more subjective assessments. Parents generally preferred the discursive approach and were more likely to volunteer relevant and thoughtful comments in the course of conversation than in response to a standard questionnaire. The early case dossiers assembled by the social workers, although containing much that was too unsystematic and subjective for research purposes, nevertheless provided much factual description, as well as yielding global impressions of parental behaviour that proved to be usefully predictive of future delinquency.

The interviews with the men at 18 and at later ages were carried out by young male research workers employed full time and selected for their ability to communicate easily with working-class subjects. Interviews with the youths, unlike those with the parents, were carefully structured with prepared questions to which the replies could usually be recorded directly in the form of prearranged numerical codes.

This permitted a ready check on bias due to differences between interviewers, but this was not in fact a significant problem (see Appendix IV, ref. 3, appendix A). The interviews at 18 and 21 were tape recorded and included open-ended questions, when the men were encouraged to express themselves freely in their own way. Their words were later transcribed for purposes of analysis.

Any research based upon interviews is open to challenge on the grounds that the informants may have been unreliable or untruthful. On matters we could verify, the members of the study proved surprisingly frank and honest and factually correct in their accounts. For example, the versions of family circumstances and school and work careers given by the same informants on different occasions, or by outside informants (that is, parents and social agencies) nearly always tallied in essentials. Checks on accounts of delinquency involvement (some of which are described in Chapter IV) confirmed our impression of the basic trustworthiness of the information. The similarity of replies when informants were questioned about the same or related topics in different ways at different times was also impressive, but the very consistent pattern of intercorrelations between items in the reports from so many different individuals was the most convincing feature. With the aid of information gained over a long period of time from a variety of sources, the field workers got to know many of their clients fairly intimately, and this doubtless helped to keep the interviews on a realistic footing and to improve the quality of the information. Repeated assurances of confidentiality and the conditions of privacy under which interviews were conducted must also have had a good effect, for hardly anyone raised objections to the use of the tape recorder.

CHAPTER II

How Much Delinquency?

Interpreting the statistics

According to popular belief and comments in the media, youthful crime has been increasing alarmingly. This is nothing new, every generation expresses similar concern. In point of fact the criminal statistics furnish material both for alarmists and for commentators who want to underplay the problem. The number of offences recorded by the police in England and Wales, as in most countries of the Western world, increased substantially in the 1950s and 1960s, and the proportion of offences attributable to teenage males also increased, but since the 1970s there has been some levelling off. At least a part of the increase has been due to changes in legislation and policing, so that people are nowadays processed through the criminal justice system for relatively trivial acts that would once have been dealt with informally. For instance, in real terms, because of inflation, one needs to destroy relatively little property in order to be charged with criminal damage. Crime reports from other sources, such as Post Office reports of vandalism, have not kept pace with the great increases shown in the police statistics.

Because the increase has been most noticeable in the statistics of recidivism, it could be that it is the persistence of the established offender that has changed, rather than the criminality of the population at large. The fact that older persons are convicted much less often than the young suggests that it remains true that much youthful delinquency is a self-limiting phenomenon which comes to an end with the achievement of years of discretion. The fact that more youngsters than ever before are being received into borstals and detention centres might be thought to point to the serious nature of their crimes, but increasing numbers are also receiving fines or cautionings, which might suggest that many youthful offences are relatively trivial.

Crude statistics of numbers of delinquents reveal nothing about the seriousness of offences or about how many young offenders go on to become adult criminals. By following closely a small sample over a sufficient length of time we have been able to obtain a more detailed picture of the extent of involvement in delinquency. The findings lend

no support to either excessively gloomy or excessively rosy interpretations of the situation.

For the purpose of this study delinquents were defined as individuals
with a criminal conviction record in the central files at Scotland Yard.
This excluded persons with only traffic or regulatory infractions. Details
of the counting of convictions are given in Appendix II.

A fifth of the study sample (84 of 411) acquired an official record
for offences committed as juveniles (that is, between the tenth and
seventeenth birthdays). By the eighteenth birthday the proportion of
delinquents had risen to a quarter (103 of 411), but after that new
recruits to the delinquent ranks became increasingly infrequent. By the
time they had reached their twenty-fifth birthdays a third of the sample
(136 of 411) had a conviction record.

The high proportion of officially ascertained delinquents in the
study may seem surprising, but in fact it is not surprising for a sample
of urban, working-class males. Power *et al.* (1974) found an even higher
prevalence of juvenile delinquents, 30 per cent as opposed to our 20 per
cent, in the London Borough of Tower Hamlets. Nils Lie (1981) followed
up a normal population of 2000 Swedish schoolboys, taken from one
large and one medium-sized town. They were aged 19–24 when their
records were searched, by which time 21 per cent had their names in
the police register, signifying that they had been found guilty on at least
one occasion of a crime committed after age 15. Marvin Wolfgang
(1974) and Wolfgang *et al.* (1972) estimated that among males born in
Philadelphia in 1945 a half would have an offence record by the age of
35. From arrest rates over the whole of the United States in the year
1965, a Taskforce of the President's Commission on Law Enforcement
calculated that the expectancy of an arrest for a criminal offence at
some point in the lifetime of an American male had reached 62 per cent
(Christensen, 1967). From the national statistics of convictions in
England and Wales in the year 1977 given in Table I (taking into
account the size of the population in each age-group and assuming that
conviction rates remain constant), David Farrington (1981) has calculated that the proportion of males who may be expected to sustain a
conviction (for standard-list non-motoring offences) by his twenty-
fifth birthday is now over a quarter (26.6 per cent). This compares with
the actual figure of one-third in the study sample. Such a large proportion of the young male population cannot all be seriously maladjusted.

Some of our delinquents were first convicted at a surprisingly early
age. Table 1 displays the numbers and proportions of delinquents first
convicted at various ages and contrasts them with Home Office estimates
of the total number of males in England and Wales in corresponding
age-groups who were convicted for the first time in the year 1977. The
figures are not strictly comparable because the national statistics are
recording persons of different ages all convicted in the same year,

Table 1 Age on first conviction

Age	Cambridge study sample (number of persons convicted for first-time offence against age)		National sample (1977) (estimated number of males convicted for first time for standard-list offences (in thousands) against age)	
	No.	Percentage	No.	Percentage
10 and under 13	20	14.7	8.2	8.1
13 and under 15	34	25.0	16.6	16.3
15 and under 17	30	22.1	22.9	22.5
17 and under 19	27	19.8	22.2	21.9
19 and under 21	17	12.5	15.1	14.8
21 and under 25	8	5.9	16.7	16.4
	136	100.0	101.7	100.0

Source of National sample (1977): Home Office, *Criminal Statistics (England and Wales)* (HMSO, 1978), table 10.2.

whereas the figures from this study are of males of a similar age convicted in different years. Even so, the comparison suffices to show that our delinquents tended to start acquiring conviction records at an earlier age than is usual today. One reason for this was that they were born too soon to benefit from the introduction in London, following the passing of the Children and Young Persons Act 1969, of a system of official police cautioning, which is nowadays used particularly extensively for very young offenders in place of prosecutions. The table also shows that relatively few of the sample were convicted for the first time after the age of 21. The pressures of life in a working-class area probably caused most of those who were vulnerable to becoming delinquents to do so at an earlier age.

How many recidivists?

The acquisition of a criminal record does not necessarily signify the start of a long criminal career. The fact that each year the number of young persons convicted greatly exceeds the number from the older age-ranges shows that there is a high drop-out rate from officially recorded criminal careers. Currently, about 7 per cent of males aged 17 sustain a conviction for a serious offence in any given year (the figure for the study sample was 9.5 per cent), compared with 5 per cent of males aged 20 and less than 1 per cent of males aged 25. Most of our delinquents had just one or two convictions in youth and then no more. Of the total of 131 convicted men (among the 397 still in the UK at age 22) 50, 38.2 per cent, were convicted only once, 21 twice, 19 three times and 41 more than three times. A minority of only 30 of the 131 offenders (22.9 per cent) acquired over half (56.6 per cent) of the total convictions recorded. This degree of concentration of offences among a hard core of recidivists is similar to what was reported in the Philadelphia cohort study (Wolfgang *et al.*, 1972) in which a minority of 18 per cent of offenders were responsible for 52 per cent of all the recorded offences. In our study, only 36 offenders (27.5 per cent) were defined as persisting recidivists (having had at least two convictions for offences committed before the nineteenth birthday and at least one further conviction for an offence committed during the succeeding five years, that is, between the nineteenth and twenty-fourth birthdays).

Most young adult offenders have begun as juvenile delinquents. In this study, a majority of the men convicted for offences committed between the nineteenth and twenty-fifth birthdays had been previously convicted. The exact figures were 53 previously convicted out of a total of 78, (or 68 per cent), which compares with a corresponding figure of about 60 per cent of a national sample of males of this age convicted in England and Wales in January 1971 (Phillpotts and Lancucki, 1979). Wolfgang (1974) estimated the chances of a man in Philadelphia offending between the ages of 19 and 26 as one in two if he had a prior offence record, but only about one in eight if he had not. We found a similar contrast. Half of the 106 men with a previous conviction record were reconvicted for offences between the nineteenth and twenty-fifth birthdays, whereas only 8 per cent (25 out of 291) of the men without previous convictions were convicted for offences during this age-span.

It is well known that being convicted at an early age is a bad sign. In a large sample of delinquents in Ohio, Hamparian *et al.* (1978) found that the younger the age at first arrest the greater the average number of re-arrests. In an earlier survey of Swedish statistics, Sellin (1958) showed that the likelihood of reconviction in later life was significantly greater the younger the age at first conviction. Our sample was no exception. Among the 131 delinquents who remained in the UK 33 had been convicted for offences committed before their fourteenth birthday. A majority of this group, 60.6 per cent, were reconvicted for offences committed in later years, that is, between the nineteenth and twenty-fifth birthdays. In contrast, of 28 first convicted for offences committed between the seventeenth and nineteenth birthdays, only 35.7 per cent were reconvicted later.

Another bad omen for the future was a high frequency of convictions for juvenile offences. Among the total of 131 delinquents, 65 had no more than 3 convictions for juvenile offences and of these only 12 (18.5 per cent) subsequently acquired 4 or more convictions for offences as adults. In contrast, of 13 delinquents with 4 or more convictions for juvenile offences as many as 10 (76.9 per cent) were convicted on at least 4 occasions as adults.

Long-term recidivism involving serious offences was surprisingly unusual. When the inquiry came to an end in 1980 only about 7 of the 131 delinquents were thought to be still active or dangerous criminals. These included a man who had been repeatedly imprisoned for robbery at knife point, 3 who had been recently involved with accomplices in a number of robberies using firearms, and 3 others who were known, through information gleaned at interviews, to have become 'professional' dealers in stolen goods. Apart from these 7, there were twice as many again who continued to sustain convictions, but mostly for minor, disorganized crimes or assaultative behaviour.

How serious were the youthful offences?

One indication of seriousness is the severity of the sentences imposed. Of the 131 delinquents who remained in the UK 13 had experienced borstal and 14 had been in detention centres, but only 12 were sentenced to imprisonment (including 5 who had already passed through borstal or detention). The fact is that the conviction careers of most young male delinquents are sporadic and short term and come to an end without the courts finding it necessary to impose any custodial sentence, and this remains true in spite of recent increases in the use of custody for young offenders. Sentences being comparatively short, the vast majority of young delinquents are at liberty in the community most of the time. In our sample, none of the delinquents was in prison or borstal under sentence on his twenty-first birthday; 2 were in prison under sentence on their twenty-second birthday and 3 on their twenty-third birthdays. These figures suggest that the offences of the generality of young delinquents are less serious and less persistent than one might expect from surveys based upon the minority who end up in penal institutions. This impression was born out by analysis of the types of offences recorded against members of the study.

Table 2 displays the numbers and types of offences leading to conviction that were committed up to the twenty-fourth birthday, grouped into those committed as juveniles (that is, under 17) and those committed later. The legal labels provide only a rough indication of the nature of the misbehaviour, but it is clear that the vast majority of offences were crimes of dishonesty. After the juvenile age-range was passed, drug offences emerged for the first time and aggressive offences, although still in a small minority, became relatively more common, but still property crime accounted for three-quarters of all the offences.

As far as official records revealed, the delinquents in the study could be succinctly described as 'thieves', some of whom occasionally committed other kinds of offences. Among the total of 136 criminal records only 11 were without some conviction for an offence of dishonesty committed either as an adult or a juvenile. Among the 32 delinquents

Table 2   Types of offences recorded against 411 males

Offence*	Offences as juveniles (between 10th and 17th birthdays) (sub-total)		Offences as adults (up to 24th birthday) (sub-total)	
Crimes of dishonesty				
Theft from shops, etc.	24		14	
Theft from and of motor vehicles	31		26	
Unauthorized taking of motor vehicles	32		56	
Theft of cycles or part of cycles	9		1	
Theft from automatic machines	11		6	
Theft by employees	1		17	
Theft on entering but not breaking in	17		17	
Other thefts	11		28	
Burglary	56		56	
Fraud, forgery, deception, etc.	6		18	
Handling stolen goods, receiving, unlawful possessions	11		20	
Equipped to steal, suspected person, etc.	20		35	
	229	(89.1%)	294	(75.4%)
Aggressive crimes				
Robbery, conspiracy to rob, access to rob	3		8	
Assault	4		22	
Insulting or threatening behaviour	5		1	
Carrying offensive weapon	4		12	
	16	(6.2%)	43	(11.0%)
Damage to property				
Arson	1		0	
Wilful, malicious or criminal damage	7		21	
	8	(3.1%)	21	(5.4%)
Sex offences				
Indecent assault on female	1		0	
Indecent exposure	1		0	
Indecent telephone message	1		0	
Importuning males	0		1	
Unlawful sexual intercourse	1		0	
	4	(1.6%)	1	(0.3%)
Drug offences				
Unlawful possession of drugs	0		19	
Attempt to procure drugs	0		1	
	0	0	20	(5.1%)
Other offences				
Obstruct police	0		9	
Breach of peace	0		2	
	0	0	11	(2.8%)
Total of all offences leading to conviction	257	(100%)	390	(100%)

Note: *Including all proved charges on each occasion of conviction, except for
breaches of probation or items not normally contained in criminal record
files. Matters taken into consideration excluded.

convicted for violence against another person (see p. 66) only 4 had been convicted solely for such offences. Individuals specializing exclusively in some type of crime other than theft — for example, violence, sex or drugs — were far too few to affect the overall trend.

The rarity of criminal specialization among young offenders has been noted by other authorities. Walker *et al.* (1967) noted that convictions for violence in English criminal records are usually incidental to recidivist careers. When young offenders commit other than property offences it is usually an expression of versatility rather than specialization. In his Philadelphia study, Wolfgang (1974, p. 86) found that the probability that a delinquent's next offence would be of any particular type was scarcely affected by the nature of his last offence. The potential versatility of youthful offending is confirmed by self-report studies showing that the admission of offences in one category carries an increased likelihood of admissions of offences in other categories also (Hindelang, 1971). Later in life, of course, a significant degree of specialization becomes apparent. An analysis of a national sample of male offenders of all ages (Phillpotts and Lancucki, 1979, table 4.4) showed that a man initially convicted of one type of offence (for example, violence), if reconvicted, was more likely to be convicted again for that same type of offence than was a man whose initial conviction had been for an offence of a different category (for example, fraud or sex or burglary).

The police descriptions of offences contained in central criminal record files were generally terse and sometimes lacking in basic particulars, such as whether the offender was alone or how much property was stolen, but the information that was given showed that the majority of offences, especially those committed by juveniles, were small scale and relatively trivial, more of a nuisance than a serious threat. Of course, these were merely the offences for which the delinquents were apprehended and convicted. It was apparent, from the youths' own admissions and descriptions of their way of life, that the officially recorded offences were merely the tip of an iceberg. A few of the delinquents, when seen as young adults, were apparently living comfortably on the proceeds of crime, although this could not have been deduced from the small scale and frequency of their officially recorded offences. But these were the exceptions. Most of the offence histories seemed to reflect petty, disorganized, impulsive and generally unprofitable crimes.

In the 90 instances in which a value was stated in the charge, or in a police report, for the total property involved in a juvenile offence by a member of the study, this ranged from 5p to £550, with an average of £30 11p. Of the 95 amounts stated, 47 were £5 or less. In the case of offences as adults (up to the twenty-fourth birthday) the 91 quoted values ranged from 10p to £7500 with an average of £222 46p. Over half were £23 or less. Even allowing for inflation, the scale of offences had clearly increased with age, although the majority were still relatively small scale.

The police reports of violent offences sometimes specified that the victim was bruised or cut or needed stitches, but more often reference was made to punching, kicking or striking without mention of injury resulting. Apparently, relatively few of the violent incidents dealt with by the police had caused serious harm to victims, although, as will be seen later, injuries from fights that had not led to prosecution were quite frequently reported by the delinquents themselves.

Do official statistics give a true picture?

If the volume of undetected offences (what criminologists delight in calling the 'dark figure') greatly exceeds the number that come to the attention of the police, then the picture of delinquency obtained from conviction records could be quite unrealistic. Many confirmed delinquents, especially perhaps the more cunning and determined offenders, may never be officially identified. In recent years criminologists have explored this issue by confidential questioning of young persons about their law-breaking habits, regardless of whether their behaviour has resulted in a conviction record. The results have tended to confirm the suspicion that delinquents identified by their own confessions are more numerous and less likely to fit prevailing beliefs of what a delinquent is like than the cases seen by the courts. Youths who talk tough, sport disapproved hair styles and mode of dress, and come from poor neighbourhoods and broken homes may attract police attention because they are of a type believed to be delinquent-prone, whereas youths who do not happen to fit this stereotype may more easily escape detection when they misbehave (Hood and Sparks, 1970).

Most studies of self-reported delinquency have been American or Scandinavian, but one important survey of a large sample of London boys aged 13–16 has been published by Belson (1975). The project was generously financed and pursued with impressive methodological thoroughness and statistical sophistication. In only 14.0 per cent of his target group of 1655 boys did Belson fail to secure a valid interview. The original sample intentionally included an over-representation of lower-class members, but this was compensated for by a 'weighting' system in order to produce estimates applicable to a normal population. Every boy admitted to at least some kind of stealing. In each of the 44 categories of theft inquired about (such as 'stealing from a shop' or 'stealing from a vehicle') admissions were made, on average, by 42 per cent of the sample. However, only 13 per cent of the boys said they had been caught, but this minority tended to include the worst cases, a half of them coming from the quarter of the sample who reported the most stealing.

Broadly similar results were obtained from our own self-report inquiries. In the course of the interviews at age 14, and again at age 16, the boys in this study were presented with 38 cards each bearing a description of an item of misbehaviour. They were asked to sort the cards into piles according to whether they had 'never', 'once or twice', 'sometimes' or 'frequently' committed the act in question. If the admissions were completely accurate the proportions of boys claiming to have committed a particular act at some time in the past should always have been at least as large at age 16 as at age 14. This proved to be the case for nearly all the 38 acts (see Appendix IV, ref. 2, p. 152). Some of the acts had clearly become more prevalent with increasing age. For instance, 'Buying cheap, or accepting as a present, anything known or suspected of being stolen', was endorsed by 57.4 per cent of boys at 16 compared with 36.3 per cent at 14. On the other hand, the more childish forms of misconduct had probably diminished. For example, 'Letting off fireworks in the street', although admitted by 86.7 per cent at 16, had already been admitted by 84.2 per cent at 14. Items of minor misconduct such as this were admitted by the great majority. For example, at age 16, 'Going to X films under age' was admitted by 89.7 per cent. The exceptional few who claimed always to have behaved with near-perfect conformity to law were, at least in a statistical sense, a highly deviant group.

The study sample was in no way unusual in the substantial proportions of boys admitting to minor delinquencies. A more recent survey of boys attending secondary schools in an English Midland town, which made use of some of the same questions, elicited even more admissions, as the following examples illustrate (Shapland, 1978). The only item admitted much more frequently by our boys was 'Going to X-rated films'. This was probably due to the greater availability of such films in London.

Another English self-report survey, this time directed to the topic of vandalism, but utilizing a few questions resembling some of those in the present study, was carried out by the Home Office Research Unit (Clarke, 1978). The sample questioned consisted of 584 boys attending maintained schools in a northern city. Table 4 sets out the comparison with the present study.

Once again it appears that boys in a comparable survey made rather more admissions than did boys in our sample. Probably our boys tended to minimize rather than to exaggerate their misbehaviour. As the interviewers knew them and had indirect contact with their families, our boys may have been motivated to put themselves in a good light. (The reliability of self-reports is discussed briefly in Appendix III.)

In view of the ubiquity of misbehaviour revealed in self-report studies, an indiscriminate selection of offenders that ignored seriousness or persistence of offending would be virtually a random sample of

Table 3   Percentage of boys (aged 14) admitting various items of misbehaviour

Description of misbehaviour	Sample of 51 boys from a Midland town (Shapland, 1978)	Sample of 405 London boys (Cambridge study)
Riding a bicycle without lights (or with no rear light) after dark	96.1	77.0
Taking money from home – with no intention of returning it	21.6	9.4
Taking an unknown person's car or motor bike for joyriding (with no intention of keeping it for good)	13.7	7.4
Annoying, insulting or fighting other people (strangers) in the street	58.8	23.0
Stealing things out of cars	9.8	8.9
Using any kind of weapon in a fight	37.3	12.1
Struggling or fighting to get away from a policeman	23.5	6.9
Stealing school property worth more than about 5p	62.8	29.1
Going to 'X' films under age	19.6	64.0
Stealing goods or money from slot machines, juke boxes, telephones, etc.	39.2	14.6
Stealing from people's clothes hanging up anywhere	15.7	3.5

Table 4   Percentages of boys admitting various acts of vandalism

	Percentage of boys admitting the behaviour
Cambridge study (at age 14)	
Smashing, damaging or slashing things in public places – in streets, cinemas, dance halls, railway carriages, buses, etc.	11.9
Breaking the windows of empty houses	68.9
Home Office survey (at age 11–15)*	
Damaging the tyres of a car	28
Broken a window in an empty house	68
Slashed bus seats	22

Note: *For source of Home Office survey, see Clarke (1978).

the young male population. Official conviction records would be meaningless unless they picked out the more important offenders. We identified as self-reported delinquents the fifth of the sample (80 boys) who gave the highest self-report scores at ages 14–16. None of this group admitted to less than 21 of the 31 items of misbehaviour about which they were questioned. (The score for each boy consisted of the total number of different items of misconduct admitted in the course of two interviews, at age 14 and at 16. For the 15 boys who could be seen only once, the score from that occasion only had to be used. A total of 409 boys were tested at least once; only 2 were not tested at all.)

By the date that they were seen and questioned at age 16, nearly half the 80 self-reported delinquents already had an official conviction record (38 out of 80, 47.5 per cent). Among the remaining 329 who were tested and not found to be self-reported delinquents, only 37 (11.2 per cent) were officially convicted delinquents. This was an enormously significant contrast ($\chi^2 = 56.5$, $P < 0.0001$). The figures show conclusively that the conviction records did indeed tend to identify those who would be considered the worst delinquents according to their own admissions. The result was not unexpected in view of similar findings from other surveys (Shapland, 1978; Erickson, 1972; Belson, 1975; Hardt and Hardt, 1977).

The self-reported delinquents who had no official record prior to testing at age 16 were particularly liable to acquire a first conviction subsequently. Among the 41 such individuals who remained in the UK, as many as 18 (43.9 per cent) were convicted later. In contrast, of the 285 individuals remaining in the UK who had been non-delinquents on both self-report and official records when examined at age 16, only 42 (14.7 per cent) sustained a first conviction subsequently ($\chi^2 = 20.3$, $P < 0.0001$). The fact that self-reported delinquency not only correlated with past convictions, but was also significantly predictive of future first convictions, showed that the overlap with official delinquency was not to be accounted for by those already convicted being readier to admit their offences.

A few self-reported delinquency questions were included in the interviews with the sample at age 18. An important conclusion from this later inquiry was that, although the occasional offender often escapes detection, most persistent offenders are caught and convicted in the long run. Of those who admitted to having committed burglary once in the past three years, 53 per cent (9 out of 17) had been convicted for it, but of those who had committed burglary six or more times 77 per cent (10 out of 13) had been convicted for that offence. Taking and driving away (as it was then known) was less often detected. Of those who admitted to one such offence 33 per cent (7 out of 21) had been convicted for it, and of those who had done it five or more times 45 per cent (9 out of 20) had been convicted. The result is in agreement with findings of American research that persistent serious offences almost always lead to conviction in the long run. Glaser (1975, p. 79) estimated that a robber has only a one in five chance of being arrested for any particular offence, but a nine out of ten chance if he commits ten such offences.

The very considerable correspondence between the acquisition of a conviction record and the admission of many different offences in self-report inquiries suggests that official processes are fairly reliable in identifying the worst offenders. The picture of delinquency revealed by official records is probably more realistic than is generally supposed by critical criminologists. The topic is discussed further in the next chapter (see pp. 32–5).

Motives for offending

The light-hearted quality of some of the subjects' declared motives for offending gave additional support to the impression gained from official records that many youthful crimes, especially juvenile crimes, were not too serious.

During interviews at age 18, and again at 21, the men were shown short descriptions of a number of specific offences. If they admitted having committed any of the listed acts of delinquency they were asked to describe their motive, or their most usual motive, for each type of offence. All accounts that were sufficiently explicit were categorized as follows: self-exculpatory (that is, making excuses, denying responsibility); purposive (nearly always for material gain); enjoyment (excitement, 'kicks', relief of boredom); group solidarity (going along with the crowd) (see Appendix IV, ref. 3, p. 35). The numbers of offenders who cited each category of motive are shown in Table 5.

The commonest reason given for youthful offending was desire for quick material gain, but offending for pleasure came next. The reasons varied somewhat with the type of offence. The common offences of dishonesty, such as stealing from slot machines and 'buying cheap', were very largely done for gain, whereas damaging property was quite often done for enjoyment. At age 18, out of 52 explanations given for causing damage, 30 (57.7 per cent) fell into the category of enjoyment, whereas of the reasons given for stealing from slot machines only 6 out of 56 (10.7 per cent) were for enjoyment.

Delinquents' explanations for their offences are apt to vary according to the way the questions are put to them, but the study results were broadly in keeping with what others have found. Love of excitement, need to keep up with peers, and the chance of gaining some money are the most frequently mentioned reasons. Analysis of the responses of juvenile offenders at Ardale Community Home for boys and at Stamford House Assessment Centre in London, when asked to cite all their

Table 5 Numbers of offenders citing various categories of motive for each type of offence

| | Motive categories | | | | | | | | | |
| Offence category | Self-exculpatory | | Purposive (material gain) | | Enjoyment | | Group solidarity | | Total classifiable | |
	Age 18	Age 21	Age 18	Age 21	Age 18	Age 21	Age 18	Age 21	Age 18	Age 21
Damaging property	11	2	3	0	30	2	8	0	52	4
Taking and driving away	5	6	11	10	32	6	4	0	52	22
Shop-lifting	3	9	28	9	16	3	4	1	51	22
Stealing from slot machines	7	3	40	1	6	1	3	0	56	5
Stealing from cars	1	1	30	10	6	2	1	1	38	14
Breaking and entering	5	0	27	11	4	2	1	0	37	13
Buying cheap*	5	–	154	–	0	–	0	–	159	–
Obtaining money from the government by deception†	–	1	–	19	–	0	–	0	–	20
Stealing from work†	–	17	–	34	–	0	–	1	–	52
Total explanations cited	37	39	293	94	94	16	21	3	445	152
Percentage explanations cited at each age	8.3	25.7	65.8	61.8	21.1	10.5	4.7	1.9	100.0	100.0

Notes: *Not asked about at age 21.
†Not asked about at age 18.

reasons for offending, showed that 80–84 per cent mentioned 'need for easy money'. Some 62–67 per cent mentioned 'boredom' and 45–47 per cent mentioned a wish 'to be part of the peer group' (Mayers, 1980, p. 5). Williamson (1978), in research centred upon an English working-class district where unemployment was high, found that boredom — expressed as 'nothing to do around here' — by creating a desire for excitement, not only contributed to the incidence of such offences as vehicle-borrowing and vandalism, but also promoted theft or house-breaking, since the gains from such exploits could be used to obtain excitements that had to be paid for, such as drink and discos. Belson (1975), from his extensive study of self-reported thieving among London boys, concluded that a permissive attitude towards stealing, association with others of similar outlook, and a search for excitement were prime causes. In an Australian study (Kraus, 1977), boys in a high-delinquency area, and delinquents in an institution, were asked their opinions as to the cause of offending. They cited as common causes the usual categories — peer influence, thrill seeking, boredom, material or monetary gain — but they also mentioned, more often than anything else, causes such as bad homelife, broken home, cruel, uncaring, unloving or neglectful parents, that fell under the heading 'parental inadequacy'. If the boys in the study had been asked to give 'causes' rather than immediate motives for offending, they might perhaps have given similar responses.

During the interviews at age 21 the men admitted to fewer recent offences. The criminal-damage category in particular had become much less frequent than at age 18. As to motives for offending, self-exculpatory accounts were more prevalent at 21 and mention of enjoyment and group solidarity was less common. For example, at age 18 many explanations for taking and driving away vehicles and for shop-lifting (48 out of 103 or 46.6 per cent) fell into the enjoyment category, but at age 21 the proportion was much smaller (9 out of 44 or 22.3 per cent). Seemingly, the men had become less delinquent, less likely to offend for enjoyment and less willing to admit responsibility for any offences they had committed. In short, the study findings supported the common-sense view that the offences of young adults are fewer, but larger in scale, than those of juveniles, that they tend to reflect stronger and more reasoned motivations, and that they should therefore be taken rather more seriously.

CHAPTER III

Who is at Risk and Why?

Identifying the important factors

By the time the boys were 10 we had tried to assess and record some
two hundred items relating to their behaviour and background. Almost
every item proved to be in some degree associated with a risk of becoming one of the group of 84 juvenile delinquents. This was gratifying
confirmation that we had been asking relevant questions, but proved to
be something of an embarrassment when it came to sorting out what
was really important.

Virtually without exception it was the adverse points of any rating
that were associated with future delinquency. It was the boys from
broken homes rather than those from intact homes, those from poor
homes rather than affluent homes, those with unhealthy mothers rather
than those with healthy mothers, and those born illegitimate rather
than those born to married parents who were more likely to become
juvenile delinquents.

Several distinct clusters of intercorrelated items emerged, each
reflecting a unitary theme, and each of which could be conveniently
reduced or amalgamated into a single assessment. For example, all the
measures of intelligence and educational attainment, obtained from
psychological testing at the primary schools, correlated closely with
each other, presumably because whatever else affected the scores these
tests all reflected one basic variable, namely general ability or intelligence. One particular test, which seemed to be the best representative
of this cluster, was chosen as our measure of intelligence. This was
Raven's Progressive Matrices, a non-verbal test consisting of a serious of
increasingly difficult spatial puzzles in which the subject has to choose,
among specimen alternatives, which one completes an interrupted
pattern. The scores on two occasions of testing, at ages 8 and 10, were
averaged. Low scores were significantly predictive of delinquency.

Another cluster reflected the financial status of the family. This
included job status of the bread-winner (using the Registrar General's
classification), family income level as estimated from interviews by
social workers, dependence on national assistance or other social

agencies, and quality of housing. In this instance family income was selected as the best measure and it proved significantly predictive of delinquency (see Appendix IV, ref. 1, p. 18).

Most previous research work has related delinquency to social class rather than to family income. 'Class' stands for a complex cluster of attributes and life-style, notably occupation, income, education and housing, all of which are inter-related. Parents' occupation is generally used as the main index of social class. The Registrar General's lists of employments are grouped into five categories, from Group I (professional and managerial) to Group V (unskilled manual). Delinquency is relatively rare in Groups I and II. For example, Rutter *et al.* (1979, table 5.6) in a London survey found that only 17 per cent of boys aged 14 had an official delinquency record (including cautions), if their parents' occupational level was Group I or II, compared with 46 per cent if their parents had Group V occupations.

In our study, because the whole sample was from a single neighbourhood, where the range of occupations was limited, and only a small proportion of occupations fell into Groups I or II, the Registrar General's scale did not provide good discrimination. Our estimates of family income provided a more realistic indication of variations in life-style and attitude associated with social class than did the classification of father's employment.

Another cluster of items, all concerned with child-rearing, included maternal attitude, maternal discipline, paternal attitude, paternal discipline, marital disharmony and parental inconsistency. These assessments, all of them made by the social workers, were closely inter-correlated and obviously reflected the social workers' general opinion of the satisfactoriness or otherwise of parental management. No single item from those above could be singled out as being more important than the rest. It seemed likely that the social workers had found it impracticable to rate all these aspects of family life independently, so all the items in this cluster were combined into a single score, representing a global rating of parental behaviour.

Although, by these means, the total number of items was reduced to more manageable proportions, that still left many isolated assessments, some of them significantly predictive of delinquency, that could not be readily combined with anything else. A typical example was the item 'born illegitimate'. We discovered 25 boys whose natural parents were not legally married to each other at the time they were born (a fact that was not always evident from birth certificates). A high proportion of these boys, 40 per cent, became juvenile delinquents. This was not a particularly useful observation for purposes of prediction, because the item affected such a small proportion (6.1 per cent) of the sample that it could not possibly help to identify many potential delinquents. It was not particularly helpful either in the search for predisposing causes of delinquency.

Illegitimacy could be a consequence of the disorderly way of life characteristic of some delinquent families, but it could also be recorded against adopted boys or boys living in stable homes where for some reason parents were not legally married at the time of the birth. The datum 'born illegitimate' was not, in itself, particularly meaningful.

Other items were discarded as unhelpful because they were unreliably recorded or too subjective. For example, in 49 cases the social workers considered that a boy's physical welfare — food, hygiene, clothing, etc. — had been seriously neglected. Although, like illegitimacy, this item was significantly predictive of delinquency, it had not been very well defined and one of the social workers found proportionately twice as many boys 'neglected' as did her two colleagues.

Ultimately, for the purposes of the main statistical analysis, the items were reduced to some twenty key measures which were thought to be important and which had been assessed reasonably carefully. These were examined, not only for their associations with delinquency, but also to determine whether each one made a contribution to the prediction of delinquency independently of others. This was done by selecting cases matched on one item, A, and seeing whether, after matching on A, items B, C, D or E, etc. still made a difference to the likelihood of delinquency. It was found, for example, that a history of separations from parents, for reasons other than death or hospitalization, although in itself predictive of delinquency, ceased to be so after matching for other more important items, such as 'parents have a criminal record'. 'Separations' appeared to make no significant contribution other than as a secondary consequence of more fundamental family characteristics revealed in other assessments.

In the end we were left with five major factors, each of which had a significant association with likelihood of delinquency, that could not be explained in terms of other, more basic, items. This does not mean that all the other factors were without interest. The vagaries of chance, the limited numbers in the sample and the differing degrees of efficiency with which items were identified and measured could have prevented the true importance of some factors from being recognized. However, the five factors which did stand out from the analysis were clearly important.

From all the items of adversity that were examined, five key factors were identified. Each was present in about a quarter of the sample. The possession of any one of these adverse factors effectively doubled the likelihood of becoming a juvenile delinquent, to about one in three for boys in an affected quarter from one in six among boys in the remaining three-quarters. The five key factors were as follows.

(1) Coming from a low-income family. Of 93 such boys, 33.3 per cent became juvenile delinquents (compared with 16.7 per cent among the rest of the sample).

(2) Coming from a large-sized family (defined as four or more other surviving children born to the boy's mother up to his tenth birthday). Of 99 such boys, 32.3 per cent became juvenile delinquents.

(3) Having parents considered by social workers to have performed their child-rearing duties unsatisfactorily. Of 96 such boys, 32.3 per cent became juvenile delinquents.

(4) Having below-average intelligence on testing (defined as IQ of 90 or less on Raven's Matrices Test). Of 103 such boys, 31.1 per cent became juvenile delinquents (compared with 15.9 per cent in the rest of the sample).

(5) Having a parent with a criminal record (acquired before the boy's tenth birthday). Of 103 such boys, 37.9 per cent became juvenile delinquents (compared with 14.6 per cent among the rest of the sample).

There was a significant overlap between these adverse factors, the presence of any one factor making the presence of others more likely. For instance, with 93 cases from low-income families and 99 from large-sized families one would expect by chance only 22 cases with both these features, but in actuality there were 56. Nevertheless, each factor contributed its own independent increment to the likelihood of delinquency. For example, on comparing cases matched on income level of the parental family the boys from large families still produced more delinquents than those from smaller families.

Because of the extensive overlap of adversities a substantial minority of 63 boys had a combination of at least three of the five predictive items. Almost a half of this group became juvenile delinquents compared with only a fifth among the sample as a whole.

The limits of prediction

From these five predictive factors it would have been possible to identify a minority of boys who were at risk of becoming delinquents, but it would not have been possible to make a confident assertion about the outcome for any given individual. Although the group of 63 boys who had a constellation of several adversities produced as many as 31 juvenile delinquents, they also produced 32 without a juvenile record. Moreover, a majority of the juvenile delinquents, 53 in fact, did not belong to the high-risk group and would not have been predicted.

The level of prediction achieved in this study compares favourably with that of other surveys, and is probably as far as it is possible to go in distinguishing high- and low-risk groups among the general population from an examination of family background factors at primary-school age. Delinquent behaviour cannot be determined entirely by past events. Contemporaneous happenings, such as variations in the methods and size of the local police force, or the number of vehicles left temptingly unlocked in the neighbourhood, must influence the likelihood of appearance before the juvenile court, but such things cannot be predicted from an analysis of the individual's circumstances in earlier years.

Exaggerated claims for the effectiveness of prediction have been made in some criminological writings, but these have usually been based upon retrospective comparisons between sharply contrasting groups, such as institutionalized delinquents (the worst of their kind) and individuals free from any taint of delinquency. We could ourselves have obtained a very effective division between delinquents and non-delinquents by selecting for prediction only the 'worst' 10 per cent and the 'best' 10 per cent and ignoring the rest.

We explored the boys' early backgrounds to try to understand how delinquency develops rather than to produce a prediction formula. For purely predictive purposes it seems that nothing works so well as observation of pre-delinquent behaviour, but that, of course, tells one nothing about how such behaviour originates. A measure of 'troublesomeness', derived from observations by teachers and classmates at primary school, was as good a predictor of delinquency as any combination of background variables. When the boys were aged 8, and again at 10, their teachers filled in questionnaires on behaviour in class — a modified version of those used in a national survey (Douglas, 1964). The questions (see Appendix IV, ref. 2, p. 107) covered application to work, scholastic performance, concentration, cleanliness, obedience, attendance and relations with other children. The boys were divided into three groups — most troublesome, average and least troublesome — according to whether their scores fell into the worst quarter, the middle range or the best quarter of their particular school class. At age 10 the boys were also divided into most troublesome, average and least troublesome groups according to their classmates' responses to a questionnaire which required them to tick off on a class list the names of the four 'most troublesome' members. A combined score of teachers' ratings at both ages and peer ratings at age 10 produced the final ratings of 'troublesomeness'. Of the 92 boys categorized as most troublesome, 44.6 per cent became juvenile delinquents, compared with only 3.5 per cent of 143 boys in the 'least troublesome' category and 21.6 of the 176 'moderately' troublesome cases. Thus, being perceived as an above-average nuisance by teachers and peers (whose ratings were significantly congruent) was much the best single predictor of juvenile delinquency. This was a somewhat depressing finding, because it implied that deviant behaviour observable at an early age is likely to persist and take a delinquent form as boys grow older. It was also slightly mysterious, since there was no logical reason why untidiness, poor concentration and the other items which made up the score of 'troublesomeness' should foreshadow the sort of activities, such as stealing or breaking in, which are the typical offences of juvenile delinquents.

The more important component of the 'troublesomeness' evaluations was the teachers' opinions, which were almost as effective predictors by themselves as when combined with the views of classmates. Teachers' ability to identify future delinquents is indisputable; it has been demonstrated repeatedly in surveys both in England and the United States (Kvaraceus, 1960; Conger and Miller, 1966; Wadsworth, 1979, p. 64; Rutter *et al.*, 1979, p. 239). It is sometimes suggested that, by damaging a boy's self-image and his status in school, thereby exacerbating his problems, teachers' adverse opinions operate as self-fulfilling prophecies. It may well be that some teachers are capable of making matters worse, but this does not mean that their initial impressions of troublesomeness were without foundation. In our study there were significant correlations between the ratings made on the same boys by different teachers on occasions separated by a period of years, but of course the teachers who came later were probably aware of their predecessors' opinions as to which were the difficult boys.

The superior predictive power of teachers' ratings of behaviour over assessments of early background does not mean that background factors were unimportant. Besides being the basic reasons for 'troublesomeness', early deprivations may have been important ingredients in teachers' impressions. Like the assessment made by social workers, those made by teachers must have been influenced by a multiplicity of clues extraneous to the items purportedly under scrutiny. Children from poor backgrounds, because they tend to be uncouth in manners, scruffy in appearance, and to speak with unmistakable slum accents, are viewed with a jaundiced eye by some teachers and may attract unfavourable ratings that reflect their origins as much as their actual behaviour.

Are early adversities valid predictors of delinquency?

In the self-report study by Belson (1975), the sons of professional and skilled men reported less stealing than the sons of unskilled or semi-skilled fathers' but the difference was insufficient to account for the large over-representation of lower-class boys among those who admitted having been caught. Among the apprehended minority, the sons of the less skilled were more often prosecuted for their first offence than the sons of the skilled. Findings such as these suggest that features that appear to predict delinquency may not predict actual behaviour so much as vulnerability to police action.

In the Cambridge study the 80 self-reported delinquents shared most of the characteristics of the 84 boys defined as delinquents because they had been officially found guilty of juvenile offences. This was hardly surprising as 41 individuals belonged to both groups. The first two columns of Table 6 show the contrasting percentages of self-reported delinquents and of official delinquents among groups affected

Table 6   Percentages of self-reported and official delinquents among boys who displayed various adverse features

Adverse features	84 youths with official record of juvenile offences	80 self-reported delinquents (defined by tests at ages 14 and 16)	83 delinquents defined by combined measure
'Troublesome' at primary school	44.6	34.1	47.3
Low family income	33.3	28.0	33.3
Large family size	32.3	27.3	31.3
Criminal parent	37.9	34.0	35.0
Unsatisfactory child-rearing	32.3	28.4	31.6
Lowest quartile of IQ	31.1	28.4	31.4

by the major adverse factors predictive of delinquency. It will be recalled that each of these features was present in about a quarter of the total sample. The figures show a substantially raised incidence among the adversely affected groups of both self-reported and official delinquents, with the prevalence of the official delinquents slightly, but consistently, higher. The difference, however, was so small that had the research been based upon self-reported delinquents rather than official delinquents the findings concerning their background characteristics would have been much the same.

In order to highlight any differences that might exist between delinquents identified from official records and those defined by self-report, the 80 self-reported delinquents were subdivided into 41 who also had an official juvenile record and 39 who did not. It was found that the former were particularly extreme, with even larger percentages displaying adverse characteristics than among the official delinquents as a whole. In contrast, the 39 who were free from findings of guilt for juvenile offences had a relatively low incidence of adverse characteristics, and were in fact closer to the non-delinquents than to the official delinquents in this respect (see Appendix IV, ref. 2, p. 160). In fact there were proportionately even fewer from large-sized or low-income families than among the boys who were neither official nor self-reported delinquents. This could be taken to suggest that self-report measures successfully identify some delinquent individuals who are missed by the authorities because they do not conform to the popular stereotype of what a delinquent is like. An alternative explanation is that these 39 individuals were the less serious delinquents among whom social deviance would be minimal. In support of this latter interpretation, the scores of these 39 individuals, although high enough to be included in the self-reported delinquency category, were on average much less than those of the 41 self-reported delinquents who also had an official record (see Appendix IV, ref. 3, p. 166).

More systematic statistical analysis, using partial phi-correlations (see Appendix IV, ref. 41, p. 99), showed that after partialling out officially recorded juvenile delinquency, only one of the five major background precursors of delinquency, namely parental criminality, remained significantly correlated with self-reported delinquency. Had the sample been larger, however, the statistical result might well have been different, for several items closely related to the key background factors (notably poor parental supervision, low occupational status of father, erratic paternal work record, poor scholastic attainment and below-average verbal ability) did produce significant correlations even after partialling out officially recorded juvenile delinquency. Since some of the background characteristics typical of convicted delinquents were less typical of unconvicted but self-reported delinquents, it might be argued (Farrington, 1979) that circumstances of deprivation have more to do with the acquisition of an official conviction record than with the genesis of troublesome behaviour, but this would be an exaggeration. Within the convicted group, those with high self-report scores had a substantially raised incidence of background adversities (such as large family size) and were more often recidivists. If a combination of self-report and conviction record gives the most valid identification of the 'true' delinquent, then the link with family background variables is confirmed rather than refuted.

The most plausible interpretation of our results seems to be that both conviction records and self-report scores are legitimate measures of delinquent behaviour. Each has a certain bias, but in neither case is this sufficient to obscure the salient characteristics of the delinquent group. Because self-report questionnaires usually ask about a variety of relatively trivial misconduct, and because they rely on conscientious respondents, a delinquent group defined by self-report alone may include some minor or marginal delinquents who lack the characteristics usually associated with delinquents. In fact, some self-report surveys have found no association whatsoever between social class and delinquency, but more recent and methodologically superior research suggests that there is an over-representation of lower-class members among the badly behaved, although the effect is less extreme than in official conviction records. This was the conclusion of Elliott and Ageton (1980) who used a self-report schedule that contained items closely corresponding to actual legal offences, avoided overweighting by trivial misbehaviour, and gave due credit to frequency of offending. An opposite bias occurs in official records, which depend upon the vagaries of detection, and which exclude the less important incidents that attract police warnings or cautions rather than prosecutions, and tend to neglect individuals whose delinquent behaviour is minor or infrequent. Official records also probably over-represent delinquents from large, poor families because they spend so much of their time in the streets where their misbehaviour is more visible than that of boys from better backgrounds.

It may be that a method of assessment combining both self-reports and official records would arrive at a more satisfactory identification of the truly delinquent minority than either method employed on its own. Accordingly, 83 delinquents were selected on criteria utilizing both convictions and self-reports. The group included all who had more than one conviction for a juvenile offence, all who had a juvenile record as well as an above-average score on self-report, and all of the self-reported delinquent group who also had a record of contact with the police as a result of their unlawful behaviour. (For further details see Appendix IV, ref. 2, p. 166.)

It can be seen from the third column of Table 6 that delinquents defined by these 'combined' criteria were just as prevalent among the disadvantaged groups as the delinquents defined by official records alone. It may be safely concluded that the deviant social characteristics of the delinquents in our study were not attributable to the fact that they were identified from official records. Possible reasons why other researchers have reached contrary conclusions are discussed in Appendix III.

Family size and family income

A statistical association between some feature in early life and the risk of becoming a delinquent years later does not in itself explain the chain of events that brings it about. One can envisage many different reasons why the misfortune of having a large number of siblings might increase the likelihood of a boy becoming delinquent. The effects of any parental shortcomings, incompetence or neglect are likely to be exacerbated if they have more children than they can cope with properly. Indeed, the mere fact of having too many children, indicative of neglect of family planning, suggests possible neglect of other aspects of parental responsibilities. Under working-class conditions parents with too many children often suffer financial hardship, if only because the mother cannot go out to work to supplement the family income. Limited spending power forces parents to live in neighbourhoods with a high incidence of delinquency and also restricts the supply of such aids to child learning and socialization as toys, room space, leisure pursuits, reading matter and school clothes. Overburdened parents have limited opportunity to monitor their children's activities or to exercise consistent control over misconduct. Then again, lack of individual attention from parents promotes reliance on peer groups who may exert pressures towards delinquency. The older children in a large family may be left to manage the younger ones, a situation known to be conducive to indiscipline and aggressive conflict between siblings and probably also to delinquency (Burgess and Couter, 1978). Large numbers of children in a family of limited income often results in overcrowding in the home, and this, in turn, may have a deleterious effect upon behaviour (Gove *et al.*, 1979).

Since boys become delinquent more readily than girls, and older brothers may set a bad example to the younger members of the family, it might be thought that the presence of older brothers would be particularly likely to stimulate delinquency. In fact in the present study, the likelihood of juvenile delinquency was associated to the same extent with the number of sisters as with the number of brothers, and to the same extent with the number of younger brothers as with the number of older ones (see Appendix IV, ref. 2, p. 32). It was a boy's actual number of siblings rather than their sex or his position in the family order of birth that appeared to matter.

Other surveys have not been unanimous on this point. Jones *et al*. (1980) studied a sample of 73 delinquent boys on probation in Ottawa, comparing them with 73 non-delinquents matched individually for age, school performance and socio-economic class. The delinquents were found to have more siblings than the non-delinquents (302 against 154), but the excess was due entirely to a superabundance of brothers. Whereas the non-delinquents had roughly equal numbers of brothers and sisters, the delinquents had nearly twice as many brothers as sisters. Furthermore, among the delinquents, antisocial behaviour scores (derived from interviews with the parents) were significantly higher for boys with several brothers and lower for those with several sisters. This conflicts with the findings reviewed by the Home Office researchers Clarke and Softley (1975) who reported that, with the exception of samples from approved schools, data from various groups of delinquents, including our own sample, showed no consistent excess of brothers. Moreover, taking self-report scores from our study, there was no consistent variation in the ratio of brothers to sisters according to the seriousness of admitted delinquency. Clarke and Softley were inclined to attribute the anomalous ratios in approved-school samples to the way the courts selected delinquent boys for this measure. A similar bias in the selection of juveniles for probation in Canada might perhaps explain the Canadian results.

The smallest size of family is the only child. Only children have been supposed to be less vulnerable to delinquency on account of closer supervision and protection by parents, but it has also been suggested that they could be more vulnerable through 'spoiling', or through the boy's need to combat maternal possessiveness and assert masculine independence. In point of fact the 46 only children in the sample included a smaller proportion of juvenile delinquents (10.9 per cent) than any other category of family size. A similar observation emerged from the National Survey of Health and Development. Boys who remained only children for three years or longer were significantly less likely than others to become delinquents, and those who remained only children up to the age of 11 were particularly unlikely to become delinquents (Wadsworth, 1979, p. 40).

In our study the influence of family size was much greater among the low family-income group. If the family had adequate living accommodation the presence of four or more children did not significantly increase the risk of delinquency (see Appendix IV, ref. 2, p. 33). This was in keeping with another of the national survey findings, that the links between family size, on the one hand, and delinquency, on the other, were greatest among boys from the lower (manual) classes. Presumably higher-status families, who have better education, housing and income can manage a larger number of children without their becoming delinquents. As with other items of information about family background, the correlation between delinquency and family size reflects a complex chain of relationships. How it works depends upon other aspects of the family set-up.

Low family income is yet another datum that reflects a constellation of influences. In the present study, as might have been expected, low income correlated not only with large size of family but also with poor parental behaviour and particularly with poor parental supervision. It is easy to see how the social alienation imposed by poverty may lead to identification with a subculture of low social standards and to the abandonment of middle-class ideals of conformity and respectability. Parents in overcrowded accommodation in poor tenements cannot protect and supervise their young children as they might wish. They have to let them out to roam the streets and fight their own battles among a similarly disadvantaged peer group.

Family poverty can be the result of extraneous circumstances that have nothing to do with individual behaviour (such as the state of the local labour market), but it can also come about through a father deserting the home, or being incompetent, work-shy, neglectful, alcoholic, sick or subject to fines and imprisonments. The effects of financial stringency upon the children will be made worse if the mother is not an efficient and prudent housekeeper.

Of course poverty is relative. People compare themselves with their contemporaries. Although not actually starving, people without a television today have reason to feel deprived, resentful and insecure. Critics of the criminologist's harping on poverty point to the increase in delinquency that has occurred coincident with a real increase in the material standards throughout society, but this argument ignores the fact (well established by the 1978 Royal Commission on the Distribution of Income and Wealth) that the distribution − or as some might prefer to express it, the mal-distribution − of incomes within the population has changed little in recent decades.

Low income, like most predictors of delinquency, connects up with, and in a sense stands for, a large collection of interlinked circumstances, each of which may reasonably be supposed to have some influence on the development of a child's attitudes and behaviour. A much larger sample than was available in this study would have permitted the use of sophisticated techniques of multiple regression and might have served to indicate some of the more salient influences. No survey, however, could hope to provide a complete map of cause and effect. The most one can expect to do is to identify, within an infinitely complex system of interacting influences, some items that make a significant contribution to the likelihood of delinquency and then go on to consider whether any of them might be modifiable by social experiments and social policies.

Intelligence, scholastic retardation and brain damage

The apparent importance of low intelligence in promoting delinquency among members of our sample was unexpected. The survey was carried out at a time when criminological writings were inclined to dismiss any observed differences in IQ between delinquents and non-delinquents as merely a secondary consequence of low social class, or as a result of the test questions being unfairly biased against the less well educated. Some surveys, notably the Cambridge Somerville Youth Study in Boston (McCord *et al.*, 1959, p. 65) had yielded results suggesting that 'no significant relationship exists between criminal behaviour and low intelligence'. In that particular instance, however, close scrutiny of the figures points to a contrary conclusion. There was a distinct deficit of boys with high IQ (more than 110), and an excess of boys in the dull—average range (81—90) among those who became delinquents (McCord *et al.*, 1959, pp. 202—3, tables 4 and 5). Most researchers have in fact discovered about the same amount of difference in IQ as we did, delinquents scoring on average about five points below the population norm (Douglas *et al.*, 1968, p. 121; Woodward, 1955). A recent scholarly review of the topic has concluded that there is good evidence for a significant relationship between low IQ and delinquency that does not depend upon social class (Hirschi and Hindelang, 1977).

Our main measure of intelligence was the non-verbal, pattern-completion test known as Raven's Matrices. The average IQ of the future juvenile delinquents (derived from the mean of their scores on two occasions of testing, at age 8 and again at age 10) was 95, only six points below the average for the rest of the sample, which was 101. This relatively small difference, because of the consistency with which delinquents appeared more often among the low scorers, that is, those of IQ not more than 90, was sufficient to make the IQ score one of the important predictors. Of the 84 juvenile delinquents 39.2 per cent were low scorers compared with little more than half that figure, 21.7 per cent, among the remaining 327 members of the sample. The relationship was especially evident in the case of the 37 juvenile recidivists, of whom 21 (56.8 per cent) were of low IQ.

In the past IQ tests made great use of language and general-knowledge questions and were largely a measure of size of vocabulary and amount of scholastic information absorbed. The scores reflected educational experience as much as potential for further learning. One reason why delinquents score poorly on tests dependent upon scholastic attainment is that their education is often blighted by attendance at the poorest schools, by truancy, by poor relations with teachers and by allocation to low-grade classes. Modern intelligence tests include many non-verbal puzzles in which children lacking in education are at less of a disadvantage. Some surveys have shown delinquents to be less retarded on non-verbal tests (Wechsler, 1958; Prentice and Kelly, 1963). It could be that on verbal tasks they fail to perform up to their true potential. In our study the delinquents performed relatively poorly on both verbal and non-verbal tests, so their retardation was not just a matter of inadequate schooling. Moreover, their scores did not seem to be artificially depressed by lack of motivation. When presented with tasks of increasing difficulty delinquents gave up no more readily than others (see Appendix IV, ref. 2, pp. 94–6).

Intelligence level, as measured by standard tests, gives a good indication of general problem-solving ability and is a significant predictor of scholastic achievement and of success in training for technically demanding work. Hereditary endowment sets limits to an individual's potential for developing a high IQ, but so also do environmental factors. A mild degree of retardation, such as is found among the majority of our juvenile recidivists, is common among children of large-sized, impoverished families living in overcrowded and generally deprived circumstances. In their analysis of the cycle of deprivation found in succeeding generations of disadvantaged minorities, Rutter and Madge (1976, p. 110) point out that the association between low IQ and low social class is: 'In part . . . a reflection of genetically determined differences in intelligence influencing social class distribution . . . but also there is evidence that the association reflects social influences on intellectual development.' Middle-class parents give their children more explicit and informative instruction than do working-class parents, provide them with educational toys, encourage and train them in language and reading and so prepare them to respond well to the academically oriented demands put upon them at school. In our study, however, the lower IQ of delinquents was not fully accounted for by their lower social-class status. After matching for family income, or for occupational status of the family bread-winner, IQ remained a significant predictor of delinquency.

In the National Survey of Health and Development it was found, as in our own study, that on both non-verbal tests and on reading and word-comprehension tests, administered at age 8, boys who became delinquents by the age of 21 scored lower than those who were non-delinquents. Boys from the lower socio-economic groups, and boys with several older siblings, also tended to have lower than average intelligence-test scores. When these two factors were allowed for, intelligence level no longer discriminated between delinquents and non-delinquents in the National Survey (Wadsworth, 1979, p. 67). It is generally accepted that the children of large families, especially the younger members, have on average lower IQs than the children of smaller families, possibly because they receive less parental attention and intellectual stimulation during their early years. In the present study, for example, the proportion of boys who were fourth or later born children within their families was significantly larger (30 per cent) among those of low IQ than among the rest of the sample (17 per cent). However, neither family income nor position in the family accounted for the whole of the difference between the IQ scores of delinquents and non-delinquents in our study. Unfortunately, we could not replicate exactly the analysis carried out by Wadsworth because of the unusual way socio-economic status was evaluated in the national survey, taking account of both parental education and occupation.

However it comes about, and whatever the relationship with other factors, the brute fact remains that boys who are below average in measured abilities are more likely than others to become delinquents. If, in fact, the effect is largely due to the environmental deprivations associated with large, poor families, rather than to innate deficiency, so much the better, since this means that remedial action is more likely to succeed.

Below-average intelligence is viewed by some theorists as a prime cause of delinquency by virtue of the difficulties it causes for pupils. Inability to meet the demands of teachers makes for loss of self-esteem and lowering of status among peers. Although the delinquent's deficiency may be only slight, coupled with the handicap of a poor background and indifferent socialization it may cause severe problems. In a survey of youths attending schools in Oregon, Frease (1973) found that inferior school performance, and not inferior social class, was the most prominent feature of those who appeared before the juvenile court. The stigma attaching to poor performance was exemplified by the high frequency with which the statement: 'Lots of people think I am a delinquent' was endorsed by boys with low school grades, regardless of whether they actually had a conviction record and regardless of whether their fathers were in white- or blue-collar occupations.

An attitude survey of adolescents in California, carried out by Polk (1969) showed that below-average performance in school (assessed on grade points) and low expectations of success were both associated with a relatively high incidence of officially recorded delinquency and a high incidence of rebellious attitudes. These relationships held true regardless of the social-class origin of the pupils concerned.

In a well-known study of secondary schools in England, Hargreaves (1967) showed that pupils who were relegated to bottom-stream classes on account of their poor scholastic performance developed hostile attitudes towards authority and manifested a high level of delinquency. Their situation appeared to have provoked a pro-delinquency subculture. Such findings lend support to the theory that low intelligence, by virtue of the difficulties it puts in the way of attaining status in school, is a significant factor in promoting delinquency.

Offord *et al.* (1978) and Offord (1981) have challenged this view. If scholastic retardation is in itself a sufficient cause of delinquency then retarded children who become delinquents should not display so many of the unfavourable background characteristics found among delinquents who are not retarded. The results of his Canadian survey showed the opposite. Compared with delinquents who passed their school grades satisfactorily, those who were school failures came significantly more often from broken homes and from homes supported by public welfare. Furthermore, the siblings of delinquents failed just as often at school, even when they were not themselves delinquents. Offord concluded that the scholastic retardation associated with delinquency was not a primary cause but, like delinquency itself, merely one of the likely consequences of early deprivation. That being so, educational programmes to combat scholastic retardation, because they were not tackling the prime cause, might not be as effective for delinquency prevention as some theoreticians have suggested.

Our own results agree with Offord's findings in pointing to early deprivation as an important factor contributing to both delinquency and scholastic retardation. The more severe the deprivation the more probable it becomes that both consequences will follow. Unlike Offord's findings, however, our results suggest that low IQ, however it arises, and whatever the level of family deprivation, makes an additional contribution to the likelihood of delinquency developing.

From a practical standpoint the question whether limited intellectual ability is an aggravating feature or a prime cause of delinquency matters less than the question whether the situation can be alleviated, and the risks of delinquency thereby lessened, by remedial action. Our research, being limited to passive observation, can only point to this possibility for constructive intervention. The literature on the evaluation of delinquency-prevention programmes gives little cause for optimism. Many efforts have been carried out without proper control groups with which to compare and assess the effects of intervention, and where valid comparisons have been possible the outcome has often been disappointing. Sometimes well-meaning interference does more harm than good. For example, in the present sample the incidence of delinquency was particularly high among those boys who had been formally ascertained 'educationally subnormal' and placed in special schools.

Since more boys than girls were thus 'ascertained', one suspects that their nuisance value had something to do with the selection as well as their intellectual limitations. Segregation of troublesome children among others of like tendency may sometimes serve to amplify rather than to reduce their problems. In one well-controlled American study, however, some under-achieving children were allocated to special classes. A follow-up over a two-year period showed that, in comparison with a control group, the children in this programme had significantly fewer recorded offences (Bowman, 1959). In a more recent follow-up study Hackler and Hagan (1975) compared groups of boys from a delinquent area, some of them being enlisted in supervised work groups, others being asked to try out simple teaching machines. The idea behind the latter procedure was to combat lack of confidence in their own abilities. The boys were asked to say whether they thought the machines would be useful for younger children, the implicit message being that they themselves were accepted as capable of scholastic work. Among the boys given practice on the teaching machines, and especially among those who were most socially disadvantaged, a smaller proportion acquired offence records during the follow-up period. Experience in the work groups seemed to have a contrary effect, producing slightly more delinquents during follow-up. The authors speculated that this may have been due to a buildup of expectations about employment followed by disillusionment when, after the experimental period was over, jobs were not available. The benefit derived from the teaching machines could have been the result of improved confidence generating better adjustment to the scholastic demands made upon the boys subsequently.

Such results confirm the intuitive impressions of experienced educationists and point the way to the kinds of scholastic reforms that might prove helpful in reducing delinquency. As Kelmer Pringle (1974, pp. 148–54) has pointed out, children have a great need for praise and recognition in order to maintain their confidence and self-esteem and acquire the favourable attitudes to learning that enable them to make the most of their abilities. In traditional schools recognition is more often given for achievement than for effort, so the bright, attractive and efficient receive praise in abundance. 'In contrast, the intellectually slow, culturally disadvantaged, emotionally neglected or maladjusted get far less . . . Whatever small successes they achieve inevitably demand far more effort and perseverance; yet they receive less reward because they achieve less.' Teachers are in a position to mitigate the problems which arise from natural disparities of intellect, physique and temperament by giving praise for 'improvements', however modest the attainment, and by recognizing effort and co-operation in a variety of contexts, including games, crafts, hobbies, punctuality, courtesy and the performance of necessary 'chores'. The brighter children need and should have the encouragement to achieve superior intellectual targets, but not at the cost of underestimating or neglecting the less able. In practice, as our study showed, few delinquents are so badly lacking in potential intellectual ability that they cannot, given favourable circumstances, learn to perform adequately in basic scholastic tasks. For instance very few members of the study remained permanently illiterate, although many had been so in their earlier years, and consequently unable to derive the benefit from their schooling that they might have had if their potential had been realized sooner.

Individuals good at one type of task tend to be good at most others, and vice versa, hence the utility and generalizability of IQ tests, such as Raven's Matrices, which measure only a limited range of problem-solving abilities. A minority of cases, however, have learning disabilities in one particular area only. For instance, so-called dyslexic children do not easily recognize or recall written words, and may therefore become severely retarded in literary tests, although in other respects they can perform well. Slight damage or malfunction in particular areas of the brain, insufficient to cause generalized mental defect, is thought to be the cause. This assumption is difficult to prove, but two symptoms of brain damage, clumsiness of movement and inability to stay still and pay attention for any length of time, are often noted in children with specific learning disabilities. Partial deafness in children, which is also a form of neurological malfunction, provides an analogy, for the learning problems so produced are apt to be mistaken for stupidity or laziness unless timely diagnosis and the provision of hearing aids proves otherwise.

It has been suggested that the scholastic retardation of delinquents, especially noticeable in delinquent boys, may quite often be due to specific disorders of cognitive function rather than to the more commonly cited factors of poor motivation, limited exposure to learning situations and generalized intellectual deficiency. Conclusive evidence on the point is hard to obtain owing to the difficulty of defining and measuring the minor disabilities in question, and the problem of finding strictly comparable groups of delinquents and non-delinquents available for testing (Murray, 1976). Nevertheless, some studies of young delinquents, employing large batteries of tests, and including tasks of specialized sensory-motor skills (such as tactile recognition of shapes, speed of tapping and complex spatial judgements) have found a characteristic pattern of slight deficits which resembles the pattern found among persons with known neurological impairments (Slavin, 1978; Fromm-Auch et al., 1980). Minor neurological disturbances, suggestive of subtle forms of brain damage, frequently accompany the so-called hyperkinetic syndrome of childhood. This consists of a combination of overactivity, restlessness, resistance to discipline and general anti-sociality. The overlap between this supposedly neuropsychiatric disorder and ordinary juvenile delinquency is very obvious (Sandberg et al., 1980; Stewart et al., 1981).

In our study, Dr H. B. Gibson (see Appendix IV, ref. 6) developed the Spiral Maze Test, a measure of speed and accuracy in a task calling for well co-ordinated movements. The boys were asked to trace with a pencil a continuous line along a printed spiral track without letting the line touch or cross the borders or any of the 'obstructions', which were represented by small printed circles dotted along the path. They were urged to go as fast as they could and were timed by stop-watch. The ratio of errors to time taken provided a measure of clumsiness. If neurological dysfunction, manifest in poor psycho-motor co-ordination, is characteristic of delinquents, a high score on this test should be predictive of juvenile delinquency – and so it turned out. A score indicative of clumsiness, obtained by combining the results of the Spiral Maze with those from two other psycho-motor tests, was very significantly predictive of juvenile delinquency. The clumsiness scores, however, were closely correlated with IQ scores. After matching for IQ, delinquents and non-delinquents no longer differed significantly on clumsiness, and after matching for clumsiness they no longer differed on IQ (see Appendix IV, ref. 2, p. 110). Seemingly, the relative inferiority of our delinquents in psycho-motor performance was not due to a specific defect, but merely reflected their lower level of general intelligence. In other words, the delinquents' clumsiness was no worse than might have been expected from their poor performance generally.

Since we did not apply tests for specific cognitive dysfunctions the hypothesis that unidentified learning disabilities attributable to brain damage play a part in promoting delinquency has not been disproved. However, our results do suggest that brain damage of a kind that might produce minor clumsiness without loss of intelligence is not a feature of the generality of delinquents. Clinical evidence suggests that the more serious degrees of brain damage (sufficient to produce physical signs of spasticity or epilepsy as well as intellectual defect) may provoke behavioural disturbance in children, but such conditions affect relatively small minorities. They might not show up in a small sample such as ours and they could not account for the generality of delinquency.

Crime in the family

Of the five key factors predictive of delinquency which were described at the beginning of this chapter, parental criminality was the most powerful. Youthful crime often seems to be part of a family tradition. Analysis of the conviction records of members of the study sample, their parents and siblings revealed a high concentration among a quite small minority of families. A count based on records available in 1974 showed that the members of 4.6 per cent of the families (18 of 394) had attracted almost a half (581 of 1217) of all the convictions recorded (see Appendix IV, ref. 3, p. 111).

A further analysis was carried out based on criminal records of members of the study up to their twenty-third birthdays, and of their presumed natural parents and siblings up to the year 1978. (Men no longer in the UK at age 22 were omitted, and so were 14 men with a younger brother also in the study. This was to avoid counting the same parents twice.) It emerged that the risk of a man acquiring a conviction by his twenty-third birthday was more than doubled if his father had a conviction record. Of 102 men in the study sample who had a convicted father, 52 (51.0 per cent) were delinquents, compared with only 67 (23.8 per cent) of the 281 men whose fathers had no known conviction record. The analysis was repeated with the inclusion of both the members of the study sample and all of their brothers who had been born before 1961. The larger numbers so obtained displayed the trend still more clearly. The 102 criminal fathers had 261 sons of whom 135 (51.7 per cent) were convicted delinquents and 91 (34.9 per cent) were recidivists. In contrast, the 281 fathers with no known criminal record had 526 sons of whom only 144 (27.4 per cent) were delinquents and 73 (13.9 per cent) were recidivists (see Appendix IV, ref. 40, p. 123).

If family members other than fathers were convicted this also increased the probability of delinquency in sons. Of 21 members of the study with a mother, but not a father, with a conviction record, 47.6 per cent became delinquents. However, because convicted fathers were more numerous than convicted mothers they influenced more boys. A delinquent brother increased the likelihood of delinquency whether or not the father also had a record. This was not explained by the fact that delinquents had more brothers than non-delinquents for the difference in delinquency held true when men with the same number of brothers were compared. It did not seem to be the case that older brothers were leading younger ones astray. The proportion of sons in the middle position in their families who became delinquents was almost the same in families with a younger convicted son as in those with an older son with a conviction record (see Appendix IV, ref. 30, p. 181). The actual number of persons in the family with a conviction record was important. The chances of a man being a delinquent were some three and a half times greater if he had more than two other family members with a record than if he belonged to a conviction-free family (see Appendix IV, ref. 3, p. 113).

One of the reasons for the concentration of criminal records among a minority of families was the phenomenon of assortative mating, criminal men being more likely than others to have criminal wives. Thus, 58.0 per cent of the members of the study sample with a criminal mother also had a convicted father, compared with only 21.9 per cent of those whose mothers were free from any known conviction (see Appendix IV, ref. 40, p. 124). Another contributary factor was the relatively large size of criminal families, which meant they had more offspring at risk.

It seems a plausible assumption that in some way criminal parents transmit to their children their own delinquent tendencies, but other explanations are possible. Labelling theorists might suggest that once the stigma of a criminal conviction is applied to someone in a family it remains indefinitely and renders the children of that family particularly likely to be convicted should any misconduct occur. Some evidence for this emerged from an analysis carried out in 1974, by which date 28 per cent of the youths in the study had been convicted (see Appendix IV, ref. 3, p. 118). The sample was divided into four groups according to their rank scores on self-reported delinquency at ages 14 and 16 (see p. 23). At each level of delinquent tendency, as judged by self-report, those with a relative convicted included a higher proportion of officially convicted delinquents. As expected, most of those in the group representing the highest scorers on self-reported delinquency were in fact convicted (46 out of 76), but the proportion was much higher (78 per cent against 33 per cent) if another family member had a criminal record than if the man came from a conviction-free family. Again, among those in the lowest quarter on self-reported delinquency, convicted delinquents were correspondingly much fewer (8 out of 85), but were relatively much more prevalent (26 per cent against 1.7 per cent) if they came from a criminal family. Thus, while confirming that the worst behaved were more likely to be convicted, the findings also suggested that, apart from the level of the individual's misbehaviour, having another member of the family with a criminal conviction record considerably increased his own chances of being convicted. In case the result might have been produced through some kind of bias in the self-report scores (perhaps boys from criminal families were less inclined to make admissions), the analysis was repeated using instead rankings on 'troublesomeness' derived from comments by teachers and classmates at primary school. Again, as troublesomeness increased so did the prevalence of official delinquency, but at each level of troublesomeness those from criminal families were much more likely to sustain a conviction.

The findings do not explain how, apart from their behaviour, youths from criminal families carried a higher risk of being convicted. Local police have records of names and addresses of criminals and suspects in their area, so it is possible that their method of dealing with a young person could be influenced by knowing he comes from a criminal family. Less direct influences might also be at work. For example, criminal records are commoner among large poor families residing in particular streets. Youngsters from such backgrounds may be watched over more closely and dealt with more sharply than those more fortunately placed. A recent research study in London (Landau, 1981) showed that an apprehended juvenile's chances of prosecution for certain offences were significantly affected by his area of residence and whether he happened to be black. Very likely the juvenile's willingness or unwillingness to co-operate with the investigating police officer has considerable relevance to the decision to prosecute. A criminal conviction is the end product of a complex chain of decisions by complainants, witnesses, police and courts. At all stages of the process, especially when the matter is not too serious and the offender is youthful, decisions are liable to be affected by issues extraneous to the nature of the misbehaviour in question. Among the many factors that help to determine the outcome are the appearance and responses of the suspect, his reputation and background, whether he denies the accusation, whether his parents protest on his behalf or join in condemning him and whether he is one of the minority who have legal representation at the juvenile court. These determinants of the likelihood of conviction are themselves profoundly affected by family characteristics, such as poverty, which in turn tend to be associated with a parental conviction record.

All this has a bearing upon current controversies as to the origin of and appropriate treatment for youthful delinquency. Social workers are apt to look upon delinquency as a manifestation of individual maladjustment rooted in family problems. Sociologists tend to see it as a natural response to the economic and political structure of society, an inevitable result of the suppression of youthful desires and aspirations, which is especially noticeable where it is most acutely felt, namely among the underprivileged sections of the community. If, in fact, the forces of social control are applying the delinquency label more readily to selected groups — the offspring of criminal parents, for example — this would serve to exaggerate the apparent deviance of such families and so provide spurious justification for regarding them as pathological. Since most of our findings highlight the deviant characteristics of delinquent individuals, and so might be regarded as supportive of psychological rather than sociological interpretations, it is right to emphasize a finding that shows how membership of a stigmatized minority may bring with it an unfair risk of being processed as a delinquent. At the same time it is plain that unfair labelling can be no more than a partial explanation of the transmission of delinquent tendency from parents to children, for delinquency, as measured by self-report independently of official records, was very significantly correlated with parental criminality.

In searching for clues as to how paternal criminality might influence sons to become delinquent a puzzling feature came to light. In keeping with the observation that criminal careers do not often extend into adult life, many of the fathers' conviction records were limited to minor offences of long ago. For example, 44 of the 102 so-called 'criminal' fathers had no conviction since the son in the study was born, and yet a high proportion of the sons of these 44 men (56.8 per cent) became delinquents.

A doubt was cast upon this result when it was realized that some of the criminal records pertaining to fathers' earlier years were not available. This applied particularly to the older men, those born before 1910, for whom scarcely any findings of guilt for juvenile offences were located. When these fathers were young, juvenile offences were not always reported to the Criminal Record Office. Other fathers had spent their youth abroad. The biggest loss of records, however, was the result of destruction of old files under rulings that allowed records containing only non-serious offences of more than ten years past to be weeded. (Fortunately for the research many such files had escaped destruction.) The net result was that fathers appeared to have had fewer youthful convictions than expected in view of the number of convictions sustained during their later years. We suspected that the link between paternal convictions of the distant past and sons' delinquency might be spurious, if early records that were particularly serious were selectively preserved, but this explanation was conclusively disproved. Most of the available records of criminal fathers who had been free from convictions since the son in the study was born were not serious. Of a total of 44 such records a majority of 31 had only juvenile convictions, or at most only one conviction as an adult, but even so as many as 58.1 per cent of these 31 men had a delinquent son in the study (see Appendix IV, ref. 40, p. 123).

The offences of members of the study sample were compared with those recorded against their fathers when they were of a similar age (see Appendix IV, ref. 42, table II). In the two generations the crimes committed by juveniles were distributed similarly between the various types of offence, with some 90 per cent falling into the category of dishonesty. In the early adult age-range (17–23 inclusive) the fathers' records included no drugs offences and a smaller proportion (5.1 per cent as opposed to 11.0 per cent) of aggressive crimes. One cannot be sure of the correct interpretation, since prosecution practices may have changed, but, such as it is, the evidence is in agreement with the commonly held opinion that violence has become more prevalent. Where the conviction record of fathers included one or more offences of violence against the person their delinquent sons were no more likely than other delinquents to have a conviction for violence. Specialization in violent crime was exceptional among both fathers and sons.

Relatively few fathers were imprisoned during their sons' lifetimes, so family disruption from this cause could not have been a factor in the generality of delinquency among sons, although it may have had serious effects when it did happen. Of the 8 members of the study who had a father sentenced to imprisonment after the son had attained his tenth birthday, 7 became recidivist delinquents (see Appendix IV, ref. 40, p. 124).

Fathers with recidivist conviction careers extending into relatively recent years were particularly likely to have delinquent sons. Counting both sons belonging to the sample and their brothers, the 90 men whose fathers had been convicted more than once since the year 1950 included a significantly higher proportion of delinquents (62.2 per cent) than the 95 men whose fathers had been convicted only once since 1950 (35.8 per cent) (ibid., p. 123).

It would seem that the minority of fathers whose continued criminal activities impinged directly upon the lives of their sons were particularly likely to produce delinquent sons. Nevertheless, the largest difference in incidence of delinquency was between men whose fathers had no traceable conviction record and those whose fathers had some kind of record, however stale or trivial. Whether or not the father had a record, rather than the quality of the record, was the crucial factor. Unless the whole of the effect can be attributed to 'labelling', which does not seem likely, one must look to some more subtle method of transmitting delinquent tendency from father to son than by father's continuing bad example.

Direct inculcation of criminal attitudes and habits by parents in their children was probably extremely rare. The records included very few instances of children being involved as accomplices in their parents' offences. Where this happened it was more likely to be a mother and daughter shop-lifting together than a father and son co-operating in house-breaking. Parental attitudes towards youthful delinquency were almost always censorious, regardless of the parents' own delinquent history.

A more plausible hypothesis was that criminal parents brought up their children less well than other parents, but there was little evidence for this. Boys with criminal fathers were not, to any significant extent, more likely than those with non-criminal fathers to have been exposed to unsatisfactory child-rearing behaviour, at any rate not according to the assessments by social workers when the boys were aged between 8 and 10. The small minorities with criminal mothers or imprisoned fathers did fare worse in this regard, but not the generality of boys with a convicted parent (see Appendix IV, ref. 30, p. 185). In one respect, however, both 'criminal' fathers and 'criminal' mothers tended to fall short of the standards of the average parent, their boys being reportedly less well supervised (Appendix IV, ref. 2, pp. 42, 55, 217). After matching for the degree of supervision exercised, a parent's criminal record made much less difference to the likelihood of a son becoming a delinquent.

Poor supervision, which was an assessment made by the social workers, meant a combination of laxity in applying rules of behaviour and lack of vigilance in watching over the child's activities and his whereabouts. Poor supervision could be one of the most important ways in which parents fail to protect their sons from delinquency.

This was certainly the opinion of Glueck and Glueck (1950, p. 261) based upon their protracted studies of cohorts of American delinquents. More recently, Harriet Wilson (1980) has arrived at a similar conclusion from a survey in the West Midlands of families affected by varying degrees of social handicap. Parents who were lax in their supervision (for instance, allowing their children to roam the streets without a set time for return and without knowing where they were) were more likely to produce delinquents, and highly likely to do so if they resided in areas of high delinquency rate. Wilson noted, however, that living in a poor neighbourhood, lacking such amenities as private yards or gardens where children's play could be supervised, the children needed to learn from an early age to stand up for themselves on their own, and their parents felt obliged to allow them more independence than they might otherwise have wished. The correlation between low family income and poor parental supervision, noted by both Wilson and ourselves, was perhaps as much the result of social pressures as the freely chosen style of the parents concerned. This could be the clue to why we found parents with a criminal record to be lax in supervision while appearing to maintain more usual standards in the personal aspects of child-rearing behaviour, such as degree of affection, methods of punishment, consistency of discipline and harmony between parents. On the other hand, it could be that some common factor in the character of parents, such as intellectual or educational deficit, contributed to both their lower standards of supervision and their liability to criminal convictions.

If criminal parents have deviant standards of supervision they might also have deviant attitudes to authority which they communicate to their children. We looked for evidence of this. At ages 14 and 16 the boys in the study were given questionnaires to test their attitudes towards the police. Delinquents expressed significantly more hostile attitudes than non-delinquents, although it was noticeable that the hostility developed for the most part after they had experience of being convicted (see p. 107). The parents were not questioned on the matter, but it is a reasonable assumption that convicted fathers would be more hostile to the police than others. If so, they failed to communicate their views to their sons. The non-delinquent sons of convicted fathers were just about the same as other non-delinquents in their opinions of the police (see Appendix IV, ref. 30, p. 184).

One characteristic of criminal fathers which appeared to repeat itself among their sons was a readiness to become dependent upon state welfare. With the help of the Department of Health and Social Security, the claims for benefits by fathers and sons were compared (see Appendix IV, ref. 35). Two criteria were investigated; first, an insufficiency of National Insurance contributions. Persons with long, unexplained periods without work are likely to contribute less than fluence of fathers upon the onset of criminal careers waned after their sons attained the age of majority, for the same proportion, about 10 per cent, of both convicted and unconvicted fathers had a son in the of less than 30 weekly contributions per year. Since leaving school, and up to the time their records were searched in 1975, the delinquent sons in the study, compared with the non-delinquents, had a similar excesss of poor contributions, 34 per cent against 11 per cent. The 'criminal' fathers with 'poor' contribution records produced a high proportion of sons in the study, both delinquents and non-delinquents, with similarly 'poor' contribution records.

The second criterion examined was a claim for unemployment benefit. A third of the criminal fathers, compared with only a tenth of the non-criminal fathers, had made at least one successful claim in the years 1955–65. Nearly two-thirds of the delinquent sons, compared with little more than a quarter of the non-delinquents in the sample, had received some unemployment benefit since leaving school and up to the time of the record searches in 1975. Furthermore, there was a clear association between claims for unemployment benefit by fathers and by their sons, which held true regardless of the son's delinquency status. Where the father had received benefit 54 per cent of the sons in the study had received benefit also, but where the father had not received benefit during the years under consideration only 32 per cent of their sons in the sample had done so.

It was clear that more than average demands upon unemployment benefit and neglect of welfare contributions (both criteria being a reflection of erratic work history) were significantly associated with criminality among both fathers and sons. Furthermore, where these characteristics were found among fathers, their sons had a significantly increased likelihood of showing similar characteristics. One plausible interpretation of these results is that fathers who give relatively low priority to regularity and self-sufficiency in employment tend to produce sons with a similar value-system and who are therefore, like their fathers, particularly prone to criminality.

Another possibility, but one which we could not explore, was that a paternal history of offending might reflect some aspect of temperament which fathers passed on to their sons by heredity, so that when the boys reached the appropriate age they began to react as their fathers had done at a similar stage of life. This is not altogether implausible. Evidence for a slight but significant genetic contribution to delinquent tendency has been obtained both from studies of twins (Christiansen, 1977) and from studies of adopted children (Hutchings and Mednick, 1977).

It is noted later (see p. 75) that latecomers to crime, those whose first convictions did not occur until after the eighteenth birthday, did not have any appreciable excess of convicted parents. Certainly

the influence of fathers upon the onset of criminal careers waned after
their sons attained the age of majority, for the same proportion, about
10 per cent, of both convicted and unconvicted fathers had a son in the
sample who was first convicted for offences committed between the
eighteenth and twenty-fifth birthdays. Seemingly, men who become
delinquents after their period of dependency upon their family of
origin is over do so for reasons other than the influence of their father's
conviction record. This is not a result that would be expected if heredity
were an important determinant of both youthful delinquent tendency
and criminality starting later.

One of the problems with a survey such as the present study is that
it raises questions which can only be answered by further research. It
brings to light not only the many influences that contribute to delinquency, but also the interactions between these influences, without
providing sufficient data to identify the complex chains of cause and
effect that are involved. The topic of family transmission of criminality
illustrates this particularly well. A process which might have been
thought relatively simple turns out to have multiple and confusing
ramifications. Without doubt a criminal record in a parent or sibling
predisposes to delinquency, but probably for many different reasons.
In the small minority of disorderly families in which everyone is in
some sort of trouble with the authorities – neighbours, schools, social
workers, housing department or police – 'criminality' is but one feature
of an ongoing saga of multiple deviance. In other cases the same neighbourhood influences and social handicaps which contributed to a
parent's criminality continue to operate on the children. In some cases
the stigma of a long past conviction may continue to exert some effect.
In other cases one suspects that subtle qualities of temperament and
attitude which encouraged youthful rebellion and delinquency in the
parents when they were young are communicated to the children, but
more likely by unwitting example than by direct instruction.

Parental behaviour

The most obvious concomitants of delinquency are external social
factors such as socio-economic status, area of residence, ethnic origin
and peer-group affiliations. It has been argued that criminologists pay
far too much attention to child–parent interactions and that social
policies are too much preoccupied with the emotional problems of individual families, whereas 'the more pressing need is to help families combat
the pressures of the external environment since it is those pressures that
impact most directly on the behaviour of their offspring' (Johnstone,
1980). I think this view is mistaken. In the earlier years of life, at any rate,
the social factors that affect children do so through the parents, who are
the main transmitters of the expectations and attitudes of their milieu.

Early upbringing is probably the most important reason why, even in the most crime-ridden localities, some youngsters successfully resist the pressures to adopt a delinquent life-style. In our study, unsatisfactory upbringing, like other key factors of early background, was significantly predictive of youthful delinquency, and of recidivism persisting into adulthood, but it did not predict criminality beginning for the first time in later years.

In view of all that has been written about the importance of parent—child relationships, it was somewhat surprising that this factor appeared to be no more important than other simpler criteria, such as paternal conviction record or large-sized family. On the other hand, parental behaviour is a complex phenomenon not easily observed or measured. Recent psychological research indicates that very prolonged observations, in which actual items of behaviour are recorded as they occur naturally in the home setting, are necessary in order to obtain a realistic evaluation (Reid, 1978). Problems of communication, faulty recollection and confused emotions interfere with parents' reports even when they are highly motivated to give accurate accounts.

As was mentioned in Chapter I, we found parental behaviour particularly hard to assess. We had to depend very largely upon the impressionistic judgements of social workers which may not have been very reliable. Nevertheless, alternative approaches, notably the use of questionnaires, proved no more useful. Parents who had been approached initially in an informal way, and had been willing to discuss topics of interest to them in the course of unstructured conversation, were less inclined to fill in forms or to answer a schedule of set questions, the relevance of which was not so obvious to them. The substantial number of questionnaires that remained uncompleted, even after repeated requests, was an indication of their reluctance, and those who did provide answers may not all have done so very conscientiously. Questionnaire assessments of parental authoritarianism (see Appendix IV, ref. 2, p. 74), maternal neuroticism (Cornell Medical Index, ibid., pp. 76, 210) and parental discipline (ibid., pp. 229—32) gave scores much less closely related to delinquency than did the social workers' impressions based upon less structured interview conversations and observations.

We used the social workers' assessments in preference to the questionnaire scores because they were more closely linked with delinquency potential, but the disadvantage of these evaluations was that they failed to focus clearly upon the different aspects of parental behaviour that they purported to measure. Each individual rating tended to be influenced by a multiplicity of impressions that were not strictly relevant to the item under consideration. This may have increased the correlations with delinquency, but at the expense of some doubt as to the precise nature of the features responsible for the correlations.

Evaluations of such items as marital conflict, style of discipline, consistency between parents in the handling of the child and emotional warmth were all so closely intercorrelated that it proved impossible to sort out one from another. The best one could do was to combine the different assessments into a single, global impression of the overall satisfactoriness or unsatisfactoriness of parental behaviour.

Doubtless these problems were caused in large part by the 'halo effect', that is, the tendency to perceive things as either all good or all bad, but there was also a real difficulty in trying to distinguish between expressed attitudes, underlying feelings and actual behaviour. For example, following the system used by McCord *et al*., (1959) mothers' attitudes were classed as 'loving normal', 'loving anxious', 'over-protective', or 'cruel, passive or neglecting' (see Appendix IV, ref. 1, pp. 73–85). Although the definitions of these descriptive categories were made as full as possible, and were thought to be well understood and consistently applied by the interviewers, these judgements did involve hypothetical distinctions between behaviour motivated by 'love' and similar behaviour differently motivated. It is arguable that such distinctions, however well made, are meaningless, since only actions count. However that may be, it would probably have been better to direct the interviewers' efforts to the recording of specific items from the parents' accounts of their actual behaviour (such as how often and in what circumstances they employed physical methods of punishment, or whether they had ever met any of the child's teachers) rather than to permit speculation as to parental feelings or to try to force complex mixtures of behaviour into a limited number of predetermined categories. Of course, it is easy to be wise after the event.

Unlike fixed items, such as the parents' past conviction record or the number of younger siblings, parental behaviour may well vary over the years. Parents who were repeatedly rated unfavourably by different social workers over a period of years were particularly likely to have delinquent sons (see Appendix IV, ref. 2, p. 50). Our main predictive assessments, however, were based on the impressions recorded when the boys were 8–10 years of age. According to psychoanalytic theories, the crucial time for character formation comes earlier in life, which suggests that parental behaviour during infancy might have been more relevant. The unfavourable features that contributed to the general rating of 'unsatisfactory' parental behaviour included marital conflict, the dominance of one parent over the other in decision-making relating to the children, inconsistency between the parents in their handling of the child, attitudes of indifference, positive rejection or neglect, over-strict or erratically varying discipline and harsh methods of enforcement. In effect, this is very much the same kind of list as other investigators have produced (Glueck and Glueck, 1968; Patterson, 1981; Delfini *et al*., 1976).

Psychoanalytic literature is almost obsessively preoccupied with events during infancy and, in particular, with the necessity for a close and uninterrupted bond, both physical and emotional, between mother and baby. John Bowlby (1951), the arch protagonist of this 'bonding' theory, suggests that separation of mother and baby during the critical early years permanently impairs the child's capacity to form loving, trusting relationships, so that he develops into an 'affectionless' character, unfettered by family ties or feelings of loyalty or obligation, and hence likely to pursue an antisocial or delinquent life-style.

Bowlby's claims about the serious results of physical separation from the mother, and the ineffectiveness of substitute mothering, have been contradicted by objective research (Casler, 1961; Rutter, 1972). The Cambridge study found that a history of separation from one or both parents for more than a month during the first ten years was significantly associated with later delinquency, but separations under age 6 were no worse in this respect than separations between 6 and 10. What was important, however, was the reason for the break. Temporary or permanent separations occasioned by illness or death bore comparatively little relationship to offending, but separations caused by the breakdown of the parents' marriage were very significant precursors of delinquency (see Appendix IV, ref. 2, p. 72). Others have found the same (Douglas *et al*., 1968). Further analysis of the study sample, counting all permanent breaks from a natural parent up to a boy's fifteenth birthday, and counting as delinquents all 131 who had any conviction for an offence committed before the twenty-fifth birthday, served only to confirm the result. Compared with the rest of the sample, the delinquents included proportionately more than twice as many from homes broken by circumstances other than death (19.9 per cent against 8.6 per cent), but just about the same proportion for homes broken by death (7.6 per cent against 6.7 per cent). It would seem that family discord is the main reason for the link between broken homes and delinquency.

The Bowlby theory suggests that family disruption would have worse effects if it occurs early in life. The Cambridge study (see Appendix IV, ref. 2, p. 71; ref. 19) found no closer association with delinquency when the breaks occurred early. The same observation was reported by McCord *et al*. (1959, p. 83) in the Cambridge Somerville follow-up study. In the much larger national sample surveyed by Douglas, however, it emerged that a significantly higher proportion became delinquents if the family break took place when the child was under 5 years of age (Wadsworth, 1979, p. 54).

As with other items of adversity, broken homes stand for a cluster of interacting circumstances. Added to the emotional stress occasioned by the loss of a parent is the stress caused by consequential loss of income and the deterioration in standards of child care that may come about through a parent being unexpectedly left to cope alone. The consequences for the child are likely to be worse when the break occurs during the early years of greatest dependency, and the emotional turmoil in the family is likely to be longer lasting if the break is the result of conflict between the parents.

In his more recent writings Bowlby (1973, p. 215) expresses views more in keeping with criminological research. He acknowledges the importance of other sources of disturbance than actual physical separation, such as 'threats to abandon the child made for disciplinary purposes', marital quarrels engendering fears that a parent may leave home, or talk of suicide. He suggests that both separations and 'instabilities of maternal care' may lead to untoward responses, and that these may take two contrasting forms, anxious attachment or aggressive detachment (ibid., p. 225). It is only children who respond in the latter way who become aggressive, disobedient, apparently neither trusting nor caring for others and potentially delinquent. Whichever of these two patterns becomes established in the first five years tends to persist into later life.

The theory that disturbed parental relationships provoke anxiety and neurotic symptoms in some children and antisociality or delinquency in others did in fact receive some support from the Cambridge study results. The social workers identified a minority of boys who were socially withdrawn (that is, shy, ill at ease in social situations, easily embarrassed, stand-offish or 'living in fantasy') or had nervous symptoms (such as tics, sleep disturbances or bed-wetting) (see Appendix IV, ref. 1, pp. 45 ff). These 'nervous-withdrawn' boys, even more than delinquents, tended to have experienced unsatisfactory parental behaviour, but, in spite of this, relatively few became delinquents (Appendix IV, ref. 2, p. 115). It would seem that a timid, shy, anxious temperament tends to deter boys from responding to family disturbance with rebellious, aggressive, delinquent reactions. They may, however, evince other forms of social maladjustment, as will be shown later when the group from bad homes who did not become delinquents is examined (see pp. 90–6). Although a broad distinction between 'neurotic' or 'delinquent' types seems possible in the majority of cases, the study findings did suggest, as have other surveys that looked into the matter (Bennett, 1960), that mixtures of the two types are not infrequent. Many delinquent juveniles display some of the traits that are also typical of the neurotic, notably unsociability, poor school performance, sleep and speech disturbance, tantrums and feelings of rejection.

The importance of an isolated trauma in an otherwise normal family setting has been exaggerated. The typical criminogenic family is beset by chronic problems. The Cambridge study found no evidence for the predominant importance of the circumstances of early life over those of later years. Delinquents tended to come from families with continuing disturbances that affected children in their school days as much as in their infancy and which manifested themselves in many different ways. For instance, parents who let their children spend most of their leisure time away from the family, fathers who never took part in their sons' leisure activities, and mothers whose expectations for their sons' future career prospects were low in comparison with his educational achievement level, were all more likely than others to have sons becoming delinquents (see Appendix IV, ref. 2, pp. 56—7).

A particularly noticeable characteristic of the parents of many of the delinquents in the study was carelessness or laxity in matters of supervision. They were less concerned than other parents to watch over or to know about their children's doings, whereabouts and companions, and they failed to enforce or to formulate fixed rules about such things as punctuality, manners, bedtime, television viewing or tidying up (Appendix IV, ref. 1, p. 74). Poor standards of supervision were not necessarily associated with lack of affection, but they were particularly prevalent among large, poor families (Appendix IV, ref. 2, pp. 55—6). Similar observations were made by Harriet Wilson (1974) in her surveys of parental behaviour among the poor. Families that tolerate low standards of social behaviour, perhaps because of the circumstances under which they are obliged to live, may be affectionate and supportive towards each other while at loggerheads with the wider society on account of the uncontrolled and delinquent behaviour of their offspring. However important a 'loving' relationship may be in shaping character, it is no insurance against delinquency unless accompanied by adequate social training.

This point is central to the conflict between social learning theorists and psychoanalysis. In attributing such predominant importance to the magic bond between mother and baby, analysts underestimate the need for consistent conditioning through the years of childhood and early adolescence. A positive and secure attachment established in early years may facilitate social learning at every stage, but unless sufficient learning situations are provided social requirements cannot be communicated, however ready the child may be to receive them. In so far as our findings have any bearing upon this controversy they favour the view that social learning via parental example and instruction is a continuous process throughout childhood.

CHAPTER IV

The Delinquent Personality

Eysenck's theory

A certain amount of rule-breaking is a normal manifestation of the excitement-seeking phase of youthful development, but the minority whose persistent misbehaviour leads to a criminal record, especially a recidivist record, are not exactly average representatives of their age-group. Many years ago a previous work by the present writer entitled *The Young Offender* appeared with a photograph on the cover depicting a tough-looking youth in leather jacket and boots clutching a belt as if about to swing it at someone. A correspondent in the *Guardian* wrote protesting at the publisher's exploitation of an image that scarcely corresponded to the delinquents described in the book. Nevertheless, this picture of an untamed beast is not unlike the stereotype of the poorly socialized, aggressive, impulsive, hedonistic character with a low frustration tolerance, a self-centred outlook and a hatred of authority that is described in many psychological texts on delinquency. In point of fact, and against the investigators' expectations, it appeared from the interviews with members of the study at age 18 that the more extreme delinquents did begin to approximate to this stereotype, while others displayed at least some of the attributes described.

On the whole, attempts to identify the essential components of the personality of the potential delinquent, and to devise psychological tests to assess them, have not been particularly successful. One of the best-known theories purporting to explain why certain personality types should be vulnerable to delinquency has been developed by Hans Eysenck (1977). If he is right, it should be possible to use his personality tests to predict convictions.

Long before he turned his attention to the personality characteristics of criminals Eysenck had identified two fundamental dimensions of temperamental variation, extraversion–introversion and neuroticism, which were supposedly based upon genetically determined variations in the functioning of the central nervous system. Pronounced extroverts are outgoing, expressive, sociable, impulsive individuals who enjoy action and risk taking. At the opposite extreme, pronounced introverts are quiet, introspective, orderly, cautious and not given to outward displays of feeling. The brain cortex of introverts is said to be in a state of greater physiological arousal than that of extraverts, which makes for easy conditioning and swift and effective social learning. Extraverts are believed to have more sluggish, less highly tuned neurophysiology. They respond less readily to conditioning and so experience greater difficulty in learning to control their primitive, instinctual impulses and are more likely to remain unsocialized and aggressive and to take to delinquency. Persons with a high degree of neuroticism are unduly anxious, worrying and prone to neurotic symptoms when under stress. Those who are low in neuroticism are placid and stable. Persons high in neuroticism are believed to have over-reactive autonomic nervous systems which makes them emotionally labile. If they are also extraverted, their excessive emotional drive exacerbates their other qualities, notably their impulsiveness and aggressiveness. Thus the theory predicts that delinquent populations should contain an excess of neurotic extraverts, that is, persons who are high on both personality dimensions.

Eysenck and his collaborators have developed several personality questionnaires for scoring individuals according to their degrees of extraversion and neuroticism. In the Cambridge study one of these, the New Junior Maudsley Personality Inventory, was given to boys at ages 8, 10 and again at 14. The scores showed no significant excess of neurotic extraverts among the juvenile delinquents, such as would have been anticipated according to the Eysenck theory (see Appendix IV, ref. 2, p. 113).

Another questionnaire for assessing neuroticism and extraversion, the Eysenck Personality Inventory, was given to the boys at age 16. Again, no significant correlation between neurotic extraversion and officially registered juvenile delinquency emerged, but there were significant correlations with the self-reported delinquency assessments, both those at age 14–16 and those at age 18. Furthermore, there was a just significant excess of neurotic extraverts among delinquents who were first convicted as adults, that is, between the seventeenth and twenty-first birthdays (Appendix IV, ref. 46).

These later results could well be artefactual. If some youths have a confessional tendency, admitting both their delinquencies and their more questionable personality characteristics more readily than most, this bias could produce a spurious correlation between high self-reported delinquency scores and high scores on neuroticism and extraversion. In fact, after controlling for self-reported delinquency scores, neurotic extraverts were no longer significantly over-presented among the delinquents first convicted as adults.

In later research, Farrington (Appendix IV, ref. 46) investigated the matter further. He found that the intercorrelations between the responses to the various questionnaire items that purportedly measured neuroticism were quite low, and those measuring extraversion lower still.

This cast doubt on the validity of the scores as measures of basic, unitary dimensions of personality. Examining the correlations between each individual questionnaire item and the delinquency measures, it emerged that only two of the 57 questions ('Do you often long for excitement?' 'Do you generally do things quickly without stopping to think?') were significantly related to both self-reported juvenile delinquency and adult official delinquency. This amounted to slight confirmation of other evidence suggesting that delinquents are impulsive and like excitement, but otherwise these additional questionnaire results did little or nothing to support the Eysenck theory. Equally equivocal or frankly contradictory findings have been obtained in other attempts to apply Eysenck inventories to delinquent populations (Farrington, 1981). It would appear that either the personality attributes of the generality of delinquents do not in fact conform to Eysenck's predictions, or that his inventories are not effective measures of the attributes in question. Certainly, our own attempts to identify a crime-prone group by means of assessments of neuroticism and extraversion proved unfruitful.

The antisocial character

In contrast to the failure of personality tests to establish delinquent characteristics, the interviews at age 18 yielded a wealth of information about the surprising differences between the life-style and attitudes of the delinquents and that of their peers.

The interviews at 18 were the most ambitious of the entire research. The vast majority took place in the office, with the young men being ferried back and forth by car where necessary. They lasted, on average, two hours, but in some instances considerably longer. The use of many prearranged questions, with a fairly elaborate instruction manual for coding the responses, permitted systematic coverage of a wide range of topics. Since many of the items were inter-related, checks on internal consistency gave some indication of the conscientiousness of the men's responses (see Appendix IV, ref. 3, p. 77), as did comparisons between answers given at this interview with information from the past (from previous interviews, home visits and school surveys) or from independent sources (for example, the reports that were sometimes available from social services, probation officers, police and other informants). The outcome of all such checks was to produce an impression of surprising frankness and substantial accuracy, but with a tendency, in most contexts, to underplay rather than to exaggerate socially deviant behaviour.

Apart from the self-reported delinquency questions (see pp. 23–4) and many open-ended questions about experiences with courts and police, the interview schedule included inquiries about employment histories, leisure activities, income and expenditure, family relationships, involvement in fights, use of alcohol, tobacco and prohibited drugs, and sexual experience. Social attitudes were assessed by a questionnaire which invited agreement or otherwise with 49 separate propositions (see Appendix IV, ref. 3, pp. 186–9) such as: 'Boys who get the chance should stay on at school' (endorsed by 84.8 per cent of the 389 respondents) or 'Pot-smokers should be left alone by the police' (endorsed by 50.9 per cent).

Some of the findings illustrated more clearly than any official statistic the kind of population from which the study sample was drawn. For example, a substantial majority, about three-fifths, had left school under the age of 16. The jobs they were doing were mostly such as required no apprenticeship, no day-release education and no protracted in-service training. In response to questioning as to whether they participated at least once a month in various leisure pursuits, it emerged that the most popular activity, acknowledged by 347 men (89.2 per cent) was 'going to pubs'. 'Reading' was acknowledged by 175 (54.0 per cent), 'going to youth clubs' by only 56 (14.4 per cent). More went to betting shops (19.5 per cent) than to evening classes (12.1 per cent). Only 20.9 per cent replied they would vote Conservative if forced to choose between Labour and Conservative. However, our purpose was not to document the life of working-class males but to explore the difference between the 101 young men with an official conviction record, for offences committed before the interview at age 18, and the other 288 men interviewed who were their non-delinquent age mates and social peers.

At least eleven separate social characteristics of a generally undesirable nature were found to be significantly more prevalent among the delinquents than among the non-delinquents. These are listed in Table 7.

As can be seen at a glance, most of these eleven characteristics were some two to three times more prevalent among the delinquents than among the non-delinquents. Only 42 of the 288 non-delinquents (14.6 per cent) compared with 68 of 101 delinquents (67.3 per cent) had as many as four of these 'antisocial' characteristics. At the other extreme, 69 non-delinquents (24.0 per cent) compared with only 3 delinquents (2.97 per cent) were free from all eleven undesirable characteristics.

As these starkly contrasting figures demonstrate, in comparison with the rest of the sample the delinquents appear consistently more rebellious and less conformist in a wide range of contexts, that is, they are socially deviant in many ways besides their occasional thieving. Some of the differences reflected a considerable degree of divergence from conventional norms on the part of the delinquents. For instance, most of the 37.6 per cent of delinquents who were 'involved in antisocial groups' admitted recent participation in group fighting or group vandalism. Most of the 45.5 per cent of delinquents (and 11.5 per cent of non-delinquents) assessed as 'high' on self-reported aggression admitted

Table 7   Contrasts between delinquents and non-delinquents on eleven social characteristics

Social characteristic	Total men concerned	Percentage among 101 delinquents	Percentage among 288 non-delinquents
Tattooed	35	22.8	4.17
High on self-reported aggression	79	45.5	11.5
Unstable job record	92	45.5	16.0
Spends leisure 'hanging about'	42	21.8	7.0
Involved in anti-social groups	81	37.6	14.9
Admits drinking and driving	85	38.6	16.0
Heavy gambler	87	37.6	17.0
Sexually experienced	164	69.3	32.6
Heavy smoker	104	43.6	20.8
Has used prohibited drugs	122	48.5	25.3
Anti-establishment attitudes	98	36.6	21.2

being involved in at least ten fights in the past three years, carrying a weapon frequently and using a weapon to injure someone. Most of the 45.5 per cent of delinquents (and 16.0 per cent of non-delinquents) categorized as having an 'unstable' job record had histories of dismissals, periods of unemployment lasting more than five weeks per year and also frequent changes of job, often without clear reason. Spending at least one evening each week just 'hanging about on the street' was admitted by 21.8 per cent of delinquents (and 7.0 per cent of non-delinquents). As many as 28.7 per cent of the delinquents (and 13.2 per cent of the non-delinquents) reported starting smoking at age 13 or less. A majority of the delinquents, 68 per cent, smoked during the interview, but only 40 per cent of the non-delinquents did so. Heavy alcohol consumption (defined as at least 20 pints of beer per week) was reported by 45.5 per cent of delinquents (and 18.1 per cent of non-delinquents). Continued use of prohibited drugs (defined as consumption on at least five occasions, including at least once in the last six months) was reported by 19.8 per cent of delinquents (and 11.3 per cent of non-delinquents), although only 3 youths had actually been convicted for a drug offence. This was an interesting illustration of disparity between assessments of the frequency of deviant behaviour from self-report and from conviction statistics. The close link between delinquency status and experience with prohibited drugs was no surprise as the connection has been frequently observed by others, including Bell and Champion (1979), who carried out a large survey in Australia.

They found, as we did, close associations between self-reported delinquency, use of illicit drugs, heavy alchohol consumption and excessive tobacco smoking.

Convictions for motoring offences — other than those incidental to taking vehicles without the owner's consent — were admitted by 30.7 per cent of delinquents and 10.8 per cent of non-delinquents. This particular contrast was all the more striking since delinquents were less likely than non-delinquents to own a vehicle or to have a driving licence. Claims to have experienced sexual intercourse at age 14 or earlier were made by 29.7 per cent of delinquents (5.9 per cent of non-delinquents). At the opposite extreme, only 6.9 per cent of delinquents, compared with 33.0 per cent of non-delinquents, said they had never had sexual intercourse. That readiness to gamble was characteristic of delinquents was confirmed by the fact that 67.3 per cent of them (and 48.2 per cent of non-delinquents) accepted the suggestion to gamble part of their interview fee (double or nothing) on the toss of a coin.

The 'anti-establishment' attitude thought to be held by 37.6 per cent of delinquents was assessed from responses to eleven items on our forty-nine item attitude questionnaire (see Appendix IV, ref. 3, p. 75). For example, 49.5 per cent of delinquents (25.0 per cent of non-delinquents) endorsed as true the statement: 'The police are always roughing people up'. An actual majority, 53.5 per cent, of delinquents (and 26.4 per cent of non-delinquents) endorsed the view that: 'School did me very little good'. As well as being prone to violent behaviour, according to their admissions of involvement in fights and weapon carrying, the delinquents also expressed aggressive attitudes. For example, 21.8 per cent of delinquents (only 6.9 per cent of non-delinquents) agreed with the item: 'I enjoy a punch up'. The 36.6 per cent of delinquents classed as aggressive in attitude were so identified by their responses to eleven such items on the attitude questionnaire.

There were indications that many of the delinquents were not finding life easy or managing their affairs effectively. An item on the attitude questionnaire: 'I have had an easy time in life' evoked disagreement by 52.5 per cent of delinquents compared with 29.2 per cent of non-delinquents. A substantial proportion of the delinquents (37.6 per cent as opposed to 16.7 per cent of non-delinquents) were not getting along in their parental homes, either they were living away or wanting to do so on account of differences with their parents, or else they frankly admitted 'not getting on well' with one or both parents. The delinquents tended to have higher incomes than the non-delinquents, because they were mostly in relatively well-paid but unskilled employment with little prospect of improvement, but they more often overspent their income, built up debts and failed to keep any money as saving.

The antisocial characteristics prevalent among delinquents at age 18 would have seemed even more striking had 39 men with only one conviction been eliminated from the comparison. For example, 25.8 per cent of the recidivists, but only 10.3 per cent of the one-time delinquents, admitted continuing use of a prohibited drug. It would be too tedious to run through all the percentages again (most of which can be found in Appendix IV, ref. 3, ch. IV); suffice to say that the clear trend was for the recidivists to deviate more extremely on all the 'antisocial' features under consideration. Whilst this result provided gloomy confirmation of the degree of deviance prevalent among recidivists, it also carried the more optimistic corollary that one-time delinquents (whose expectation of further convictions was relatively low) were considerably less deviant.

The observation that delinquent behaviour is but one item among the characteristic cluster of attributes and life-style that make up the typical antisocial personality is far from new. A similar conclusion emerged from a longitudinal study of schoolchildren and students in Colorado (Jessor and Jessor, 1977). In that example, the cluster included marijuana use, high alcohol consumption, high score on a self-reported delinquency schedule, precocious sexual activity, low commitment to academic achievement, a critical attitude to conventional social values, and tolerance of deviance. The interest of the present findings lay in the degree to which the delinquent characters stood out among a predominantly working-class, English population.

Aggressiveness and violent offences

In the area where the study was carried out the level of overt aggression among teenage youths was surprisingly high. At age 18 a majority of the sample described involvement in recent fights, many of which sounded serious. Many of the informants admitted to carrying a weapon, allegedly necessary for self-protection, and many dwelt with evident satisfaction upon the damage they had done to opponents. These were not isolated impressions. In an anonymous self-report survey of a large sample of London boys aged 12–17 Belson (1978) also found that reported violent behaviour was widespread. About 12 per cent of his total sample admitted to at least ten violent acts classed as 'serious'. Among certain groups the percentage was significantly higher, 27 per cent among truants and 23 per cent among boys whose fathers' occupations were of the lowest grade, but only 8 per cent among grammar-school boys.

In our study, notwithstanding the violent behaviour reported by some non-delinquents, outstanding aggressiveness (reflected at age 18 in the number of fights described and the number of aggressive opinions endorsed on the attitude questionnaire) was the most prominent and distinctive feature of the delinquent minority. Observations from earlier years had shown that aggressiveness was a significant character-istic of the boys destined to become official delinquents, and that aggressiveness was a particularly persistent trait. There was a statistically significant tendency for the same individuals to be picked out again and again on measures of aggression applied at different times. The point is illustrated in Figure 1 (from Appendix IV, ref. 37) which shows how boys who were assessed as 'high' or 'low' at age 8—10 were categorized in later assessments at age 12—14 and again at 16—18.

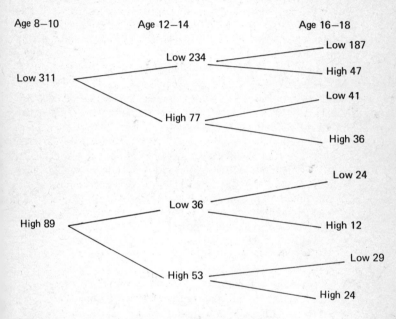

Figure 1   Aggression assessments at various ages

The first of these aggression measures came from teachers' ratings at ages 8 and 10 combined, when they were asked to nominate the boys most difficult to discipline. The second measure was derived from teachers' responses at ages 12 and 14 combined, when they were asked to score boys on disobedience, indiscipline, roughness at playtime, quarrelsomeness, or punishment (see Appendix IV, ref. 24). The last assessment was based on admissions at the interviews conducted when aged 16 of getting into fights, carrying and using weapons and fighting policemen, coupled with admissions at the interviews when the youths were aged 18 of frequent fighting, starting fights and using weapons. Over half of all the boys rated were put in the same category of aggres-sion at all three ages. Of those rated 'high' on aggression at 16—18,

30 per cent were also rated 'high' at 8—10, but of those rated 'low' at 16—18 only 16 per cent had been assessed as 'high' at 8—10. This stability of aggressive characteristics is entirely consistent with findings from many other studies. Lefkowitz *et al.* (1977, p. 101), in a longitudinal study in New York State, found great consistency in ratings of aggressiveness by various methods (including both peer ratings and self-reports) when the same individuals were assessed and reassessed at ages 9 and 19 respectively. Among personality attributes aggressiveness is second only to intelligence in its constancy over long spans of time (Olweus, 1979).

Evidence that overt aggressiveness is a characteristic of delinquents in general leaves open the question whether there remains an important minority who are prone to violence much more than to other kinds of offences. Convictions for personal violence arouse great public concern. A total of 32 members of the study (all from the 397 who were still in the UK at age 22) were at some stage convicted of offences of violence against another person. (The offences counted were actual or grievous bodily harm, wounding, robbery and assault on police. Carrying an offensive weapon, obstruction, disorderly behaviour and common, non-indictable assault were not included.) These 32 violent offenders were often to be found in the worst categories on various assessments of aggression. For example, of the 31 who had been assessed by teachers at age 14 as many as 58 per cent had been scored in the most aggressive category (compared with only 38 per cent of the non-violent delinquents and 14 per cent of the non-delinquents). Similar contrasts were obtained when the self-reported delinquency schedules at ages 14 and 16 were rescored, counting only those items referring to actual or potential violence (see Appendix IV, ref. 2, p. 170).

The aggressiveness of the delinquents who were convicted for violence reflected the fact that they were particularly persistent delinquents from particularly bad backgrounds, rather than that they were qualitatively different from other delinquents. Only 4 of them had been convicted solely on charges arising from violence. Most of them (20 out of 32) were recidivists. Among delinquents who had no conviction for violence much fewer (38 out of 99) were recidivists.

Those formally convicted for violence were not always the ones who were most violently behaved according to their own and other people's descriptions. The great majority of the 77 boys rated aggressive on their self-report responses at 14 and 16, and the great majority of the 79 men rated aggressive on the admissions they made about fighting, etc. when interviewed at 18, remained free from any actual conviction for a violent offence. One reason for this was that youths found fighting among themselves were not often prosecuted and those who resisted arrest, after being apprehended for a non-violent offence, were not necessarily charged with assault on the police.

Violence is the outcome of interaction between the aggressor and his situation. Some acts of violence result from external pressures. For example, in order to maintain status among delinquent groups a boy may have to show readiness to attack anyone who proffers an insult to himself or his friends. Other acts of violence may occur because the aggressor has an explosive temperament and is easily provoked to anger. At age 18, the youths who admitted to involvement in fights were asked to describe the most vicious incident in which they had been involved over the past three years. Out of a total of 255 'most vicious' fights, 117 were group fights in which the boy had fought alongside others. Different situations and motives characterized the group and individual fights.

Descriptions of the group fights were suggestive of a culturally determined strategy for coping with particular social situations (that is, instrumental aggression), whereas the solitary fights were more often the outcome of personal situations and anger (that is, expressive aggression). The group fights more often took place in pubs or in the street and the youths more often said they had become involved through an opponent making an unwelcome comment to themselves or their girlfriends, or because they had to go to the aid of a friend. The youths reporting individual fights were more likely to admit to being angry at the time and to initiating the fight themselves. Group fights were more likely to involve the use of weapons and to lead to injury and to attract the notice of the police.

Further analysis (Appendix IV, ref. 48) revealed little tendency for youths to specialize in either group or individual fights; those who reported several fights were likely to describe both varieties. Youths reporting a large number of fights were particularly likely to be recidivist delinquents, to express a large number of aggressive attitudes (including hatred of racial minorities), to come from large, poor, criminal families and to have other antisocial traits in addition to their aggressive propensities. Persistent aggression of both an 'instrumental' and an 'expressive' kind is significantly associated with persistent delinquency.

Even more clearly than the statistics, the actual life histories of some of the aggressive members of the sample conveyed the picture of traits of attitude and behaviour, clearly noticeable in childhood, continuing into adulthood and associated with persisting criminal careers. The following example is a case in point.

Case 590

This was a 'persisting recidivist'. Two of his six convictions were for offences involving personal violence. The first arose from an incident at age 20. He was a passenger in a friend's car when their progress was halted by a car stopped awkwardly in front of them. He got out and an altercation began with the other driver. In his own words he 'pulled him out and threw him all over the place'. He was convicted of assault occasioning actual bodily harm. The second such incident leading to a conviction was when he was 24. He said he had just parked his car when another motorist drew up and accused him of 'cutting in'. An argument and fight developed involving the companions of both men, during the course of which he drew a knife and slashed his opponent's car tyres. Initially charged with causing grievous bodily harm, he was finally convicted on this occasion of criminal damage.

He was a recidivist whose deviant life-style and delinquent habits were still prominent when he was interviewed for the last time at age 26. The interviewer described him as 'a total hedonist who drinks heavily, is a regular drug user, sexually promiscuous and does whatever suits him'. He had a child by a former cohabitee. 'He pops in to see the child when he feels like it, but regularly breaks arrangements to take the child out.' 'He is living with two mates who share his life-style and dislike for responsibilities. They are regularly getting into trouble: mainly fights and drug dealing. During the interview his mate came into the room and phoned to arrange to buy £160 of cannabis . . . He has no qualms about stealing. One of his favourite activities is "walk-in", that is nipping in when he catches sight of an open door and walking out with whatever comes to hand.' At this same interview he described a brawl at a large party in which he had been recently involved. There were many injuries and the police arrived and arrested some of his friends, but he escaped without hurt and without arrest.

Although not particularly young on the occasion of his first official finding of guilt at age 14, like most persisting recidivists his offences had in fact begun much earlier. At age 9, he was already known to our social workers as a stealer from information given to them by his parents.

This man had one juvenile conviction for taking a car. He was soon after arrested for theft, but released for lack of corroborative evidence. His adult offences were mostly for possessing or dealing in cannabis. As a child he had been described as sturdy, wilful and independent. His parents, who were both busy working, often had no idea what he was up to. He disliked school and was a persistent truant, sometimes covering up with forged notes. He was in the most aggressive category according to teachers' comments at age 12 and again at 14.

He was the product of a broken home, his mother having left and been divorced when he was aged 5. When interviewed at age 19 he said he had left home to join the army because he did not get on with his father and step-mother. Not long after the interview, however, he was discharged after receiving a sentence of imprisonment. He reported numerous fights, mostly in public houses, in which he had participated both before and during his army service. Seen again at age 21 he once more described various affrays in which he had been involved, but he was resolved to stay out of trouble with the law, or at least so he said, commenting 'I couldn't go back inside, I'd fucking top [hang] myself'.

In the next example an official criminal career came to an end at age 18, but there was evidence of aggressive behaviour continuing much longer.

Case 731

This man's fourth and last conviction was for assault on the police and being drunk and disorderly. His previous convictions were for thefts from cars and breaking and entering, but numerous episodes of fighting and drunkenness were known to the interviewers. When seen at age 18 he admitted to involvement in numerous fights over the previous three years and was ranked among the worst 10 per cent of the sample on self-reported aggression. The incident leading to his conviction was a fight with his brother, followed by assault on the police who tried to intervene. Less than a month earlier he had hit a policeman in the course of a similar family fracas, but on that occasion he was not prosecuted.

His aggressive propensities had been apparent from an early age. When he was 9 his mother reported to the social worker that he 'liked a fight' and that he had a very severe temper which broke out almost every day. He would pick up a knife and throw it. At those times 'he doesn't know what he is doing'. His brothers were said to be scared of him. In later years he was a persistent truant and a very difficult boy to control. At both ages 12 and 14 he had been placed in the most aggressive category according to teachers' reports. At a court appearance for theft when he was 17 he was said to have been 'aggressive and arrogant'.

In his earlier years he had suffered at the hands of his physically violent father, a man who had been diagnosed as an aggressive psychopath and who terrorized the family. The whole family was noted for violent outbursts. At one point both his father and elder brother were convicted following a knife fight with black neighbours.

At age 21 he was already married, working regularly and leading a much more settled life. The interviewer found him 'extroverted and charming, but still aggressive, with hostile feelings towards the police'. He described various recent fights. In one of these he had hit a man who accused him of cheating during a card game. 'I only hit him about twice. He went down and that was that.' On another occasion he was himself beaten when he went to the aid of his father-in-law who was being 'got at' by two Irishmen. He had tried but failed to grab a piece of wood with which to strike his opponent's head.

When last seen at age 26 the interviewer described him as a friendly, charming man who remains 'a bit of a lad'. 'He takes his marriage and his children very seriously indeed and is concerned for their welfare.'

He was working regularly and had a nice home. 'He is very happy with life and only involved in minor delinquencies.' He admitted to fairly regular stealing from work and to a recent escapade of stealing lead from roofs. Nevertheless, his aggressive ways had not subsided altogether. He admitted to 'about four' fights in the previous two years. The last was said to be only a brief scuffle with a man in a pub when 'we were both pissed'. The argument arose over comments on the National Front, an organization with which he sympathized.

CHAPTER V

Varieties of Delinquent Career

Persisting recidivists

The small group of young delinquents who appear before the courts repeatedly and persistently, because of the frequency of their offending, are responsible for a disproportionately large share of the social disruption associated with delinquency. They include a high proportion of offenders with serious social and personal problems. Only a minority of the juvenile offenders in the study (37 out of 84) were convicted more than once for a juvenile offence, but this minority included proportionately twice as many individuals who had been exposed to unsatisfactory parenting (19 out of 37 versus 12 out of 47) and over twice as many from poor-income families (20 out of 37 versus 11 out of 47).

The ability to identify at an early age those who are at risk of becoming long-term delinquents is of greater practical importance than the identification of potential juvenile delinquents, most of whom will be no more than a temporary nuisance. As mentioned previously, 36 men in the study were convicted at least twice for offences committed before the nineteenth birthday and reconvicted at least once for further offences in the next five years, that is between the nineteenth and twenty-fourth birthdays. We re-examined the data to see how many of these persisting recidivists might have been picked out from the items investigated at age 10 or earlier. Since they comprised less than a tenth of the sample, we looked to see how many were drawn from the 10 per cent of the sample who were most badly affected by early adversities. It was truly surprising how many of the persisting recidivists were in fact to be found among those who had in the past attracted the more extreme ratings on measures of adversity. The figures displayed in Table 8 (which are extracted and updated from ref. 40, table I) show, for example, that 36.1 per cent of the persisting recidivists, compared with only 5.8 per cent of the rest of the sample, had been rated extremely troublesome by class teachers when they were aged 8–10. Again, 41.7 per cent, compared with only 8.9 per cent in the rest of the sample, came from very large families (defined as six or more children born to a boy's mother before his tenth birthday).

Table 8   Early variables as predictors of long-term recidivism

Adverse features identified at age 10 or earlier	Among 36 persisting recidivists		Among 361 others still in UK at age 22	
	No.	%	No.	%
Extreme categories on key background adversities previously identified as predictors of juvenile delinquency				
(1) Very poor parental behaviour (score 6 or 7 on rating scale combining PSW assessments up to age 10)	8	22.2	31	8.6
(2) In lowest 10 per cent of sample on IQ (effectively IQ 83 or less on averaged scores on progressive matrices at ages 8 and 10)	10	27.8	31	8.6
(3) Very large family size (six or more brothers and sisters at proband's tenth birthday)	15	41.7	32	8.9
(4) Large family (five or more brothers and sisters) and also low family income at proband's tenth birthday	15	41.7	29	8.0
(5) Both parents convicted before proband's tenth birthday	11	30.6	13	3.6
(6) At least four of five background adversities on assessments completed at age 10	12	33.3	19	5.3
(7) Exceptional troublesomeness (score 20+ on teachers' ratings at 8 or 10)	13	36.1	21	5.8

From among the early assessments which appeared predictive of long-term recidivism we selected three criteria: (a) *very* troublesome according to teachers' reports; (b) father with at least two criminal convictions in adult courts before the boy was 10; (c) mother with an adult conviction record, or a sibling with a conviction record (juvenile or adult) before the boy was 10.

There were several reasons for selecting these particular criteria as indices of risk. They were all rather simple items likely to be readily available or easily replicated in any future survey. Two of them were measures of criminality in the family, the background feature which — after troublesomeness in the classroom — was the one most strongly predictive of future delinquency, both adult and juvenile. The definition of parental criminality used for this purpose excluded juvenile convictions, not because they were thought to be irrelevant, but because juvenile conviction records of the parental generation were so incomplete. However, the exact criteria for assessing criminality in the family were unimportant since past convictions of family members were strongly predictive regardless of the method of counting adopted.

Among the 397 men who remained in the UK, 35 had had at least two of the three specified items of serious adversity recorded against them before they were aged 10. Out of this high-risk group, 18 (51.4 per cent) in fact became persisting delinquents and many more showed varying degrees of social disturbance. For example, a further 8 (22.9 per cent) were recidivist delinquents who fell outside our strict definition of 'persisting'. In contrast, of the 362 men not in the predicted high-risk group only 18 (5.0 per cent) became persisting recidivists. This level of contrast probably represents about the maximum efficiency with which persisting recidivists can be identified predictively from information available before the age of 10. It would appear that for purposes of purely statistical prediction one or two salient and readily measurable items serve as well as a much larger range of background items.

As will become apparent very soon, the social histories of most of the persisting recidivists proved little short of disastrous. If boys at high risk of developing so badly can be picked out at primary school by a few simple pointers, then the urge to do so with a view to prevention becomes very strong. It cannot be emphasized too strongly, however, that the persisting recidivists were a fairly small minority. There is some truth in the idea that troublesome infants become troublesome adults, temper tantrums, bed-wetting and lying in pre-school years giving way to lying and truancy at school and finally to violence and crime later on, but fortunately the dominant trend is towards improvement, growing out of deviancy being more typical than persistence into adult sociopathy. The considerable contrast between a persisting recidivist and other, more ordinary, delinquents is best illustrated with actual examples.

Case 941

Classed as a persisting recidivist, this man showed a particularly malignant progression. He was first found guilty of crime as a juvenile aged 15, when he threatened another boy with a stick and robbed him of £1. He had earlier been arrested for keeping a look out while another boy tried to break into the coin box in a telephone kiosk, but on that occasion he was released for insufficient evidence. He had also been taken to court for persistent truancy. From age 16 onwards he acquired various convictions for traffic offences, such as driving without insurance and driving while disqualified. At age 18 he was reconvicted for crime, but only for a minor theft, although he admitted at interview that he had been involved in numerous delinquencies around that time. Re-interviewed at age 21, he claimed to be a reformed character and was apparently embarked at last on a successful work career. However, at age 22 he was reconvicted for taking a car, his accomplice being the same who had been involved in the telephone incident over seven years previously.

Marriage to the girl he had been living with brought only a worsening of his behaviour. His drinking began to get out of control, he began to take prohibited drugs and he was spending all his time away from home with delinquent companions in pubs and clubs. He gave up his job to join in with an 'organization' involved in robberies. When interviewed for the last time at age 25 he was in prison. Eventually he received a long sentence for participating in a serious robbery and possessing a firearm. The incident concerned an old couple who had been tricked into letting the thieves into the house, overpowered and tied up, and robbed of a substantial amount of cash and jewels.

Typically, this man came from a large, conflict-ridden family living in impoverished circumstances; his father and siblings also had a criminal record.

Case 791

This man was a recidivist, but like many of those so classed his offences were not particularly serious and his criminal career was short-lived. His first conviction, at age 17, was for carrying an offensive weapon, a lock knife. He and his companions had been stopped one evening in the street and searched by the police when the knife was found. Later in the same year he was convicted a second time for stealing petrol from unattended cars. His third and last conviction was at age 18 when, in company with another young man, he burgled a shop and stole a large number of cigarettes.

He came from a normal, non-criminal family with no particular financial problems. There was some tension between himself and his elderly father. At the time of his last conviction he had left home after a quarrel with his parents and was sharing accommodation with the friend with whom he committed the burglary. He returned to his parental home subsequently and was still there when interviewed at age 21. He was placed on probation. His supervising officer, with whom he formed a good relationship, felt he would not reoffend.

Case 260

This man was one of a substantial number of delinquents with no more than a single conviction. He had no juvenile findings of guilt, although he had once been warned by the police for breaking into a sweet shop. At age 17 he was convicted of a burglary, together with his brother-in-law, a man six years older than himself. In an attempt to steal, they gained access to a store during half-day closing by pretending to be painters. They had been drinking together immediately prior to this escapade and the older man, who had a previous criminal record, was almost certainly the instigator.

This man came from a non-criminal family. He had somewhat indulgent parents and suffered no particular deprivations. Interviewed at age 21, there was no hint of continued delinquency. He was described as a contented labourer of rather dull personality, living a life of strict routine and content to let his wife be the dominant partner in their marriage.

Latecomers to crime

The men who acquired their first criminal conviction after reaching years of maturity formed an interesting group whose characteristics differed sharply from those of the persisting delinquents, most of whom had conviction histories extending back to a very early age.

Most young adult offenders are 'juvenile delinquents grown up'. Over half (57 out of 106) of the members of the study who sustained convictions for offences as adults had had a previous finding of guilt for a juvenile offence. As was shown in an earlier published analysis (see Appendix IV, ref. 3, table VIII(1), pp. 142–3), most of the items that predicted becoming a juvenile delinquent predicted even more successfully those who acquired convictions for both juvenile and young adult (that is, up to age 21) offences. This was only to be expected, of course, since all of these men were necessarily recidivists, and recidivists had already been found to be particularly deviant.

In the later stages of the study it became possible to examine the group of 33 latecomers to crime whose first convictions were for offences committed between the eighteenth and twenty-fifth birthdays. The age of majority, 18, was chosen as the criterion of late entry into crime because we knew it was at that stage that the incidence of first convictions begins to fall sharply and the character of offences to change towards a more adult pattern. The 33 latecomers were compared with the remaining 98 delinquents (still in the UK at age 22) who had convictions for offences committed under age 18. It became at once obvious that the latecomers shared only to a slight extent the five major early background features that had been found typical of other delinquents. Thus 24 per cent came from large families (compared with 40 per cent among the remaining 98 delinquents), only 21 per cent (compared with 36 per cent) came from low-income families, only 27 per cent (compared with 50 per cent) had a parent with a criminal record, and only 22.6 per cent (of 31 cases assessed) had been exposed to unsatisfactory parenting (compared with 38 per cent among the other delinquents). The only exception was that as many as 33 per cent (compared with 37 per cent) had been placed in the lowest quarter of the sample on IQ testing at ages 8 and 10.

Since each of these five items of early adversity had been found in 17–20 per cent of non-delinquents, it was clear that in most respects the latecomers were nearer to non-delinquents than to the generality of young offenders. For example, only 12.1 per cent of the latecomers had more than two of the five key background adversities, compared with 38 per cent of the younger offenders and 7.5 per cent of the non-delinquents. Early adversities other than the five just mentioned — for example, illegitimate births and broken homes — were also relatively rare among the group of latecomers to crime (see Appendix IV, ref. 39).

Although they had less early deprivation than the majority of delinquents, there was some evidence that the latecomers had shared, at least to some extent, in the troublesome childhood behaviour typical of future delinquents. For instance, 27.3 per cent had been in the most 'troublesome' category on ratings of behaviour at primary school (as opposed to only 13 per cent of those who remained non-delinquents). On self-reported delinquency (scores at ages 14 and 16 combined) 24.3 per cent had scored high (compared with only 9 per cent of the non-delinquents). Again, on the scale of 'antisocial' habits and attitudes, derived from interviews at age 18–19, the latecomers to crime scored rather nearer to the rest of the delinquents than to those who remained non-delinquents.

Since expectation of reconviction is less for persons first convicted at later ages, many of whom remain one-time offenders, it might have been anticipated that the latecomers to crime would be less committed to a delinquent way of life and less likely to be involved in serious offences than the generality of delinquents. Actually, the sort of offences for which the latecomers were convicted were not noticeably different from those committed by other delinquents of similar age. There was some slight suggestion, inconclusive owing to the small numbers available, that the latecomers were less likely than other adult delinquents to engage in illegal entry or breaking in. Descriptions of their first conviction were obtained from some of the latecomers. An unusually high proportion of them (8 out of 21) denied their guilt to the interviewer, although most of them had pleaded guilty in court. The latecomers were also more likely than other offenders to complain that their sentence was unfair, possibly because they were reluctant to identify themselves as criminals.

The impression that latecomers tend to be less deeply committed to crime than offenders who have started their criminal careers earlier receives support from a recent American self-report survey among prisoners. Men who had committed their first serious offence after the age of 19 had committed fewer recent offences, went in for a more limited range of offences, and expressed fewer criminal attitudes than did the men who had started as juvenile delinquents. In agreement with theorists who 'argue that serious adult criminals are socialized into crime when they are young', the group reporting the most crime were those who had become involved in offences before they were 13 (Peterson *et al.*, 1980, pp. 141, x).

Our finding that the latecomers were not a particularly deprived group suggests that the compensatory and rehabilitative efforts that are beneficial to the juvenile recidivist may not be appropriate or necessary for most young adult first-offenders.

Distinguishing temporary from persisting delinquents

The prospect of repetition of offences by known delinquents is of more direct concern to officials of the criminal justice system than the identification of potential delinquents among the general population. A variety of theories have been advanced to explain why certain offenders are so persistently badly behaved. Eysenck (see pp. 58–9) blames inborn neurophysiological characteristics which render those affected ill-equipped to adapt to social restraints. Learning theorists (Lickona, 1976) emphasize the deficiencies of early child training (conditioning), or the absence of suitable role models with which the child can identify. Psychoanalysts (Friedlander, 1947; Bowlby, 1973) point to the failure of some parents to provide consistent and uninterrupted love and attention during the critical years of an infant's emotional development. Despite their differences, all these theorists are committed to a belief in the importance of a cluster of persistent traits of personality which develop early in life and bring about the chronically deviant behaviour of the recidivist delinquent.

Assuming that the occasional, opportunistic offender is less likely than the recidivist to have such characteristics, it should be possible to identify the potential recidivists among a sample of convicted offenders by assessing the extent of their personality deviation. The 'antisociality' score, derived from the youths' descriptions of their attitude and behaviour when they were interviewed at age 18 (see pp. 61–2), served to do just this. A high score very significantly increased the prospect of reconviction. Among the interviewed men 102 were convicted for an offence committed before the nineteenth birthday (and were still in the UK at age 22). Dividing these 102 delinquents into 52 who had high antisociality scores (that is, having at least five out of the eleven undesirable characteristics) and 50 with smaller scores, the proportions who were reconvicted for offences committed in the next five years (between the nineteenth and twenty-fourth birthdays) were significantly different, 63.6 per cent and 34.0 per cent respectively ($\chi^2 = 7.71$, $P < 0.01$, $\phi = 0.275$).

Much the same degree of discrimination was obtained on comparing the percentages reconvicted among men with three or more previous convictions and among those with less than three (see Appendix IV, ref. 39, p. 110). In fact, antisocial life-style and number of previous convictions were about equally effective as predictors of a continuing delinquency career. This contradicts a common criminological assumption that nothing predicts future convictions so well as the number of previous convictions (Buikhuisen and Hoekstra, 1974).

At first sight this result might seem to support the depressing, but at one time popular, view that many recidivist delinquents are incorrigible because their behaviour stems from permanent and ineradicable flaws of personality. It is important to note, however, that our 'antisociality' score was derived from descriptions of current attitudes and behaviour; it did not purport to measure supposedly immutable characteristics such as 'intelligence'. In fact, the results of interviews at age 21 showed that many of the deviant characteristics so noticeable at age 18 had greatly decreased with increasing age.

When the men were 21 an attempt was made to interview all 125 members of the study who were living in the United Kingdom and who had been convicted for offences committed before reaching the age of 21 years 6 months. A comparison group of 116 non-delinquents was also selected for interview. In the event, 114 (91.2 per cent) of the delinquents and 104 (89.7 per cent) of the largest group of non-delinquents were successfully traced and interviewed. The non-delinquents were fairly representative, although not strictly a random selection (see Appendix IV, ref. 36, p. 349). Both the delinquent and the non-delinquent groups reported less deviant behaviour at 21 than they had done at age 18. Criminal offences were admitted much less often. Anti-establishment attitudes were endorsed less often. Reports of involvements in fights were strikingly less frequent. Whereas, at age 18, 9.5 per cent of the men interviewed admitted involvement in 25 or more fights (in the last three years), at age 21 only one of the 218 questioned admitted this number of fights (in the last two years).

The lessening of deviance was particularly obvious among the delinquents, so that some of the previously observed contrasts between delinquents and non-delinquents were no longer present, and others were considerably reduced. For example, there was no longer any tendency for delinquents to have a higher take-home pay than non-delinquents or any tendency for delinquents to accumulate heavier debts. Debts occasioned by hire-purchase commitments, especially on household goods in the case of the married men, were spread throughout the interviewed sample, regardless of delinquency status. Only the recidivists stood out, in that they were somewhat more prone than others to pick up debts in the form of unpaid fines. The incidence of admitted convictions for motoring offences was no longer significantly higher among delinquents (25.4 per cent) than among non-delinquents (18.3 per cent). The habit of going around in a group of four or more male companions was much less frequently reported at 21, especially among the married men, and it no longer discriminated between delinquents and non-delinquents. The items that remained more prevalent among the delinquents included admitted use of a prohibited drug in the last two years (33.3 against 18.3 per cent), some period of unemployment in the last two years (43 against 19.2 per cent), spending heavily — more than £8 per week on drink (37.7 against 25.0 per cent) and regular smoking habits (78.9 against 58.3 per cent). Although there were fewer endorsements of hostile and aggressive comments about police at 21 than at 18, the delinquents remained significantly more likely than the non-delinquents to express such views. For example, the comment 'I enjoy a punch up' was endorsed by 31.6 per cent of delinquents and 14.4 per cent of non-delinquents (compared with 45.5 and 25 per cent at age 18). 'The police are always roughing people up' was endorsed by 12.3 per cent of delinquents and 6.7 per cent of non-delinquents (compared with 29.7 and 9.4 per cent at age 18).

The lessened contrast in life-styles between the delinquent and non-delinquent groups when seen at age 21 undoubtedly reflected the fact that by that time many youthful conviction careers had come to an end. The remaining differences between delinquents and non-delinquents were mostly attributable to the minority of persisting recidivists. The cessation of conviction careers appeared to coincide with the abandonment of other forms of social deviance, whereas persisting criminality was associated with a continuation of general antisociality. Confirmation of this conclusion was obtained from interviews with persisting recidivists and former recidivists at age 24.

At a relatively late stage of the research an effort was made to trace and re-interview at age 24 the 36 men classed as persisting recidivists, together with 25 men defined as temporary recidivsts (consisting of all those with at least two convictions for offences before the nineteenth birthday but no more over the ensuing five years up to the twenty-fourth birthday) and a comparison group of 34 randomly selected non-delinquents. As might have been predicted, the persisting recidivists proved to be the most elusive group, prone to frequent changes of address and loss of contact with relatives. Of the three groups, the numbers finally interviewed were 22 (out of 36), 22 (out of 25) and 28 (out of 34) respectively. Of the 14 persisting recidivists whom the investigators failed to interview, only 3 refused co-operation; 11 were untraceable. It is unlikely that the ones who were not seen were any less deviant than the ones who were seen (see Appendix IV, ref. 45).

The contrasts between the three interviewed groups are set out in Table 9. Every comparison we could make showed that the persisting recidivists were a disfavoured and deviant group, whereas the temporary recidivists were much closer to and often indistinguishable from the non-delinquents. The incidence of unemployment was some six times higher among the persisting recidivists than among the other two groups and the prevalence of substandard home conditions (for example, overcrowding, damp, absence of basic amenities and general delapidation) was some four times higher. Long-standing unemployment

Table 9   Some contrasts between persisting recidivists, temporary recidivists and non-delinquents when interviewed at age 24

	Percentage of 22 persisting recidivists	Percentage of 22 temporary recidivists	Percentage of 28 non-delinquents
More than eight weeks' unemployment in last two years	59.1	9.1	10.7
Spends over £4 weekly on tobacco	50.0	31.8	3.6
Spends over £20 weekly on alcohol	31.8	18.2	0.0
Home conditions poor	40.9	9.1	10.7
In home owned by self or relatives	0.0	27.3	17.9
Unpaid debts (other than negotiated credit)	54.5	4.5	3.6
Cohabiting	36.4	18.2	7.1
Separated from children (for reasons other than illness)	36.4	9.1	3.6
Uses no contraceptives	22.7	0.0	0.0
Involved in at least one fight in past two years	59.1	22.7	10.7
Admitted at least two items of self-reported crimes in last two years	36.4	0.0	7.1
At least three out of six possible points on 'antisociality' scale	50.0	18.2	0.0

(defined as six months or more out of work in the last two years) was reported by 7 persisting delinquents compared with only 2 of the non-delinquents and none of the temporary recidivists. The persisting recidivists who were working had higher take-home pay than was usual among the other two groups, but only because they were more often self-employed and evading taxes. A majority of 13 persisting recidivists (compared with only 5 temporary recidivists and 5 non-delinquents) admitted involvement in one or more fights over the past two years. Asked about their most recent fight, 10 of the persisting recidivists (compared with only 3 of the temporary recidivists and 2 of the non-delinquents) admitted having struck the first blow, and 3 admitted using a weapon (whereas none of the non-delinquents and only one of the temporary recidivists said they had done so). Most of the fights described by the persisting delinquents took place when they were out drinking. Failure to meet family obligations on the part of the persisting recidivists was indicated by such items as neglect of contraception, cohabitation without marriage, debts (unpaid rent, bills and fines) and separations from children. Of the fathers responsible for maintaining children only 3 out of 15 among the persisting recidivists (compared with 17 out of 23 among the other two groups) were thought to be providing adequate care. In fact, 6 persisting recidivists had left their children following marital rows and 2 others were separated from their children as a result of imprisonment. All 72 men interviewed were rated on a modified 'antisociality' scale. In order to adhere as closely as possible to previous assessments one point was given for each of the following items: over eight weeks' unemployment; spends over £4 weekly on tobacco; spends over £12 weekly on drink; claims sexual intercourse with more than one partner; use of a prohibited drug; involvement in one or more fights. As many as 8 of the persisting recidivists (but only 2 temporary recidivists and none of the non-delinquents) scored four or more points.

The absence of recent criminal convictions among the temporary recidivists really did correspond to a vast decrease in delinquency involvement in comparison with the persisting recidivists. It was not just a matter of evading detection. The interviewed men were presented with eight cards bearing descriptions of different criminal offences (for example, stealing from work goods, money, tools or other things worth £5 or more together). These were the same cards as had been used at age 21. The men were asked to say if they had done each of the specified acts at any time over the past two years. A majority, 63.6 per cent, of the persisting recidivists (compared with 18.2 per cent of the temporary recidivists and 7.1 per cent of the non-delinquents) admitted at least one of the specified crimes. Altogether, the 22 persisting recidivists made 28 admissions, the 22 temporary recidivists and the 28 non-delinquents each made a total of four admissions (see Appendix IV, ref. 44, p. 109).

Apart from their own admissions, official police records revealed that persisting recidivists (but none of the other two groups) had been convicted during the past two years for minor offences (such as 'drunk and disorderly') but these were not 'criminal' convictions as ordinarily defined and had not been included in our conviction counts.

The differences between the persisting recidivists and the other two groups were very substantial, consistent and significant, but they would have been even greater had the groups been defined slightly differently. It appeared that a gap of five years free from convictions was not quite long enough to identify those whose criminal careers had really ceased, for 4 of the men defined as 'temporary' recidivists were actually reconvicted for offences committed between their twenty-fourth and twenty-fifth birthdays. If these cases had been classified as 'persisting' recidivists, 10 out of a total of 26, but none of the 18 remaining temporary recidivists and none of the non-delinquents interviewed, would have scored highly (four or more points) on the 'antisociality' scale. This further strengthened the conclusion that, at age 24, the persisting recidivists continued to be significantly socially deviant, whereas men whose conviction careers had definitely ended had become as conformist in life-style as men who had never had a criminal record.

The reformation of the temporary recidivists by the time they were aged 24 was remarkable, but it has to be noted that they started off from a less extreme position than those destined to become persisting recidivists. For example, over a half (19) of the total 36 persisting recidivists in the study, but only a fifth of the 25 temporary recidivists, had as many as four convictions for offences committed under the age of 19. Furthermore, as pointed out in the discussion earlier (see pp. 71–3), the men destined to become persisting recidivists came from particularly adverse backgrounds, frequently characterized by poverty, family criminality and unsatisfactory child-reading, and were correspondingly extreme in their behavioural deviations. The temporary recidivists, however, had also been at one time, if not quite so extreme, then certainly very significantly deviant, so that their subsequent reversion to the norm was still impressive.

Looking back at the responses that the recidivists who were seen at age 24 had made when they were interviewed at age 18, the temporary recidivists had been in many respects much closer to the persisting recidivists than to the non-delinquents. For example, at age 18, only 14.2 per cent of the 288 non-delinquents interviewed reported substantial periods of unemployment compared with 41 per cent of the 22 temporary recidivists and 67 per cent of the 21 persisting recidivists who were seen in the interviews at both ages 18 and 24. Again, at age 18, heavy drinking, admitted by only 25 per cent of non-delinquents, was admitted by 32 per cent of temporary recidivists and 43 per cent of persisting recidivists. The proportions who attained high scores on 'antisociality' at age 18 were 9.4 per cent, 36.4 per cent and 85.4 per cent, among non-delinquents, temporary recidivists and persisting recidivists respectively (see Appendix IV, ref. 45, table 3).

The shift to normality on the part of the temporary recidivist group, which was more or less completed at age 24, took place relatively slowly. According to their responses when interviewed at age 21, the temporary recidivists were still in a midway position between persisting delinquents and non-delinquents in 'antisociality'. Of the 22 temporary recidivists, 32 per cent were rated high on 'antisociality' at age 21, compared with 63 per cent of the 22 persisting recidivists and only 8.7 per cent of non-delinquents. The movement away from involvement in criminal offences, however, was already apparent. The proportions scoring high on self-reported delinquency at age 21 were 72.7 per cent, 36.4 per cent and 26.9 per cent, among persisting recidivists, temporary recidivists and non-delinquents respectively (ibid., table 3).

The reasons why some recidivists reform and others do not remain unclear. Like most criminological research this study was directed more towards the exploration of influences that promote delinquency than to the discovery of factors that may exert a restraining effect. The general trend is towards a lessening of delinquency with increasing age, and the likelihood of reform is greater among those with fewer convictions, those who do not come from criminal families and those who do not share the 'antisocial' life-style of the committed recidivist. But given equally bad records and backgrounds, are there identifiable circumstances or events that make one individual more likely to reform than another? Brown and Gable (1979) have proposed exploring this question by interviewing reformed delinquents and questioning them about significant turning-points in their lives.

We did, in fact, in the course of the interviews at age 18, ask the men who claimed to have given up delinquency to explain what had brought about the change. Several reasons were cited. Withdrawal from delinquent associates ('I don't go around with them any more'), the fear of further punishment, the benefits of training while in an approved school and the influence of girl-friends were all mentioned (see Appendix IV, ref. 31).

These opinions could be mistaken, nothing more than plausible 'after-the-event' interpretations. Some confirmation that withdrawal from delinquent associates really was associated with the cessation of a delinquency career was obtained from the predictive value of the answers given when interviewed at age 18. A substantial minority of the men (38.5 per cent of the non-delinquents and 25.7 per cent of the delinquents) replied negatively to the question whether, in the past year, they sometimes went around in groups of four or more male friends. Those who subsequently became persisting recidivists scarcely ever made this assertion. The difference was still apparent after allowing for previous conviction history. As many as possible of the persisting recidivists who had been seen at 18 were matched, one by one, with 'temporary' recidivists who had had the same number of convictions for offences up to the nineteenth birthday. Among the resulting 21 matched pairs, only one of the persisting recidivists, as opposed to 8 of the 'temporary' recidivists, had claimed at 18 that he had not been going about in male groups.

Other developments reputedly linked with the reduction of delinquency, notably getting caught and getting married, are considered in the next chapter.

Examples of contrasting criminal careers

The statistical comparisons described in the earlier sections of this chapter show that officially recorded delinquency careers of young males might be roughly classified into four rather similar-sized groups.

(a) Juvenile, one-time offenders who differ only slightly in background and behaviour from their unconvicted peers.

(b) Latecomers to crime (also often one-time offenders) who tend to come from unremarkable backgrounds but who have been rather more troublesome than average as schoolboys.

(c) Temporary recidivists, who have multiple convictions in youth, but no more after passing the age of 18. They tend to come from relatively deprived backgrounds and to have been troublesome as schoolboys and significantly deviant in life-style up to the age of 18 or later, but subsequently to reform and become socially conformist and non-delinquent.

(d) Persisting delinquents, who tend to start their conviction careers at a particularly early age, to sustain frequent convictions as juveniles and to continue to acquire convictions in their twenties. They generally are from the worse, most deprived family backgrounds. They stand out as the most conspicuously deviant group, both during school years and in early adult life.

The examples which follow illustrate, more vividly perhaps than the statistics, the very varied patterns of development included within the all-embracing category of 'delinquent'. The first three are from the group of 'temporary' recidivists.

Case 852

This was an intelligent boy from a materially satisfactory but emotionally fraught home background. The school authorities were concerned about his progress, but unable to prevail upon his parents to come to discuss the problem. He was a repeated offender as a juvenile. For an offence of house-breaking, committed while truanting, he was put on probation at the age of 12. Later, he spent 18 months in approved school following a conviction for another house-breaking, in which a flat was completely ransacked and a considerable amount of valuables taken.

According to his mother, he was branded as a trouble-maker and a ringleader from the moment he started junior school at age 7. From then until he was committed to approved school at age 14 he was continually in trouble, cheeky, defiant, getting into fights and constantly truanting. A probation report quoted his headmaster as saying he was 'amoral and subversive'.

The parents refused, at first, to co-operate with the study. The boy himself complained that they were not interested in him and spent all their time out drinking, leaving him to be looked after by his elder sister. Interviewed at age 18, when he was still living in his parents' home, he commented about his father: 'He's never really cared for me', and went on: 'I'm getting my own back at me father and mother now for what they done to me ... Whereas before they used to shout at me and all that they can't now because I'm a bit bigger ... I swear at my father and tell him where to go and all this if he tells me to do anything or says anything to me.'

Interviewed at age 18, he carried a noticeable stab scar and admitted to involvement in various quarrels and fights. After describing an incident in which he had to be pulled away to stop him throttling an opponent, he commented: 'I don't like getting aggressive 'cause if I do,· if I get into a temper, I don't actually go senseless, but I don't know what I'm doing . . .' He said he had had to have a number of fights in the approved school because 'if you didn't show who you was, you used to get knocked all over the place'.

In spite of his continuing aggressive attitude, he claimed to have given up delinquency and given up the friends with whom he used to commit offences. He admitted 'buying cheap' from his workmates articles he knew were stolen, but he said that since coming out of approved school he had stopped stealing, breaking in or taking cars. He had got engaged and thought this the main reason for 'going straight', but he thought that if this relationship were to break up he would go back to his old ways and his old mates.

He did not go back. Seen for the last time at age 25, he was married with two children, working in a job he enjoyed, and living in a privately rented house. He had by now apparently given up his fighting proclivities as well as his delinquency. The interviewer commented: 'He seems to have settled down to a quiet existence. He goes out drinking, but generally takes his wife with him.'

Case 872

This man barely qualified as recidivist, having only two convictions, one for breaking and entering a shop when he was 12, and a second for burglary at age 18. In addition, he had one official police caution for attempting to steal a car mascot.

Signs of 'trouble' began early and were more serious than his relatively minor official offence record suggested. When he was 9, his mother reported that he lied, wandered off on his bicycle for hours on end, was sly and disobedient, pilfered from home, tormented his small sister and was reported by his teacher for taking small items from the classroom. His behaviour in the classroom eventually caused the school to refer him for a psychiatric opinion. In his last year at school he became particularly troublesome and a persistent truant.

His parental home, a delapidated house shared with another family, was described by interviewers as overcrowded and 'incredibly squalid'. His parents had a very stormy marriage. His mother left home on several occasions and finally, when he was 14, she left altogether and set up house with another man in the country and he went with her.

The move to the country suited him and his home life became more settled. Whereas he described his own father as having 'more time for his [hobby] than he did for the family', he said of his 'stepfather':

'He does the things I'm interested in and helps me with everything.'
By the time he was seen at age 18 he was already engaged to be married.
He admitted to traffic infractions, such as driving a friend's car without
a licence, but said he was 'keeping out of trouble'. He married soon
after. The couple continued to live for a while in his mother's home,
but following a family argument they moved out and had no further
contact with his parents. Seen at age 21, he was still attracting frequent
convictions for traffic infractions, but he was otherwise non-delinquent
and concerned to preserve the marital home he had acquired. He said:
'I've got more responsibilities now. You can hardly go to clink when
you've got this over your head . . .' Asked about delinquent acts he
said: 'Definitely London, this sort of stuff isn't it! I wouldn't go back
to London. This place is small, but I wouldn't want it any different . . .
You know everyone, not like London.' Seen for the last time at age 25
he was still happily married, with two children, a cottage on mortgage,
a car and a well-paid job which he had held for several years. He expressed himself well contented with life.

Case 791

This was a 'temporary' recidivist whose offences were not very serious
and whose criminal career was short-lived. Except for the fact that he
came from a more secure background than most recidivists, it was not
at all obvious why he should have reformed so quickly. His first conviction, at age 17, was for carrying an offensive weapon, a lock knife.
He and his companions had been stopped one evening in the street
and searched by the police. Later in the same year he was convicted,
with others, of siphoning petrol from unattended cars. His last conviction, at age 18, was for shop-breaking and stealing a large quantity
of cigarettes.

He was the youngest in a large but non-criminal family. They were
not in any particular financial stress. His father, who had been married
before, was quite elderly. The atmosphere was of a normal, caring
home, but not without its tensions. His mother was a forceful character
who expressed some resentment at her husband's passivity and habit
of leaving the family responsibilities to her.

In early life he had suffered some serious illnesses. He was of limited
intelligence and quite backward at school. His mother commented to
the social workers on his efforts to appear tough, brash and unconcerned.
She became increasingly anxious, during his adolescence, about his
association with a 'leather-jacket gang' whose habit it was to carry
knives. Also he became increasingly rebellious, voiced provocative racist
views and sported disapproved hair-style and clothes in defiance of his
parents. Finally, following a quarrel, he left home to go 'living rough'
with a friend. It was at this stage and with this friend that he committed

the shop-breaking offence for which he was convicted, and placed on probation. After that crisis he returned home.

At the interview when aged 18 he admitted to several items typical of the delinquent way of life, including sackings from work, delinquent companions, fighting while drunk and use of prohibited drugs. Nevertheless, he claimed to have quietened down. He said that he now got on 'reasonably' with his parents — 'we tolerate each other'. He said he had given up weapon carrying, referred to his convictions as 'a phase you go through', and spoke of his probation officer as an 'alright' person. In fact, he and his girl-friend formed a close relationship with the probation officer who felt, at the end of the supervision period, that he would be unlikely to offend again.

When last seen at age 25 he was still in the parental home and working regularly. He denied all offences in reply to the self-report questions. He was still single, his engagement having been broken off. He had long since given up his delinquent friends and was now spending most evenings at home watching TV. He admitted to feeling bored with his life, and for that reason the interviewer felt that he was at risk of being tempted back into delinquent excitements should the opportunity arise.

The next two examples are from the group of 'persisting recidivists'.

Case 941

This man came from a large, conflict-ridden family living in impoverished circumstances in very delapidated housing which the occupants were struggling to maintain in habitable condition. Father and siblings had a criminal record. The parents were unwilling to co-operate with the research. The father's work took him away from home a lot, and when the son was interviewed at aged 16 the parents were said to be separated.

He performed badly at school and was taken to court for persistent truancy. The probation officer found his mother cold and less than co-operative over the issue of school attendance. At school he was said to be 'indifferent to teachers, overbearing to other children and indulging in cruel bullying'.

On leaving school at the earliest permitted age, he worked off and on as an unskilled labourer, but with numerous job changes and periods of unemployment. When seen at age 18 he was talkative and slightly drunk. He admitted to having got into trouble on various occasions for drunken driving and driving while disqualified and without insurance. He complained of heavy debts from unpaid fines. He was living with a girl whom he had made pregnant, but mentioned other sexual adventures 'on the side'. He said he had been 'a bit of a skinhead' and reported a recent head injury from fighting.

His conviction history began with a finding of guilt at age 15. He had threatened another boy with a stick and robbed him of £1. He had earlier been arrested for keeping look-out for another boy who was trying to break into a telephone coin box, but on that occasion was released for insufficient evidence. His many convictions for traffic offences started at age 16. At age 18 he was reconvicted for crime, but only for a minor theft, although he admitted at interview that he had been involved in numerous delinquencies around that time. Re-interviewed at age 21, he claimed to be a reformed character and was apparently embarked at last on a successful work career. However, at age 22 he was reconvicted for taking a car, his accomplice being the same who had been involved in the telephone incident over seven years previously.

Marriage to the girl he had been living with brought only a worsening of his behaviour. His drinking began to get out of control, he began to take prohibited drugs and he was spending all his time away from home with delinquent companions in pubs and clubs. He gave up his job to join in with an 'organization' involved in robberies. Eventually he received a long sentence for participating in a serious robbery and possessing a firearm. The incident concerned an old couple who had been tricked into letting the thieves into the house, overpowered and tied up, and robbed of a substantial amoung of cash and jewels.

When interviewed for the last time at age 25 he was in prison, where he was again in trouble for fighting, this time with fellow prisoners of another race whose toilet habits he disliked.

Case 743

This persisting recidivist's criminal convictions began at age 12 and continued with little interruption during the whole of the research until, when almost 25, he was convicted for crime for the thirteenth time. He had graduated from approved school, to borstal and finally to prison. All his offences were thefts and break-ins.

Both his father and an elder brother had been convicted, but in each case on only one occasion. He was outstandingly the 'black sheep' of the family and always felt rejected by his parents. Their material circumstances were not particularly poor, although both parents were unhappy about the neighbourhood in which they had to live. His mother complained of irritability and depression and felt she had too many children to cope with.

His troublesomeness began with habits of 'wandering off' as an infant. At school his performance was always poor. A school report when he was 14 described him as follows:

Habitual truant, not at all interested, makes no real effort, very rude and insolent when rebuked, frequently causes disturbance, a destructive influence on others.

When interviewed at age 18 he said he had been sacked from nearly every job he had tried and was now just working as a casual labourer while drawing unemployment benefit. He had left the parental home and was sharing accommodation with 'mates' because it was 'more of a laugh'. He had an illegitimate child and a maintainance order against him, but of course he was not paying it while out of work. He admitted to heavy drinking and a tendency to get into fights after drinking: 'I get mad if someone says anything I don't like. I just hit them. I'd be the first one to start [the fight].' He had numerous endorsements for driving offences and had received a two-year disqualification.

Seen again at age 21 he was thinking of marrying, having got another girl-friend pregnant. He was still engaging in fights occasionally. 'Well you don't just stand there and watch some mates get a hiding, do you?' He had had to have an operation on a broken nose following one fight a year previous. He was 'able to walk away', but his opponent was knocked out from a head blow delivered with a pole. He was still mixing with a delinquent crowd and, although claiming to be a changed character, he failed to impress the interviewer that he had genuinely given up crime.

As a 'persisting recidivist' he was wanted by the researchers for interview at age 24, but he could not be found, his relatives asserting that he had gone abroad.

The following two examples are of men who were by definition included in the delinquent category, but whose involvement in crime was very limited and whose backgrounds and development were quite unlike those of the typical recidivist.

Case 260

He was the youngest child and only son of doting parents, and considered to be over-indulged. He was his father's favourite. The social worker visiting for the study noted that he was overloaded with lavish toys and presents, was not required to do any chores, and was rarely punished. Both parents worked extra hard to provide material comforts. No one else in the family had a criminal record.

He was not a bright scholar, and was keen to leave and start earning, but he liked his school and no particular behaviour problems were reported. He had no more than a single conviction, and no juvenile findings of guilt, although he had once been warned by the police for breaking into a sweet shop. At age 17 he was convicted of a burglary, together with his brother-in-law, a man six years older than himself. In an attempt to steal, they gained access to a store during half-day closing by pretending to be painters. They had been drinking together immediately prior to this escapade and the older man, who had a previous criminal record, was almost certainly the instigator.

In his earlier years he had taken part, with his mates, in various delinquent episodes, mostly minor vandalism. By the time he was seen at 18 he claimed to have given up such things. 'It was the sort of thing you do for a laugh. The sort of thing everyone does, but you get a bit more intelligent as you get older.' He admitted to continuing 'buying cheap' (stolen goods offered for sale) but denied any involvement with drugs, remarking that he had refused the offer to try some pot because 'I suppose I'm frightened, really, of the way it might affect me'. He had had various brushes with the police for unruliness at football matches, where he had been involved in several fights, but 'not a lot 'cause you go to enjoy the match'. He used to go around with a crowd of boys who occasionally got into fights with rival groups. However, by the time he was interviewed at 18 he referred to all this as 'in the past'. He was presently working regularly and engaged to be married.

Seen for the last time at age 21 he was married, working regularly and settled contentedly into a life of strict routine. He reported that when he went out it was usually with his wife. He never bet money or smoked and he had no debts. He still drank regularly and reported involvement in one recent fight. He had been out drinking with the older brother-in-law when a quarrel broke out and 'I had to help him out'. The interviewer formed the impression that his wife was a sensible woman who was the dominant partner in the marriage, but that he was quite happy to have it that way.

As regards offences, he admitted taking home materials from work, like most of his mates did, but denied doing anything likely to get him into trouble with the police again. 'I suppose 'cause I'm a bit more sensible now. I think you realize that it ain't worth doing like, but when you see others doing it you say "cor, look at him!" Then suddenly you realize you used to do that.'

Deprived non-delinquents

Few of the men from seriously deprived backgrounds remained free from criminal convictions, but these exceptions proved as interesting a subject for inquiry as any of the groups of actual delinquents. A delinquent-prone group, consisting of men with more than two of the five key background adversities predictive of delinquency, had been identified at an early stage of the study (see p. 30). There were 61 of these men still in the United Kingdom at age 22, but only 20 remained free from convictions.

That particular group of 61 was the by-product of an exercise in statistical prediction, in which the identifying criteria were necessarily limited to a small number of commonplace items recorded by the age of 10. In order to obtain a more realistic sample of the most seriously deprived members of the study, all the family background data that had accumulated were re-examined, noting which cases fulfilled each of the following criteria.

(1) Has a parent or sibling with a criminal record acquired before the boy in the study reached his seventeenth birthday (161 cases).
(2) Born illegitimate (25 cases).
(3) From a family known to have had support from state welfare (during the survey period 1961–5) (61 cases).
(4) Spent some period in the care of a local authority (other than on an approved-school order) (46 cases).
(5) From a broken home (that is, permanently separated from one or both parents before the fifteenth birthday for reasons other than death) (48 cases).
(6) Lived (at age 8–10) in very poor housing (that is, slum conditions) according to social workers (68 cases).
(7) From a large family (that is, four or more other children born to his mother before his tenth birthday) (99 cases).

From among the 397 still in the UK at age 22 a minority of 54 with a history of serious deprivation were identified on the grounds that each had experienced, in addition to the first item in the above list (that is, criminality in the family), at least two of the other six adversities. As anticipated, most of these 54 deprived individuals were delinquents, in fact 17 of them were among the minority of 36 defined as persisting recidivists. Nevertheless, at the time this analysis was carried out (when the men were aged 22) 18 of them had no criminal conviction.

In an effort to discover how these men had managed to avoid becoming delinquents an attempt was made to re-interview all 18 when they were aged 23 or 24. One man's immediate whereabouts could not be found, but in his case some information was available from his separated wife and from a health visitor's notes. Two others refused to be interviewed, but the foster-father of one of these was seen and was able to provide most of the basic particulars required, while in the other case some information was available from the social services. The situation of the deprived non-delinquents was compared with that of a control group of 26 non-delinquents who were interviewed around the same time. (This was the same control group of non-delinquents that was used for comparison with persisting recidivists (see pp. 79–80) except that two cases were excluded because, although non-delinquents, they belonged to the deprived group.)

The first point of interest to emerge was that, although the deprived group had been selected for the absence of an official criminal record, some of them evinced considerable delinquent tendencies. Questioned as to whether they had committed one or more of eight specified offences in the past two years, 6 of the 15 interviewed men (40.0 per cent) admitted to at least one, in contrast to only 1 such admission (3.8 per cent) among the 26 non-delinquent control group. Similarly 5 out of the 15 (33.3 per cent), compared with only 2 (7.7 per cent) of the control group, admitted to having been involved in at least one fight in the past two years. Two of the deprived group of supposed non-delinquents were in fact convicted after they had been selected for interview, one for an offence at age 22 and the other for one committed at age 24. In addition, two others had convictions for minor offences not normally included in criminal records, namely 'disturbing the peace' and 'drunk and disorderly'.

The most prominent characteristic of this group of 18 deprived men, who were still non-delinquents at age 22, was their social failure, manifest in unemployment, poor living conditions and social isolation. For example, 6 out of the 17 about whom information was available (35.3 per cent) were permanently or chronically unemployed, whereas only 1 out of the 26 non-delinquent controls (3.8 per cent) had been unemployed for any length of time in the past two years. Of those who had been employed most had been in low-status jobs and few had achieved a take-home pay of more than £50 per week. Unlike any of the controls, at least 5 of the deprived men were living in damp, dirty or overcrowded conditions with very poor facilities. The social contacts of the deprived non-delinquents were surprisingly circumscribed. Unlike any of the controls, 5 of them, all unmarried, had no sustained social contacts other than their own parents or siblings. Fewer of the deprived group said they frequented local bars and fewer of them (7 of 17 compared with 22 of 26) had driven a motor vehicle in the past two years. Fewer were married (7 of 18 against 15 of 26), and of the 7 deprived men who had married one was in the process of divorce, another was separated and a third had had a temporary separation of six months' duration. Of the 10 unmarried men in the deprived group who were interviewed 8 said they had no current girl-friend, a circumstance not often reported by the unmarried controls.

Low intelligence may have made some contribution to their poor social performance, since 10 of the 18 deprived non-delinquents had been placed in the lowest quarter on IQ testing at ages 8 and 10, but their odd and withdrawn personalities were a more important factor. Indications of this had been evident early in life. At age 8–10, when our social workers were visiting the boys' homes, 41.2 per cent of the deprived group (7 of 17 whose parents were seen), compared with only 10 per cent of the sample as a whole, were described as having few or no friends. At the same time a similar proportion were placed in the worst quarter of the sample on the social workers' assessments of 'nervous–withdrawn' characteristics (see Appendix IV, ref. 2, p. 115). Then again, when seen at 18, 47.1 per cent of the group (8 of 17 interviewed) were among the quarter of the sample who reported going out least often during evenings or weekends (Appendix IV, ref. 3, p. 68). Both at age 18, and again when interviewed at age 23—4, the deprived non-delinquents included proportionately more heavy smokers, and this notwithstanding their relatively impoverished circumstances.

To sum up, the results of this analysis confirmed that in this working-class sample circumstances of deprivation in early years usually resulted in the affected boys developing a strong delinquent tendency that almost always led, eventually, to an officially registered criminal record. Although the numbers were too small to permit a firm conclusion, the results also pointed to a high incidence of other forms of social maladjustment among the small minority of males from deprived backgrounds who did not become delinquents. The following example was one of the very few deprived individuals who achieved a good adjustment.

Case 880

Although born illegitimate this man was subsequently reared by his natural parents, but his father deserted the home when he was only 9. After this his mother managed very badly, falling into debt and being evicted, complaining to the police of her children's misbehaviour, suffering health problems and attempting suicide on several occasions. Like his siblings, he spent long periods away from home in the care of the social services, but unlike them he did not acquire a conviction record and caused no particular problem at school, save for occasional truancy. At one point, however, he was referred to a child psychiatry clinic on account of obstinacy and a tendency to fantasy. He was above average in intelligence but left school at 15 having taken no exams. Even before this he had tried to get away into the army. When seen at 16 he had secured a job which involved some training and he was already expressing lofty ambitions.

Interviewed at age 18 he was in a still better paid post and was described as hard-working, self-confident and egocentric. He said he had left home around 16 because of his mother's messy circumstances, which were affecting him so that he could not give of his best at work. The interviewer noted that he had apparently escaped totally from his chaotic background and was carrying off his changed circumstances to the point of affectation, with references to 'dinner at the Café Royal' and visits to the theatre. He was considered boastful and prone to exaggeration.

When interviewed at 24 he was married and living with his wife and child in 'plush' surroundings in a well-placed house acquired by mortgage. Although without formal training, he had a well-paid job in an accounts department, to which he devoted very long hours. He had no contact with his family of origin and commented: 'I left home when I was 16, but in spirit I left home long before.'

Satisfactory social adjustment among the deprived men was too rare to permit any generalization as to how these exceptional achievements came about, so the question that initiated this inquiry remained unanswered. Each case was unique, with no particularly outstanding factors that might explain it.

As has been explained, some of the unconvicted men in the deprived group had definite delinquent tendencies and were in many ways akin to the official delinquents, as the following example illustrates.

Case 782

He had been a 'troublesome' boy at primary school and was rated high on antisocial tendency when interviewed at 18 (due to his very poor work history — long unemployment, frequent job changes and sackings — and reports of heavy gambling, sexual promiscuity, drug taking and anti-establishment attitudes). He had narrowly escaped a conviction record, having a finding of guilt for indecent exposure quashed on appeal, and later having a charge of handling stolen goods dismissed.

He came from a fairly notorious criminal family, his father having a long and continuing conviction career including several imprisonments, his elder brother being a recidivist and his mother and elder sister having been convicted for an offence committed in concert. In his early years the social worker noted that the family had spent long periods in half-way houses, institutions and furnished rooms. There was great tension and numerous fights between his parents. His father was quick tempered and a heavy drinker. When seen at 16 the boy was living with an elder sister having left home 'to let them get on with it' following a fight with his father.

When seen for the last time at 23 he was sharing a flat with an elder brother and was still single. He seemed quite unconcerned that he had been unemployed for a long time. The interviewer thought him young for his age and not very bright and described him as a 'delinquently inclined extravert'. There was reason to suspect he was involved in some way with his recidivist brother's illegal activities and therefore unlikely to remain unconvicted indefinitely.

The more typical members of the deprived but non-delinquent group were social misfits or isolates. The following two examples are fairly representative of such men.

Case 004

In his early years, that is 8—10, the family was living in very poor circumstances. The father was away in the military a great deal and the mother was described by social workers as apathetic, with little rapport with her children and little knowledge of this boy. He was backward, timid, lacking friends and suffering from a speech defect. His older brothers were all delinquents. A few years later his mother divorced and remarried. He was placed in a special school where he was quiet and easily controlled, but often absent through illness.

Seen at 18 he was again considered shy, backward and unresponsive, with little interest in anything. He had a phobia of death and worried about going to sleep for fear of not waking up again. Seen again at age 24 he was still living with mother, stepfather and numerous siblings in ramshackle and overcrowded 'temporary' accommodation allocated by the local authority. He was in regular but low-paid work at a job where he felt unhappy and out of place. He was single, had never had a girlfriend, and spent most of his leisure hours in seemingly aimless wandering the streets because, he said, 'I can't stand being shut in'. He had been visiting a youth club for a long time but had no friends there.

Although he had no criminal record he claimed to have been convicted for an attempted break-in. In actuality, as was known from other sources, the offence was of a 'peeping Tom' variety, charged as 'conduct liable to cause a breach of the peace', a matter that would not attract a criminal record entry.

Case 011

This man's childhood was marred by impoverished conditions and extreme conflict between his parents. His father, who was chronically unemployed, was described as 'something of a hermit', hardly communicating even with his wife. He was 11 when his father died. His mother was an aggressive, quarrelsome woman with a long history of psychiatric disorder, diagnosed as 'paranoid psychosis with depressive features in a woman of low intelligence'. She made a number of suicide attempts.

At school he was no disciplinary problem, but was a poor attender and was taken before a juvenile court on that account. He was thought to be under his mother's domination. She would excuse his absences by complaining, falsely, that his classmates were picking on him. His mother and two of his siblings sustained criminal convictions.

He declined to be interviewed at 18, his mother writing on his behalf to order the interviewer to stay away, commenting that there were plenty of delinquents among the ignorant lot living in the same building who needed 'surveying'. She was at the time in great conflict with the housing authority who would not re-house her because she was such a troublesome tenant. When he was aged 20 the social services became involved with the household because his mother had attacked him with a knife. He was noted then to be an unemployed labourer who rarely went out in the evening.

At age 23 he did agree to an interview. He was still living with his now aged mother, but his siblings had all left and he no longer saw them. The home was in a very neglected state with the living-room floor partly eaten away by rats, the banisters and several doors fallen off and the sink almost permanently blocked. He had been continuously unemployed for eighteen months. He never went out in the evenings and his only two regular excursions each week were to collect social-security money and to window gaze. He had no outside human contacts apart from repair men and council officials. Asked about offences he replied pathetically: 'I can't get into trouble, I never go out.'

The conclusion that deprived boys rarely make good, even when they manage to avoid an official criminal record, has important practical implications. This and other studies have shown how easily individuals at risk can be spotted at an early age, but the desirability of inter-vention has been questioned on the grounds that a delinquent outcome, though probable, remains uncertain, so that some who do not require preventive measures would have to be subjected to them unnecessarily. However, if most deprived non-delinquents are social misfits of another kind, then the case for always attempting to intervene before it is too late is considerably strengthened.

CHAPTER VI

Changing the Course of Delinquency Careers

Going to the wrong school

The limited success of prediction formulae based on circumstances in early years suggests that events in subsequent life play an important part in determining the onset and course of criminal careers. Is choice of secondary school one such event?

The six primary schools from which the boys in the study were drawn each produced much the same proportion of delinquents (see Appendix IV, ref. 2, p. 127). In contrast, the local secondary schools, which the boys attended from age 11, differed markedly in this respect. Most of the study sample (335 boys) went to one or other of thirteen different local secondary schools, the rest being split up between a large number of different schools, including schools for the educationally retarded. The education authority gave us data on the numbers of boys aged 11–14 attending each of the thirteen schools and also the numbers of appearances in juvenile courts by boys of this age from each of the schools over a one-year period. From this information three of the schools were identified as having a high delinquency rate, six as having a low rate and four as being intermediate. The high delinquency-rate schools contributed nearly four times as many court appearances, in proportion to the number of boys in the schools, as did the low delinquency-rate schools. Among the latter group were two grammar schools, and these contributed almost nothing, only three court appearances in a whole year from a schoolboy population of 702 (see Appendix IV, ref. 26, p. 496).

At first sight these stark contrasts suggested a powerful influence by the schools, for better or worse, on the potential delinquency of their pupils. The figures were not unexpected as previous surveys had revealed large differences between the delinquency rates of London schools serving the same or similar neighbourhoods (Gath *et al.*, 1977). An investigation in the London Borough of Tower Hamlets had yielded particularly startling contrasts in the delinquency rates of the schools in that area, contrasts which the investigators felt could not be explained by variations in the populations of the streets served by the different schools (Power *et al.*, 1972). In the Cambridge study, however, it emerged on closer examination that the differences between the schools were more closely connected with the different kinds of boy joining each school than with anything that may have happened to them at school.

As mentioned in Chapter III 'troublesomeness' in primary schools, rated from comments by teachers and classmates, was highly predictive of becoming a juvenile delinquent. Nearly half of the most troublesome boys (44.6 per cent of 92), about one in five (21.6 per cent of 176) of the average-rated boys and only about one in thirty (3.3 per cent of 143) of the best-behaved boys became juvenile delinquents. These proportions held surprisingly constant regardless of which category of secondary school a boy attended.

Given the proportion of delinquents in each category of 'troublesomeness' and knowing the numbers of boys from the study in each category who were attending each school, it was possible to calculate the percentages of delinquents to be expected in the three groups of schools, assuming that nothing happened in the schools to alter the boys' delinquency potential. The expected percentages compared with the actual percentages of boys who became delinquents were as shown in Table 10.

Table 10   Comparison of expected and actual percentage of delinquent boys according to the delinquency rate of secondary school

	Expected percentage of delinquents	Actual percentage of delinquents
High delinquency-rate schools	31.3	35.7
Medium delinquency-rate schools	22.9	22.9
Low delinquency-rate schools	15.2	12.8

Although there were slightly more delinquents than expected at the schools with high delinquency rates, much the larger part of the differences between the high and low delinquency rates of schools was accounted for by differences at intake, the former schools suffering the consequences of the high proportion of troublesome boys sent to them. How the secondary schools came to have such contrasting populations at intake was something of a mystery. Their catchment areas were often overlapping, which permitted a certain amount of choice by parents. Probably those most concerned about their sons' education were the first to apply to and fill up the schools with the best reputations, leaving the rest to take up the vacancies in the less desirable schools. The grammar schools, naturally, admitted only those of relatively high intelligence and scholastic achievement who were most unlikely to become delinquents.

If some schools have the effect of promoting delinquency one might expect them to promote as well the closely related phenomenon of truancy. High delinquency-rate schools usually have poor attendance rates. From the questionnaires completed by their schoolteachers when the boys were 12, and again when they were 14, it was possible to identify 73 boys who were considered truants from their secondary schools. (The teachers were asked the direct question whether the boy had played truant frequently. They were also asked to state whether the boy's attendances amounted to less than 90 per cent of the total possible attendances, and if so whether the reason was truancy. Boys listed as truants on either or both questions were counted.) A similar number of truants were identified from their own admissions in response to the self-report inquiry at age 14. Troublesomeness at primary school was just as predictive of truancy at secondary school as it had been of delinquency. Accordingly, on the basis of the 'troublesomeness' ratings that had been made prior to entry to secondary school, Dr Farrington worked out expected rates of truancy (either teacher-identified or self-reported or both) in just the same way as he had worked out expected delinquency rates (see Appendix IV, ref. 43). The figures were as shown in Table 11.

Table 11   Comparison of expected and actual percentage of truants according to delinquency rate of secondary school

	Expected percentage of truants	Actual percentage of truants
High delinquency-rate schools	37.4	42.9
Medium delinquency-rate schools	29.6	30.6
Low delinquency-rate schools	22.7	18.3

The result was much the same as before. Most of the differences in incidences of truancy were accounted for by differences in 'troublesomeness' that had been present before the boys entered their secondary schools. There were slightly more truants than expected in the high delinquency-rate schools, but there was little to suggest that these schools had had any more effect upon truancy than they had had upon delinquency. (The relatively small differences between expected and observed percentages of both delinquents and truants could have been the result of early background factors other than troublesomeness, as well as being the result of later influences at the secondary schools.)

Although in this study most of the differences in the proportions of delinquents attending different schools could be attributed to the kinds of boys the schools had to deal with, it would be rash to conclude that these schools had no effect. A larger sample might have yielded more significant differences. It would be still more foolish to assume that schools elsewhere do not, or could not, make an impression upon their pupils' delinquent tendencies. A larger scale study by Michael Rutter *et al.* (1979), which included some of the same schools as in our own research and utilized a more sophisticated method of statistical analysis, indicated that although background factors present at intake were the main determinants of delinquency, still the schools did appear to make some difference. Farrington subsequently applied the same method of statistical analysis to our own data; the results were unchanged. Rutter did not have the same behavioural ratings of boys as we did, so one possible reason for the difference in results is that his assessments of delinquency potential at intake were less efficient.

In view of the very large differences between neighbouring schools found by Power, it was unfortunate that the Inner London Education Authority would not permit him to pursue research within the schools to find out the reasons. In another area of the country Reynolds *et al.* (1976) compared schools which appeared to have a similar intake, as judged by the mean IQ at intake of their pupils (on Raven's Matrices) and their social-class distribution, but found massive, unexplained differences in academic achievement, prevalence of delinquency and attendance records. It could be that in some places schools vary in policy much more than in the area where our study was carried out, and that some policies do have a significant effect upon delinquency. In particular, the amplification of delinquency problems that comes about through segregation of the less fortunate in low-stream classes is fairly well established (Hargreaves, 1967; Corrigan, 1979). The topic remains wide open for further research.

Getting married

Getting married is an indisputably crucial event which may be expected to have an effect upon life-style and delinquent habits. Since convictions of females are relatively scarce, and females are believed to be more conforming than males, one would expect marriage to exert a restraining effect upon delinquents. Moreover, if a decision to marry marks a psychological turning-point in a delinquent's career, an indication of readiness to settle down and accept social responsibilities, remaining single may be a bad sign. Save for the observation that prison populations sometimes include an unduly high proportion of single men, criminological research has contributed almost nothing to confirm or refute the common belief that marriage is a cure for male delinquency. In the present study we were fortunately able to obtain some pertinent information.

In the particular subculture in which the study was carried out, cohabitation without the obligations of a legal marriage contract was relatively unusual, but noticeably more frequent among delinquents. Among 17 men who, when interviewed at age 21, were living with a woman without being legally married, a majority of 13 were delinquents. In spite of this, delinquents were no more prevalent among those who were still unmarried at age 24 than among those who married earlier. Of the 397 men still in the United Kingdom at age 22, 77 married under 21, 104 married between the twenty-first and twenty-fourth birthdays and 210 had not married by the twenty-fourth birthday. (Owing to the length of time that elapses before a marriage appears in the records at the General Register Office, information on marital status after the twenty-fourth birthday was not available. The status of 6 men could not be ascertained because their current addresses were unknown and their names were too commonplace for adequate checking in the register.) The proportions of delinquents among these three groups were virtually the same, 33.8, 36.5 and 31.9 per cent respectively.

If the supposed beneficial effect of marriage is due to the influence of the wife, rather than the delinquent's prior readiness to reform, it would not produce an association between marital status and delinquency status, for the simple reason that the latter is generally established before marriage. Furthermore, the delinquent's reluctance to assume marital responsibilities may not have shown up in these figures because of the counterbalancing effect of pressure to marry if a girlfriend becomes pregnant. Men who married pregnant brides (identified by comparing date of marriage and date of birth of the first child on the respective registration certificates) were significantly more prevalent among the delinquents.

Since marriages take place at a time of life when the frequency of convictions is decreasing anyway, in order to demonstrate that marriage hastens the process one needs to compare the incidence of convictions after marriage with the incidence among men of similar age who remain unmarried. The statistics yielded a faint suggestion that delinquency less often persisted into adult years when men were married. Of the 181 married men, only 17, 9.4 per cent, were convicted for an offence committed between the twenty-first and twenty-fifth birthday, compared with 13.8 per cent of the 210 unmarried men, but this difference was not statistically significant.

More information about the possible effects of early marriage was obtained from interviews at age 21, when 59 of the 218 men seen were in fact already married. The married men, much more frequently than the single men, described their present life-style as having become more conformist. As many as 90 per cent of the married men, compared with 56 per cent of the single men, endorsed the claim that, in the past two years, they had become less likely to do things that might lead to trouble with the police. In addition, a number of social habits characteristically associated with delinquency were reported less frequently by the married men. For example, going around regularly in a group of four or more male companions was admitted by only 22.0 per cent of the married men compared with 49.7 per cent of the unmarried men. Use of a prohibited drug in the past two years was admitted by 13.6 per cent of the married men compared with 30.8 per cent of the unmarried. Heavy drinking (defined as expenditure over £8 weekly) was also reported by 18.6 per cent of the married men against 36.5 per cent of the unmarried men. On the other hand, some habits and attitudes, which were reported significantly more often by delinquents than by non-delinquents, were reported just as often by the married as by the unmarried. Admissions of involvement in fights, for example, were about equally common in both groups. In response to an attitude questionnaire, just as high a proportion of the married as of the unmarried expressed hostile attitudes to the police and aggressive attitudes generally. Recent unemployment was also about equally prevalent in both groups.

It seemed that the changes that tended to follow getting married were most noticeable in such matters as use of leisure time, but much less evident in more fundamental respects, such as aggressive attitudes and behaviour. Indeed, some of the changes brought about by marriage might be thought conducive to delinquency rather than the reverse. Married men were experiencing greater financial problems. Many of them had never before had to find money for rent. Contributions to the parental households in which most of them had stayed until marriage had been less than what they now had to spend to set up a new home and meet basic living costs. Indeed, married men were noticeably worse off in regard to debts. Thus, 52 per cent of married delinquents, as opposed to only 31 per cent of unmarried delinquents, reported having debts exceeding £50. In so far as the motivation for crime becomes increasingly instrumental in adult life — the felt want of money or goods weighed against the risks of getting caught — the newly married may feel under pressure to take more risks.

In contradiction to their more frequent claim to a lessening risk of the kind of behaviour that might get them into trouble, the married men's responses to the more detailed and specific self-report delinquency inquiry showed no such contrast. The admissions of offences by the married men were only slightly and quite insignificantly less than those of the unmarried. Of course, some men had not been married for long, and the self-report inquiry asked about delinquent acts over the past two years. However, the mean self-report scores of the 23 men who had been married for at least two years was no less than that of the more recently married men and was not significantly less than that of the un-married men (see Appendix IV, ref. 36, p. 355). The implication was plain: according to their own detailed self-reports, both groups had reduced their involvement in delinquency since last interviewed three years before, but still the married men were no less delinquent than the unmarried.

A comparison based on actual conviction records rather than on self-report might be more convincing. To increase the validity of the comparison, the married delinquents should be contrasted with single delinquents whose past conviction records were similar. Accordingly, each of the 52 men who married at age 22 or earlier, and who had a conviction record prior to marriage, was matched individually with the man nearest to him in birth date who was known to have remained unmarried for at least a further two years and who had had a similar number of convictions prior to the date of marriage. These 52 married delinquents were compared with their matched unmarried counterparts on reconvictions during the two-year periods following the dates of the marriages. Only 9 of the married men compared with 19 of the matching single men were reconvicted during the two-year follow-up. This was a just significant difference (see Appendix IV, ref. 42). How-ever, the 9 reconvicted married men averaged 2.0 reconvictions per man during the follow-up, compared with only 1.5 convictions per man among the reconvicted single men, so the total numbers of convictions sustained by the matched groups, 18 and 29 respectively, were not significantly different.

In order to test whether a longer period of marriage might produce a more definite reduction in reconvictions 25 delinquents who married under 21 were compared with 25 matching, unmarried delinquents on reconvictions during the subsequent three and a half years. The differ-ences were not statistically significant: of the married men 7 were reconvicted on a total of 16 occasions, of their single counterparts 11 were reconvicted on 22 occasions.

One may conclude that there probably was some tendency for marriage to be followed by a slightly greater reduction in reconvictions than was the case among men of a similar age who remained single, but the effect was small, too small to be conclusive given the limited size of the study sample.

The absence of any marked general trend towards swifter reduction of delinquency following marriage does not exclude the possibility that in individual instances a marriage may have a decisive effect for better or worse. The quality of the relationship and the kind of person chosen as a partner may be more important than the formal change of civil status. There was evidence, for example, that among delinquents who married under age 23, the proportion reconvicted at age 23 or 24 was higher among those whose wives had some conviction record. The figures (4 out of 10 against 5 out of 42) were too small for the contrast to be statistically significant, but a similar and very significant trend was apparent on examination of the records of the fathers of the study sample. Among 33 fathers who had a criminal record before they were married, 8 had wives with a conviction record and 7 of these 8 men were reconvicted. In contrast, less than half (11 out of 25) of the convicted fathers who married unconvicted women, were themselves reconvicted. Among those reconvicted, the average number of reconvictions per man was 4.43 for the fathers with convicted wives, and 1.73 for those with unconvicted wives (see Appendix IV, ref. 36, p. 352). These contrasts were not accounted for by any significant difference in the pre-marital conviction records of the two groups of fathers.

If male delinquents have a tendency to marry wives who are themselves delinquent-prone (the phenomenon of assortative mating), this might provide some clue to our otherwise puzzling findings. If most marriages have a restraining effect, as generally believed, that would explain the slightly lower incidence of persons reconvicted among married delinquents. If, at the same time, a minority contract unsuitable marriages, which exacerbate rather than diminish their delinquent habits, that would explain why reconvicted married men are on average reconvicted more often than the reconvicted single men. In support of this speculation, there was clear evidence that delinquents were more likely than non-delinquents to marry a girl who herself had, or later acquired, a conviction record. Of 16 wives with a conviction record (out of 188 names searched), 13 (81.3 per cent) were married to a delinquent, whereas only 39.0 per cent of the conviction-free wives were married to a delinquent. Marriages that were soon cut short by separation or divorce were distinctly more frequent among the delinquent section of the sample. Of course, the quality of the delinquents' marriages may not be a matter of their own deliberate choosing. A young man with a delinquent life-style, which includes an erratic work record, delinquent companions and heavy drinking habits, is unlikely to encounter or be accepted by the 'right kind' of young woman.

To sum up, the explanation that makes most sense of our findings is that marriage sometimes has a restraining effect upon delinquents, but less often than might be expected because of the tendency of delinquents to marry females who are themselves socially deviant.

Getting caught

Does a finding of guilt by a court serve to restrain youngsters from further offending, or does it aggravate their antisocial tendencies? The so-called new criminology, with its emphasis on the labelling perspective and the deleterious effects of stigma, would predict a worsening of behaviour, an 'amplification of deviance'. One can easily imagine how this might happen. The relations between a rebellious youth and his family, already strained, are likely to be further taxed by the unpleasantness of police inquiries, attendance at court and the prospect of unwelcome and shaming visitations by social workers or probation officers. The juvenile courts require reports from the offender's school, which draws the teachers' attention to the delinquent and may provoke further alienation from the school. Denunciations by magistrates, teachers and parents may contribute to a lowering of self-esteem and promote identification with the delinquent minority and with their antisocial attitudes and life-styles.

The criminal justice system acts upon opposite assumptions, namely that apprehension, conviction and deterrent punishment promote improvement, whereas misconduct that attracts no penalty promotes a softening of attitudes towards rule-breaking (Mills, 1958) and an amplification of deviance. The theory may be correct, but if the courts fail to punish severely enough delinquents may learn from the experience of being convicted that the consequences are not so bad as they feared and increase their offending subsequently. The theory propounded by Van den Haag (1975, p. 249), that 'delinquents are the products of the leniency of the law', predicts that offenders dealt with lightly should get worse while those dealt with more harshly should improve.

In this study, as analyses carried out by David Farrington clearly demonstrated, the general trend was towards a worsening of behaviour following the first finding of guilt. As this was contrary to his expectations, Farrington tried hard to discover an alternative explanation for the results, but found none. The evidence for an escalation of offending following conviction came from the self-reported delinquency scores obtained from interviews at successive ages — 14, 16, 18 and finally 21 years. Individuals convicted for the first time between one interview and the next tended to show a change for the worse in their rank positions within the total sample. For example, the 53 youths who were found guilty for the first time between interviews at 14 and 18 began with an average percentile rank of 59.5 (that is, rather worse than the 50th percentile, which would be the average for the sample as a whole), but by age 18 their average ranking was 69.3, a very considerable worsening (see Appendix IV, ref. 3, p. 129). These 53 convicted delinquents were individually matched with 53 others who had similar self-reported delinquency scores at age 14 (mean rank 59.4), but who had not been found guilty officially by the time they were retested at age 18. The matched group who escaped conviction, instead of becoming worse, improved so much that by 18 their average rank-score was 51.3, close to the average for the whole sample. At age 18 the difference between the mean rank-scores of the 53 convicted men and their 53 unconvicted counterparts was statistically very significant ($P = 0.002$). The same effect reappeared in a similar analysis of the scores of 21 young men first convicted between interviews at 18 and 21. Their mean self-reported delinquency rankings worsened significantly from 44.6 at 18 to 58.6 at 21 (Appendix IV, ref. 38).

The first doubt that arises is whether these increases in self-reported delinquency followed the court appearances or whether they began beforehand and were the cause rather than the consequence of being found guilty. Further analysis showed that the significant increases invariably occurred between interviews when a first conviction intervened, but not between interviews that preceded a first conviction. Thus, the mean rank-scores of men first convicted between interviews at 16 and 18 showed only a marginal and quite insignificant increase (from 55.2 to 59.1) between 14 and 16, but a very large increase (up to 74.0) between 16 and 18. Again, between 14 and 18 there was no increase, in fact a slight decrease, in the scores of those first convicted between 18 and 21. Since the interval between interviews was two or three years, and the self-report questions asked about behaviour in the previous two or three years, these figures fail to pinpoint the exact moment when the increases occurred. The increases might conceivably have all happened immediately before the convictions. However, bearing in mind that offences continue often for a long time before a conviction ensues, and that no significant worsening took place before the interval during which a first conviction occurred, it seems highly probable that the increases followed rather than preceded the convictions.

The accuracy of self-report scores as a measure of actual delinquent behaviour might be doubted. If some boys answered the questions unthinkingly or haphazardly they might, on occasion, give meaningless high scores by chance, whereas on retesting they would more likely produce ordinary responses. This would cause deviant scores to diminish or disappear on retesting, a phenomenon statisticians call 'regression to the mean'. This phenomenon could perhaps account for some of the apparent improvement of the high-scoring but unconvicted boys who gave near-average scores when retested subsequently. However, in view of all the evidence for the validity of self-report measures cited earlier, it seems very likely that some of the improvement was real. More important, the worsening of the scores of the convicted groups could not be explained in this way.

In order to make still more certain that the 53 youths first convicted between 14 and 18 were being compared with non-convicted youths who really were as badly behaved as themselves at age 14, the matching exercise was repeated. This time the non-convicted group was chosen so as to match not only on self-reported delinquency at 14 but also on 'troublesomeness' (ratings derived from independent comments by teachers and peers when the boys were 8 and 10) and on how many of the five key delinquency predicting factors were recorded from the survey of early backgrounds. The outcome was the same, the improvement of the unconvicted youths was just as striking and the contrast with the worsening of the convicted group just as large.

Further evidence that the worsening in self-reported delinquency scores reflected a real change in behaviour was obtained by noting how the convicted youths changed in other respects. Two attitude questionnaires, one concerned with hostile attitudes to the police (see Appendix IV, ref. 2, pp. 177–80) and another concerned with overt aggressiveness (ref. 3, pp. 74–5) were given to members of the sample, the first at ages 14 and 16, the second at ages 18 and 21. The police questionnaire invited agreement or disagreement with a series of statements such as: 'The police are always roughing people up', or: 'The police ought to get more support from the public'. The aggression questionnaire invited endorsement of such statements as: 'I enjoy a punch up', or: 'Anyone who insults me is asking for a fight'. Hostility to the police and overt aggressiveness were both very significantly correlated with being or becoming a delinquent, especially a recidivist delinquent. One might expect, therefore, if the apparent increases in delinquent tendency following conviction were real, that they would be accompanied by corresponding increases in these characteristics. In point of fact, the 27 youths first convicted between interviews at 14 and at 16 did show a significant increase in their rank positions on hostility to the police when tested at the latter age (see Appendix IV, ref. 34, p. 120), and the 21 youths first convicted between ages 18 and 21 became significantly more overtly aggressive in attitude at the later age (ref. 28, p. 281).

These findings echoed an observation made some years earlier, before any plans for an inquiry into the effects of conviction had been made. At age 14 the boys had been asked to rate themselves on a series of four-point scales. For example, each boy had to describe his degree of toughness as 'gentle', 'fairly gentle', 'fairly tough' or 'tough'. Seven scales reflecting an 'aggressive self-concept' were included. The scores from these indicated that the boys who already had a conviction record before taking the test were significantly more aggressive in their own self-estimates, but this characteristic was much less apparent among delinquents not convicted until later. From this it was concluded that aggressive self-concepts probably developed most noticeably with the experience of being convicted (Appendix IV, ref. 2, p. 185).

One alternative explanation still remains. Being convicted might have the effect of making youths readier to admit their delinquencies and so to produce higher scores than before without actually changing their behaviour. Farrington (Appendix IV, ref. 33, p. 121) tried to investigate this by comparing the self-reports of youths first convicted between 14 and 16 with those of unconvicted youths who had given similar self-report scores at age 14. As the boys had been asked when each admitted act was committed, he was able to identify acts said to have taken place before the 14-year interview which were recalled at 16 but had not been mentioned on the earlier occasion. If being convicted reduces concealment the convicted boys might be expected to recall more such acts than their unconvicted counterparts. There was in fact some such difference, but it was insufficient to account for all of the very marked increase in the self-report admissions of the convicted men.

In this study sample the numbers of youths reconvicted at various ages were insufficient to provide a secure basis for comparing the effect of reconviction with that of first conviction. There was some suggestive evidence, however, that reconvictions produced little or no further amplification of delinquent tendency. There was also some evidence that the worsening produced by a first conviction was not necessarily permanent. For example, the 39 youths who were already convicted when interviewed at 14 gave high self-reported delinquency scores on that occasion (mean rank 70.8), but by age 21 this had decreased significantly (mean rank 54.3). However, the previously mentioned complication of regression to the mean casts some doubt on the interpretation of this decrease. It is interesting to note, however, that, in contrast to the improvement shown by most of the 39 early convicted youths, the 13 among them who received institutional placements as a result of reconvictions between ages 14 and 21 retained high self-report scores (mean rank 61.5). Seemingly the experience of custody had not improved their offending habits.

The limited size of the study sample precluded a clear answer to the question whether the type of punishment awarded by the courts had relevance to the degree of amplification of delinquency that followed a first conviction. Of the 21 youths first convicted between 18 and 21 (none of whom were reconvicted in the period) 7 were discharged, either absolutely or conditionally, without punishment. By age 21 these 7 men had increased their self-reported delinquency scores much more than had the 14 men who received more punitive measures. This could be interpreted as slight evidence for the theory that initial leniency by the courts promotes further delinquency.

The finding that being convicted makes delinquents worse is not new (Klein, 1974). Two previous investigations by Gold (1969) and Gold and Williams (1969), in which young delinquents were questioned in confidence about their detected and undetected offences, both arrived at a similar result. Apprehended offenders were matched individually with offenders of a similar age who had never been apprehended, but who admitted to an offence committed within six months of the date the apprehended youngster was caught, and who also admitted a similar number of previous offences. The apprehended offenders committed more offences subsequently, according to their own reports, than did the similarly delinquent youths who had avoided being caught. Since,

as in our own study, only a small minority of the apprehended delinquents received a custodial sentence, the worsening behaviour could
hardly be explained as an adverse reaction to excessive penalties.

Accepting that a first conviction does result in an escalation of
delinquency, the reasons remain obscure. At age 18 the delinquents
in our study were asked how being convicted had affected them. Their
answers did not help. Very few mentioned any serious adverse consequences, such as expulsion from home or school or loss of employment.

Contrary to the deterrence theory, most previous research suggests
that severity of punishment, and especially commitment to a penal
institution, is more likely than leniency to produce an escalation of
delinquency. For example, in a substantial survey of juvenile offenders
convicted for violence in Columbus, Ohio, Dinitz and Conrad (1980,
p. 150) demonstrated that, 'with all else controlled', institutionalization,
as opposed to lesser penalties, was associated with shorter intervals at
liberty before re-arrest. In the Philadelphia cohort survey (Wolfgang
et al., 1972, pp. 226–9) it was noted that harsher penalties were
associated with greater likelihood of further offending. Penal regimes
that make little effort at rehabilitation are likely to have worse effects.
Farrington and Nuttall (1980), for example, were able to demonstrate
a link between overcrowding in prison and the likelihood of recidivism.

Some evidence in support of the deleterious effects of heavier penal
sanctions was presented in an official handbook for English magistrates
(Home Office, 1970, pp. 67–8). Juvenile offenders, both those first
convicted and those with previous offences, who were awarded fines
were less often reconvicted over the following five years than those
given probation or a custodial sentence. Unfortunately such observations are inconclusive. Even first-offenders vary in character. Those
given the severer penalties will usually be the ones considered by the
courts the worse behaved and the worse risks, and this fact, rather than
the penalty awarded, could explain their higher reconviction rate.
Police and courts in England rarely conduct, or allow, systematic
experiment. Decisions continue to be made in ignorance of the likely
effects. A deliberate experiment in which a series of not-too-serious
juvenile first-offenders were randomly allocated to different disposals
(for example, no action, caution without conviction, conviction and
discharge, conviction and fine, or conviction and supervision) would
provide swift answers to many of the otherwise unanswerable questions
raised by surveys such as ours. Such research as has so far been carried
out on the effects of sentences upon young offenders, mostly conducted
in America, provides no clear guidance and merely serves to emphasize
the urgent need for proper experiment (Farrington, 1978).

In one British experiment (Berg et al., 1978), worth quoting because
it did exceptionally make use of random allocation, evidence emerged
that firmer action can sometimes reduce delinquency more effectively

than apparent leniency. The sample consisted of 96 children brought before the juvenile courts in Leeds under care proceedings because of failure to attend school. The magistrates agreed to deal with these cases in two ways, either by adjournment and repeated recall to court, or by placement under the supervision of a probation officer or social worker. A predetermined sequence of random numbers decided which of the truants were to receive supervision.

A previous study, based upon retrospective comparisons, had suggested that adjournments were superior to supervision in discouraging further truancy. The random-allocation experiment confirmed that this was so. Furthermore, during the six months following their court appearance, the truants dealt with by adjournment committed significantly fewer offences leading to conviction or caution than did those placed under supervision. The authors did not discuss why adjournments should work better than supervision, but one may suspect that being made to come back to court repeatedly, with the prospect each time of being sent away from home under a care order, was a greater deterrent than the more nebulous requirement to report to a supervisor.

Contrary to the evidence from analysis of their own detailed admissions, the delinquents appeared to suscribe to the popular belief in the deterrent effect of being caught and convicted. Questioned on the point during interviews at age 18, 37.0 per cent of the 81 delinquents who made some specific comment implied that their last conviction had had a restraining effect (for example, 'I'll never do that again'). Only 14.8 per cent described reactions compatible with further crime (for example, 'I'll be careful not to get caught another time'). The remainder gave neutral responses implying that conviction had had no effect upon their delinquency. A similar conclusion emerged from the survey by Belson (1975). The great majority of his sample, 85 per cent, endorsed the reply that they would 'care very much' if the police caught up with them for stealing. Of those who reported having been caught by the police, 71 per cent thought that the effect, at least the first time it happened, was to make them steal less; only 4 per cent thought it had made them steal more. The most common reasons they gave for the decrease in stealing were risk of being 'put away' or fear of the consequences of being caught again. Belson noted that the great majority of those caught had not been punished with a custodial sentence, but his tentative conclusion was that getting caught appeared to work as a deterrent to further offending, provided that the consequences of apprehension were not so trivial that a boy could easily laugh them off. It may be, however, that this is just one more example of the frequent incongruity between what people say, or believe, about their behaviour and how they actually do behave.

To sum up, notwithstanding opinions to the contrary, including those of the delinquents themselves, the study findings were unequivocal in revealing an increase of deviant attitude and behaviour following first conviction. No firm conclusion could be reached as to the reasons for this, or whether the type of sentence passed made much difference. The number of offenders in the study who received custodial sentences was too small to permit confirmation of the result of other research suggesting that severer penalties produce greater amplification of deviance.

Moving away

Inner-city areas and their immediate surroundings are regularly reported to have higher crime rates than elsewhere (Baldwin, 1979), so it was reasonable to investigate whether members of the study who moved away would have a lessened risk of delinquency. The issue was complicated because the most socially disadvantaged and delinquent-prone families were apt to change their address frequently, although usually remaining within the city, whereas more distant moves were probably more characteristic of the better-placed and socially mobile families with less delinquency potential (Rutter and Madge, 1976, p. 156). In our study we tried to find out if those who moved away were already less delinquent-prone, or whether they became so as a result of leaving behind the crime-producing influences of the city.

Of the 397 men alive and in the UK at age 22, only 14.6 per cent were living at addresses outside the London postal districts at the time of interviews and inquiries at age 18, while 22.6 per cent were at addresses in London outside the immediate area of the study and a majority of 62.7 per cent were either still at the same address that they had been when first recruited (at age 8–9) or at an address nearby. Delinquents were more likely than non-delinquents to have moved from their original intake address. At the 18-year inquiry, of the 101 who were by then delinquents, only 20 (19.8 per cent) were still at their original address compared with 97 (32.8 per cent) of the 296 non-delinquents. Recidivists were particularly frequent movers. On the four occasions when inquiries were made as to the whereabouts of the whole sample (at intake and at ages 14, 16 and 18), 36.1 per cent of the recidivists, compared with only 15.8 per cent of the rest of the sample, had as many as three or four different addresses recorded.

Although as a general rule changes of address were correlated with delinquency, the reverse was the case for moves to places outside London. On the occasion of each inquiry at ages 14, 16, 18 and finally at 21, fewer of those who were living outside London were found to have been convicted for offences committed in the interval since the previous inquiry. For instance, at 14 years, only 5.4 per cent of the 37 who were then living outside London postal districts had been convicted for offences committed since intake, whereas among the other 360 members of the sample more than double this proportion,

11.7 per cent, had been convicted during this time. Again, of the 47 outside London at the 16-year inquiry, only 6.4 per cent, compared with 11.7 per cent of the other 350 members of the sample, had been convicted for an offence committed in the interval since the 14-year inquiry. A similar trend was apparent among the 58 who were outside London at the 18-year survey; only 12.1 per cent of these had been convicted for an offence in the interval since the 16-year survey, compared with 17.4 per cent of the 339 at that time in London. Finally, at age 21 (when a total of 232 men were traced) 51 were outside London, of whom 15.7 per cent had been convicted for an offence since the 18-year inquiry, compared with 33.1 per cent of the 181 men known to be still in London. (Only half the non-delinquents were interviewed at age 21, hence the higher proportions of delinquents in that survey.)

This clear and consistent trend, which held true at whatever age the moves took place, was not accounted for by any tendency for the non-delinquents in the sample to be more likely to move out of London. The proportions with previous convictions (that is, for offences prior to the interval during which a change of address was recorded) were similar among those who moved out of London to what they were among those who did not. The reduced incidence of convictions appeared to be a consequence rather than a cause of the moves. To confirm this, 13 delinquents who moved out of London were matched individually with 13 men who had a similar number of previous convictions, but who remained in London. The group who moved out sustained significantly fewer subsequent convictions (see Appendix IV, ref. 44, p. 38).

The reduction in convictions following moves out of London might be explained by a reduction in the proportion of detected offences, supposing that there is less police surveillance in other areas. Evidence of an actual change in behaviour was obtained by examination of self-reported delinquency scores. There was a definite reduction in the mean rank-scores on self-reported delinquency admissions (from 54.1 at 14 to 40.6 at 21) among the 32 men who had moved out of London meantime. No such reduction was observed among another group of 32, matched individually on self-report at age 14, who remained in London.

A reduction in delinquent behaviour could have come about through the break-up of delinquent associations and the lessened scope for crime outside London, rather than through any change in the delinquents' propensity for bad behaviour, given the opportunity. Indeed, this interpretation was favoured by the observation that at age 18 many of the items of behaviour that sharply differentiated delinquents from non-delinquents (such as unstable employment record, aggressive attitudes, excessive drinking and smoking and above-average sexual activity) were about equally prevalent among those who had moved out as among those who stayed in London.

Whatever the explanation, the fact remains that moving out of the city makes the continuation of a delinquency career less likely than would otherwise have been the case. The effect was more substantial than, for instance, the effect of getting married. The result could have implications for decisions about placements for delinquents after release from institutions. A Dutch survey of older delinquents released from detention showed that there was more recidivism among those who returned to their old haunts than among those who went elsewhere (Buikhuisen and Hoekstra, 1974).

CHAPTER VII

What Should be Done?

The need for caution

The task of interpreting research findings, and the further task of translating them into prescriptions for the prevention, control and treatment of delinquency, call for the exercise of considerable caution. Criminological surveys are inevitably somewhat parochial. The Cambridge study was limited to young, working-class urban males growing up in London in the 1960s and 1970s. The findings might not apply to females, to the middle classes, to immigrant groups with different attitudes and standards, or even to present-day youths in the same area, now that the pressures of unemployment have become so much more acute. If the Cambridge study had been more recent, and carried out in areas smitten by economic recession, the association between delinquency and personality deviation might have been less. New recruits to the ranks of the delinquents, produced when families who have been socially successful and industrious are plunged into poverty and welfare dependency, and their jobless adolescent children rendered idle and disaffected, may not have the same characteristics as the hard-core recidivists of the past.

It would be even less justifiable to attempt generalizations from the present survey to places and cultures with vastly different traditions and economic circumstances, where poverty and a rigid class hierarchy appear more acceptable and permanent, where individual competitiveness is an alien characteristic, where social rules are more strictly enforced with harsh sanctions and where possessions are in short supply and less temptingly available to the opportunistic thief. The thesis that most delinquents must be psychologically deviant, or the product of broken homes or faulty parental upbringing may be tenable only where it can be claimed that the social system is sufficiently stable, democratic and economically successful to provide reasonable opportunities for all normal, law-abiding youngsters. The gangs of violent and politically motivated black youths in Cape Town, for instance, or the juvenile ancillary terrorists who have been indoctrinated in the sectarian schools in Northern Ireland may be the products of social, not necessarily individual, unrest. A working paper on juvenile justice, prepared by the secretariat for the 1980 United Nations Congress on the Prevention of Crime, observed that 'in many cities of the [African] continent, children and young persons were swarming in the streets by the hundreds, without any goal except to survive, without support, without hope, subject only to peer group pressure'. The desperate characters generated by such conditions can have little in common with the average London delinquent.

No single delinquency survey can examine everything that might prove relevant, or measure everything with equal efficiency. The Cambridge study concentrated on socio-psychological data. Had we been able to include more physical measures, such as electroencephalographic recordings, tests for chromosome abnormalities, bone X-rays (to identify precocious developers), or tests of specific neurophysiological functions (such as judgement of spatial relationships) it is conceivable, if rather unlikely, that important new causative factors might have been discovered. Had it been possible to observe more closely and measure more realistically attitudes and behaviour within the family, parental influence might have appeared even greater than our results indicated. Observations of the real-life situations in which delinquent acts take place might have shown that tempting circumstances are as powerful as individual attributes in determining who breaks the law. Research findings are inevitably coloured by the predilections of the designer. One does not find what one does not search for and it is all too easy to give spurious emphasis to factors, such as size of family, which are relatively easy to document and quantify. In evaluating the implications of a particular research, the findings have to be set against the wider background of data and conclusions from other work. Where findings conflict judgement has to be suspended pending further inquiry.

The Cambridge study, like most survey research, was an exercise in passive observation, monitoring the statistical correlations between delinquency and a wide range of background variables. The interpretation of such correlations in terms of chains of causation is highly problematic. Surveys supply useful leads and provide data which any successful theory must accommodate. A theory of delinquency which failed to take account of the demonstrable importance of family criminality and relative social deprivation could no longer be taken seriously. On the other hand, surveys may not help to decide between, for instance, the several theories of transmission of criminality from father to son which were discussed in Chapter III. More decisive evidence can be obtained by experiment. For example, if one wants to know whether criminality is transmitted from father to son genetically, or by some aspect of child-rearing, one needs to look at what happens to sons separated from their natural parents. This cannot be arranged deliberately for the benefit of experimental research, but much can be learned from the quasi-experimental situation created when the son of a criminal father is adopted from birth by a new set of parents.

Some influences are more susceptible to experimental testing because they can be artificially manipulated. The theory that opportunity is an important factor can be tested by experiments in increased surveillance, or improved physical protection of property, which provide some measure of the amount of reduction in delinquency that can be achieved by making offences more difficult. The simple device of the self-locking steering column, which gives no great inconvenience to the driver, demonstrably reduces the probability that his car will be taken. The substitution of tough steel coin boxes in place of the weaker aluminium variety effected a dramatic reduction in thefts from English telephone booths (Mayhew *et al.*, 1976; Clarke, 1980).

In formulating ideas for social action, survey findings have to be taken in conjunction with results from these other methods of investigation. Even then, research conclusions do not translate readily into recipes for policy. Wherever possible, it is advisable to begin with small-scale pilot trials to evaluate the practicability and relative merits of different courses of action and to discover unanticipated side-effects. For example, it would be of little use to equip all new cars with steering locks if (as some evidence suggests) this served to increase thefts of older cars, and it would achieve little to equip all cars with the device if this merely resulted in more house-breaking instead of car theft. Likewise, there would be no advantage in reducing the number of prosecutions, in order to prevent the amplification of deviance consequent upon conviction, if in practice the benefits were outweighed through more youngsters becoming delinquent from an awareness that risk of punishment had been lessened.

Early deprivation a key factor

The concept of a recurring cycle of 'transmitted' deprivation, manifest in successive generations of problem families, was propounded by Sir Keith Joseph when he was Minister of Health, and inspired a number of research contracts, including the extension of the Cambridge study. In truth, the surprising concentration of delinquent individuals, especially recidivists, among a small minority of families in our sample, and the strong tendency for criminal parents to have criminal sons were among the most important observations to come out of the study. The additional years of follow-up, made possible by continued funding, enabled us to show that, among all the background factors investigated, criminality in the family was the most powerful predictor of recidivism persisting beyond the age of 18. Furthermore, the constellation of unfavourable features, present from an early age, that was characteristic of juvenile recidivists was found in greater frequency and in even more extreme form among the young recidivists whose criminal careers were destined to continue into adult life. The worse the background the worse the likely outcome.

Persisting recidivists came typically from large-sized, low-income families in which several other persons also had a criminal record. Additional adversities, such as illegitimacy, welfare dependency, broken homes, frequent changes of residence, neglectful parents and exposure to harsh or abusive punishments were frequently noted. Social disturbance was evident at every stage of their lives, in disruptive behaviour in primary-school classrooms, in truancy and aggression at secondary school, in serious academic under-achievement and, after school, in unstable work record and antisocial life-style. When persisting recidivists were interviewed at age 24, their irresponsible behaviour, poor living circumstances and unstable sexual relationships gave every indication that their own early experiences of deprivation would be repeated in the lives of their unfortunate offspring.

Such observations are far from new, but they serve to confirm that what has been found in the past and in other places remains true of an urban, working-class sample in England today. The classic survey conducted by Lee Robins (1966), in which 524 former clients of a St Louis child-psychiatry out-patient clinic were followed up and interviewed thirty years later, arrived at almost identical conclusions. Those with pronounced antisocial features as adults (typified by arrests, divorce, low occupational status, social alienation, belligerency, sexual promiscuity, welfare dependency, excessive drinking and 'the transmission of behaviour problems' to their children) were drawn very predominantly from those whose childhood backgrounds and behaviour were similar to the backgrounds of the persistent recidivists in the present study. Robins found that the degree of juvenile misbehaviour, whether measured by variety, frequency or seriousness, was the best predictor of persistent adult antisociality. Broken homes, especially those associated with divorce or separation, poverty, large-sized family and antisocial fathers, were the most powerful background predictors. Other longitudinal studies have yielded similar findings (Robins, 1978; Cline, 1980), and research in other countries confirms the near-universality of the link between family deprivation and delinquency (Friday, 1980).

Of course, early deprivation does not account for all crime. A history of social adversity would be untypical of older, white-collar criminals such as embezzlers, corrupt officials or fraudulent business executives. In our sample, the early adversities common among persisting recidivists were rarely found among latecomers to crime or among one-time offenders, and were less prominent among young recidivists who sustained no further convictions after passing the age of 18. Deprivation and its aftermath, the antisociality syndrome, was associated with the hard core of persisting delinquents whose conviction careers usually started at an early age and continued into their twenties. They were predominantly lower class, poorly socialized, often impulsive and ineffectual in the crimes they committed, the kind of delinquent who is highly visible to police, public and the media and extremely trouble-some to social agencies. In our study few of the boys exposed to severe early deprivation developed satisfactorily. Even those who did not become official delinquents were peculiarly liable to social isolation and inadequacy and neurotic complaints. In short, the study confirmed what others have repeatedly reported, the existence of an easily identi-fied group from problem families whose prospects of becoming contented and effective citizens are poor and who are all too likely to act as transmitters of deprivation to their own children.

Our findings constitute a challenge for theory and for social policy, but they provide no ready explanation and no easy solution. Deprivation applies only to a section of delinquents, and how deprivation operates to produce delinquents is far from clear. Deprived youngsters may steal because they lack money, but that does not explain why they should also fight each other or use prohibited drugs. The observation that boys from criminal families are at special risk of prosecution for any offences they may commit (see pp. 46–7) calls attention to the role the auth-orities may play in concentrating upon, and possibly exacerbating, the problems of the less fortunate sections of society. The fact that teachers often dislike and anticipate trouble from the children of deprived families may accentuate their alienation and contribute to their anti-sociality. The resemblance between criminal fathers and their sons in their demands upon state welfare (see pp. 50–1) leads to the suspicion that some parents may subtly influence their children away from firm commitment to honest work. The delinquent's tendency to marry a delinquent female may be thought to amplify any genetic predisposition to aggressiveness and antisociality. At this point a brief review of current theories of delinquency may help to clarify the issues.

Delinquent theories

Suggestions for coping with the delinquency problem should follow from some rational theory of causation. Unfortunately for the peace of mind of academics delinquency theories have been incorporated into political ideologies (Radzinowicz, 1966), and this encourages polemics based upon the sort of simplistic explanations that have mass appeal. Themes favoured by the 'law and order' lobby include the pusillanimity of the courts in failing to pronounce properly severe sentences and the lack of discipline in the modern family. Softer-hearted 'wets' still prefer to think of delinquents as the victims of broken homes, unsympathetic schools or an insufficiency of facilities for constructive use of leisure. Left-wing radicals see delinquency as a by-product of the class conflict inseparable from a competitive, capitalistic economy.

Although slightly more in keeping with the philosophy of the 'wets' and 'do-gooders' than with those of the other factions, the study findings did not come up with any one salient influence upon which to build a unitary theory. Indeed, the academic quest for a general explanation of all delinquency, what Walker (1977) dubs the search for 'the criminologist's stone', no longer enjoys much credibility. Indeed, as Walker so forthrightly concludes, 'the quest for a general theory which will account for all instances of crime or deviance or misbehaviour makes no more sense than would a search for a general theory of disease'.

It may be possible to construct theories to account for general trends and for certain characteristic patterns, such as the behaviour of the 'hard-core' persisting recidivist from a bad background. Less usual forms of conduct (an unexpected house-breaking by an Oxbridge man, for example) may never be predictable from any general scientific law, but only understandable by after-the-event historical analysis, what Walker calls a narrative type of explanation. Even in relation to the commoner forms of delinquency, the available theories are no more than probabilistic, indicating circumstances which make delinquency likely, but leaving a residual uncertainty. The Cambridge study found delinquency most likely to occur where there was an agglomeration of interacting adversities, but no one item of adversity was in itself a necessary or sufficient cause and many delinquents, especially those with only brief conviction records, had no significant background adversities.

According to their particular expertise and interests, different theorists seek the origins of delinquency in different places, in the environment (for example, unguarded property, 'indefensible space'), in the social system (for example, class conflict, economic and social discrimination), in delinquent affiliations (for example, 'differential association', the delinquent subculture), in unsatisfactory upbringing (for example, broken homes, parental neglect), or in the peculiarities of offenders (for example, delinquent personality, hereditary predisposition, risk-takers). It seems to me, both from common sense and from the results of this study, that these different explanations are not totally incompatible, and that an eclectic mixture of some or all of these concepts is likely to depict reality better than any single doctrinaire approach. Contemporary thinking lays most emphasis on environmental and social influences, but in relation to the more persistent 'career' delinquents individual characteristics may assume greater importance.

Bio-social theories, which seek explanations for deviant behaviour in an interaction between environmental circumstances and genetically determined temperament or neurological functioning of the individual, have recently enjoyed something of a renaissance (Wilson, 1975; Mednick and Christiansen, 1977). For a long time such theorizing fell out of fashion. Criminologists have never quite recovered from the colourful excesses of Lombroso's early theories, according to which the criminal type can be recognized by misshapen skulls and other deformities indicative of a biological throw-back to a primitive and pre-moral stage of evolutionary development. Proponents of the bio-social approach have been subject to vitriolic abuse from the ideologically committed young who like to believe that men are born equal and that bad environments account for all human failings. Sociologists have been particularly scornful. One well-known American authority (Gibbons, 1970, p. 75) dismissed the topic in his textbook with the brief comment that 'many years of biogenic exploration of delinquency have not yielded any valid generalisations . . . Although it cannot be unequivocally claimed that there are no biogenic influences in delinquency, it is undeniably true that none have been shown to exist.' Writing a decade later, however, Gibbons (1980) concluded, less confidently, that the question of biological forces 'remains open for further examination and study'. Some of the neurophysiological disorders associated with childhood behaviour problems may be preventable through environmental measures — control of lead pollution, for example (Rutter, 1980) — and realization of this may reduce the opposition to biogenic theories.

Recent work, utilizing sophisticated techniques of electroencephalography, taking into account the functional dominance of one cerebral hemisphere over the other, has yielded fresh evidence for a neurological factor in criminal behaviour (Yeudall and Wardell, 1978). There has even been some renewed interest in some of the 'stigmata' of criminality described by Lombroso. Such minor abnormalities of development as asymmetrical ears, absent ear lobes, unusual head circumference and furrowed tongue, which occur with moderate frequency among normal people, are reportedly found with particular frequency among children who are impulsive and restless and likely to develop behaviour problems (Waldrop et al., 1978). If these minor anomalies are associated with corresponding developmental deficiencies in the brain this might account for the link with troublesome, hyperactive behaviour.

The possibility that delinquency may sometimes be associated with subtle bio-physical peculiarities in no way contradicts the observation, on which all investigators seem agreed, that the vast majority of delinquents do not suffer from any gross or readily identifiable abnormality such as *grand mal* epilepsy or mental deficiency. Chronic physical illness or diagnosed neurological conditions were much too rare in the study sample to have made any substantial contribution to the incidence of delinquency. It has been suggested (Stott, 1962) that congenital weaknesses and childhood ailments are features of delinquents, but we found no significant correlation between delinquency status and reports of illnesses in early life (see Appendix IV, ref. 2, p. 118).

Mortality among teenage males, which is largely attributable to accidents or violence, is probably higher among delinquents on account of their life-style. The 5 study members who died before the twenty-second birthday were all delinquents. Only 2 died naturally of cancers.

One drowned trying to escape from custody, one was killed in a fall occasioned by drunkenness, and one darted out into a road and was run over. We found, as have others, that delinquents are accident-prone. At age 18, the delinquents reported significantly more injuries, especially injuries sustained in fights and traffic accidents, than did the non-delinquents (Appendix IV, ref. 3, p. 72; Lewis and Shanok, 1977).

Most of the bio-physical variables investigated in our study yielded no tangible links with delinquency. Reports of birth injuries and abnormalities during maternal pregnancy were obtained from hospital records (Appendix IV, ref. 1, pp. 110 ff). Measures of height, weight and strength of grip were taken in the hope of confirming previous reports of a correlation between muscular, athletic, mesomorphic physique and delinquency (Glueck and Glueck, 1956; Gibbens, 1963; Cortes and Gatti, 1972). Neither line of inquiry yielded any palpable results, but considering the limited size of the sample and the fact that these investigations, which were incidental to the main project, used rather crude assessments, one cannot conclude that birth trauma and body build are irrelevant, merely that, in so far as these factors may have been operative, they were less powerful than other more obvious influences. Wadsworth (1979, p. 77), in his analysis of the results of the National Survey of Health and Development, also concluded that body shape, as indicated by height—weight ratio, was unimportant in relation to delinquency, such small associations as were found being accounted for by the social class and ordinal position of birth of the delinquents. On the other hand, in view of all the evidence linking premature or protracted births to a raised incidence of minimal brain damage and consequential behaviour problems (Bonnell, 1980), it seems surprising that no significant relationships emerged from our scrutiny of obstetric histories of delinquents and non-delinquents (see Appendix IV, ref. 1, pp. 110 ff).

Indications that constitutional differences between individuals made some contribution were not entirely lacking. After all, intelligence, which proved an important factor (see pp. 38—40) is to some extent an innate, genetically determined attribute. One physical measure that yielded a significant relationship with delinquency was resting pulse rate, which was taken during the interviews at age 18. A fast pulse, which might reflect greater reaction to the stress of being interviewed, was marginally commoner among the non-delinquents (see Appendix IV, ref. 3, p. 71). This confirms findings from the national survey (Wadsworth, 1979, p. 101), in which pulse rates were noted during school medical examinations at age 11. Atypical under-reactivity of the autonomic nervous system in response to stress has been repeatedly put forward as a characteristic of delinquents and particularly of psychopaths (Loeb and Mednick, 1977). This under-reactivity is possibly connected with the parallel phenomenon of resistance to aversive conditioning, which has been held to account for the delinquent character's lack of response to punitive restraints (Trasler, 1962). Wadsworth argues that the cardiac responses of delinquents need not be an innate physical characteristic, and that they could be the result of habituation to severe stresses in early life. He noted that slow pulse rates were particularly prevalent among delinquent boys from broken homes.

In conclusion, it seems likely that subtle constitutional factors and physiological peculiarities may favour the development of the antisocial personality attributes found among many delinquents, but save in exceptional cases these do not amount to identifiable pathological conditions.

Turning now to sociological explanations, according to one set of theories delinquent behaviour is not so much a matter of individual choice or individual temperament, but rather a response to pressures to conform to the expectations of a criminal milieu or delinquent sub-culture. In modern pluralistic society groups with very different values and allegiances can coexist. For instance, some groups, supported by traditional religious values, believe fervently in obedience to rules restricting sex to marital relations, while others adhere to the opposite principle of the right of the individual to sexual self-determination. Underprivileged sections of the community are especially likely to develop a subculture supportive of delinquency. Because they are cut off from the good life enjoyed by those better placed in the class hierarchy, middle-class ideas of hard work leading to just reward are inappropriate. Imbued with the futility of lawful striving, the sub-culture supports the idea of living for the moment, using physical aggression when it pays off and seizing any chance to steal or cheat. In these groups, behaviour condemned as antisocial by the rest of society is tolerated, even admired, especially when committed at the expense of anonymous strangers or representatives of the more privileged classes. In these subcultures youngsters are brought up to norms of behaviour that inevitably bring them into conflict with the law. The more they conform to the expectations of their milieu, the more deviant they appear on middle-class standards. A frequently quoted example is the offence of thieving by employees, an activity frowned upon by employers but totally acceptable to the workforce, at least when conducted on a scale that does not attract too much unfavourable attention.

The credibility of the notion of subcultures committed to a criminal ideology has been attacked both on logical grounds and on the absence of empirical evidence for their existence (Kornhauser, 1978). Although our study demonstrated the prevalence of anti-establishment attitudes among delinquent youths (notably hostility to police, disillusionment with school and readiness to resort to physical violence) there was no indication of any widespread adherence to dishonesty as a chosen way of life. Stealing was recognized as wrong and was more likely to be concealed, or admitted with mitigating excuses, than boasted about. In comparison with descriptions contained in official records, youths who reported participation in acts of dishonesty or violence leading to a conviction were more likely to minimize than to exaggerate the seriousness of their offences (Appendix IV, ref. 3, p. 25). Parents were almost always condemnatory of their children's delinquency. Of course, delinquents, like other people, find it difficult to summon up the same degree of condemnation for the particular infractions which they admit to having committed themselves (Hindelang, 1974), but this amounts to no more than a lessening of disapproval, a lowering of standards rather than a reversal of principles. Delinquents are as ready as other people to complain when they find themselves the victims of theft. Even among school populations delinquents are less popular than their non-delinquent fellows (Appendix IV, ref. 2, p. 106; Roff *et al.*, 1972).

The subculture theory implies that the groups from which delinquents come, not just the delinquents themselves, are supportive towards their behaviour, but evidence from attitude surveys suggests the contrary. Conklin (1971) found that people living in an urban area with a high crime rate were as condemnatory of most criminal offences as were the residents of a middle-class suburb. Rossi *et al.* (1974) found little difference between classes or racial groups in Baltimore in their estimates of the seriousness of various crimes. The assumption that people living in delinquent neighbourhoods, who experience the unpleasant consequences at first hand, should refuse to condemn crime does not seem plausible. Kornhauser comments dryly (1978, p. 218): 'the persistence of this belief . . . owes much to its use as an ideological weapon in the war with the Establishment . . . By refusing to confront the harsh facts that shape the lives of those without power these theories betray their ignorance of, or indifference to and contempt for those in whose names they profess to speak.'

According to an alternative set of explanations, the so-called 'strain' theories, delinquent-prone groups within society do not choose freely or conform happily to deviant values opposed to those of the establishment. Instead, they strive after the same goals and are attracted to the same values as the middle classes, but from their disadvantaged position they find their way continually blocked. The nature of the class structure, with its inequitable distribution of wealth, education and power, ensures that however hard they work at honest pursuits their desires for money and status will never be fulfilled. The goals of material advancement extolled by the media can never be reached in legitimate ways. This incongruity between targets put before them and their limited means of access strains their commitment to conventional values. If they are not to be just pushed around and left behind they have to abandon customary social restraints and take illegal short cuts, which they are forced to try to justify to themselves with various mitigating excuses and rationalizations.

Subculture theory and strain theory depict delinquents as individuals who adhere to, or are forced by adversity to adopt, attitudes that permit them to commit antisocial acts. Their nonconformist stance can become second nature to them, a facet of their personality. Control theory, which is a rival sociological interpretation, envisages delinquent behaviour arising in a more passive way, not from intolerable pressures or grievances impelling people to become deviant, but from an absence of social restraints which leaves people free to indulge their greedy or predatory impulses unchecked. According to control theory, the main force responsible for producing well-socialized citizens guaranteed to follow the straight path of conformity with the law is the strength of social bonds, the dependence of individuals upon collaboration with others, and especially with authority figures, in order to secure their basic needs. Alienation from the mainstream of society, on the other hand, means a loosening of bonds and freedom to deviate because, if one has little stake in society to begin with, one has little to lose by being caught and convicted of a delinquent act.

Most studies, including our own, find that even among the poorer classes children perceive their parents as disapproving rather than applauding delinquency. If no strong parental attachment exists loss of approval carries no great threat, so alienated children feel free to go their own way in defiance of the wishes of their elders. Most schools, like most parents, try to uphold accepted standards of behaviour. The pupil who is doing well and has a good reputation at his school will be less inclined to nonconformist behaviour than the poor performer who has much less to lose by truancy and indiscipline. Of course, alienated individuals may still be restrained to some extent by the impersonal deterrents provided by the criminal law, but these are not so powerful because the delinquent always hopes to evade detection.

These differing sociological interpretations are united in one respect, in that they all trace the origins of delinquency to faults of social organization which provoke oppositional subcultures, deprive sections of the population of a fair share of goods and status, or permit the alienation of the less fortunate. They suggest that a cure for delinquency should be sought through social policy rather than by treating the individual offender. Strain theory points to the need to make circumstances easier for groups vulnerable to delinquency, but control theory could be interpreted to favour a stricter, more disciplined approach in the home, at school and by the justice system. None of these theories contradicts the fact that, whatever the predisposing social situation, certain individuals, by virtue of their personal characteristics, are more likely than others to react in delinquent ways.

An eclectic approach

Granting that delinquency has a multiplicity of causes, the many different theories appear to complement rather than to contradict each other. R. E. Johnson (1979) took this as a starting-point for research and set out to measure a diversity of variables derived from different concepts. He included, for example, both parent–child relationships and perceived risk of being caught. He wanted to construct an explanatory model that would combine the virtues of several theories. In particular, he wanted to integrate the ideas of the social-control theorists with the concept of 'differential association', that is, the notion that deviant personal values develop through selective interaction with deviant peer groups. He postulated a causal sequence beginning with parent–child bonding. Parental love and concern and a strong child–parent attachment encourage the child to identify with adult (that is, non-delinquent) social values. This, in turn, promotes a favourable attitude to school, good performance, and an identification with the conformist values which teachers support, at the same time diminishing the influence of peer groups and discouraging associations with delinquents. Conversely, lack of parental attachment and school failure will decrease commitment to educational and occupational aspirations, while increasing the likelihood of association with delinquent peers and the acquisition of such delinquent values as the belief that getting caught is a remote risk.

The Cambridge study was not designed to elicit these particular pathways to delinquency, but the interlocking processes pictured in Johnson's model would explain some of the findings rather well. For instance, parental behaviour, which might be taken as a measure of parent–child bonding, was related to school performance, and both were correlated with delinquency. Having delinquent associates was very closely correlated with being a delinquent. In the self-report inquiry, before mention of their own behaviour, the boys were asked whether any of their friends had commited the acts listed (see Appendix IV, ref. 2, p. 56). The extent of boys' self-admitted delinquencies and that attributed to their friends corresponded extremely closely. A preference for delinquent friends may mean alienation from the majority. In the Cambridge study the boys who became delinquents had been relatively unpopular among their classmates at primary school, in that they were not often named by others as 'one I'd like as a friend' (Appendix IV, ref. 2, p. 101). Similar results have been reported in a more recent study by Hardt and Hardt (1977), in which boys who named convicted delinquents as their 'best friends' themselves produced very high self-report delinquency scores. It would seem that potential delinquents, being poor school performers and to some extent outcasts, tend to mix with each other, thereby increasing deviant behaviour.

In an effort to validate his causal model Johnson carried out a survey of 734 high-school students using an anonymous questionnaire that included questions about delinquent acts, relations with parents, feelings about school and performance in school-work, occupational expectations and aspirations and attitudes to law-breaking. The responses to the different groups of questions were translated into scores meant to measure such characteristics as delinquent values, delinquent behaviour and attachment to parents. By means of elaborate statistical computations, using standardized regression coefficients in a 'path' analysis, it was shown that the patterns of correlations between these different measures were broadly compatible with the causal factors and causal sequences envisaged in the theory. However, in comparison with delinquent values, delinquent associates and school experiences, parent—child relations appeared to be much less important than was expected. Social-class membership and concern about poor occupational prospects, which would have been expected to be important according to subculture and strain theories, made no significant contribution.

This work, which is a good example of its kind, illustrates the many problems that confront the delinquency theorist attempting to interpret survey results. Even Johnson's complex multi-factorial model lacked the precision needed to predict delinquency very efficiently. The significant 'paths' identified in his analysis accounted for only 27 per cent of the variation in frequency of self-reported delinquent behaviour. As Johnson himself stated (p. 116): 'it should be admitted that none of the major theories appear to be doing very well'.

The Johnson model was not claimed to be necessarily valid outside current American society (p. 43). In England, for example, social-class membership, or at any rate family income, appeared to have considerable importance according to our own results. The model was not claimed to account for delinquency outside the range of commonplace social behaviour, since it expressly ignored biogenic and psychopathological considerations, which were assumed to have importance only in exceptional cases. Specifically excluded from the theory, therefore, were 'those adolescents — only a small minority — beyond a very broad range of "normal" intelligence, emotional development, and socialization' (p. 45).

The attempt at empirical verification rested on the belief that the scores derived from questionnaire responses fairly represented the concepts they were supposed to measure. The assumption seemed reasonable in relation to such matters as: 'What has been your most common grade in school — A, B, C or D?' It seems more doubtful whether the quality of an adolescent's childhood relationships with his parents can be judged by putting such propositions as: 'It has been hard for me to please my father — Always? Usually? Sometimes? Seldom? Never?' As Johnson (p. 141) pointed out, questions put to adolescents, even in the past tense, 'cannot really recapture a specific earlier time.

Perhaps there is some crucial period in a child's life during which his experiences with mother and/or father are quite predictive of later behavior'. The Cambridge study, being longitudinal rather than cross-sectional, was able to show this to be true. This is, of course, no reflection on the Johnson survey, for no one research can encompass everything.

The decision of what to include in a survey is necessarily subjective. Johnson thought that the notion of parental deviance 'does not seem to merit inclusion in a general model of delinquency causation on a par with parental attachment' (p. 21). He felt that parents' deviance would attentuate their children's attachment to them and thus prevent the passing on of their deviant value-system, but this seems questionable. In the Robins (1966) survey, for example, parental deviation was found to be a particularly powerful predictor of adult antisociality. Even if parents do not directly communicate criminal value-systems to their children, there are many other ways in which the children may be affected, as was shown in the discussion in Chapter III (see pp.49–52). Had the Johnson survey, like the Cambridge study, included measures of parental criminality, a different pattern of correlations, indicative of different pathways to delinquency, might have emerged.

All survey-type research has its limitations. The attempt to detect and explain general trends may lead to the neglect of contrasts between different types of offending. Johnson stated frankly that his aim was 'to uncover reasons why young people violate legal norms, not specifically why one steals and another destroys' (p. 93). Accordingly, he combined self-reports of theft, vandalism and assault, which were in any case highly intercorrelated, to produce a single global assessment of delinquency. A similar decision was taken in the Cambridge study, justified by the preponderance of theft offences, the close correlation between self-report scores on different groupings of offences, and the fact that most of the violent or destructive offenders also committed acts of dishonesty (see Appendix IV, ref. 27, p. 103). The versatility of most young delinquents' misbehaviour makes it reasonable to study an entity of 'generalized' offending, but even so it is unlikely that all categories of law-breaking, including such minority offences as domestic violence or deviant sex, and including all degrees of seriousness or persistence, can be accounted for by a single causal model, however comprehensive.

Recognizing the artificiality of ignoring all subcategories of offender, Johnson did in fact analyse separately data from the two sexes in an attempt to decide whether male and female delinquency had similar causes. The numbers were small, and the conclusions uncertain, but it appeared that poor school performance and delinquent associates were more important influences towards delinquency in boys than girls, and that attachment to school was a more important restraining influence for girls than for boys.

Surveys rooted in a particular time and place cannot chart the efforts of environmental changes, although these are probably extremely important (Council of Europe, 1979). Some of the social changes that have been blamed for promoting delinquency include a lowering of social standards (for example, lessened respect for authority and for property rights, altered relationships between the generations allowing youth greater self-determination, more permissive attitudes towards nonconformity, the stimulation of material desires through television commercials, etc.), greater opportunities for law-breaking (for example, more unattended vehicles, less protection of property because it is insured, more homes left unoccupied because man and wife both go out to work, more self-service shops that facilitate stealing, longer hours during which youngsters remain unsupervised, etc.) and increased risk of arrest (associated with an expanded and more active police and criminal justice system aided by more anti-drug laws and powers to stop and search).

The Cambridge study was no more able than other surveys to investigate these suggestions. The minority who moved away from London did provide a means of demonstrating that the environment of different areas influenced significantly the incidence of officially recorded offences, but the reasons for this (for example, level of police surveillance, opportunities for crime, changed work prospects) could not be determined.

Further advances in the understanding of delinquent behaviour and the possibilities for control may well come about from small-scale experiments. Large observational surveys tend to throw up again and again the old, familiar generalizations about social background, which provide very partial explanations. So-called action research seeks to modify circumstances, such as scholastic regimes, which surveys are obliged to take for granted. Testing the effect of specific interventions is useful not only for eliciting 'causes' in the abstract, but also for identifying where and how the causal chains may be broken or modified in the interests of both delinquents and victims.

In view of all the limitations of research, the multiplicity of infuences upon behaviour, the complex interactions between different factors, the effect of changing social conditions, the difficulty of measuring items that may be of crucial importance, and the enormous margin of unexplained variation left over in every prediction exercise, any attempt to integrate available data and theories must be highly speculative. The diagram in Figure 2, freely modified from a scheme produced by Dr R. V. G. Clarke, a leading exponent of the broad approach to crime causation (Clarke, 1977), is an attempt to represent my own suggestions as to the major influences that may contribute to delinquent behaviour.

The diagram illustrates likely causal pathways to delinquency and locates points at which intervention might be helpful. It represents a

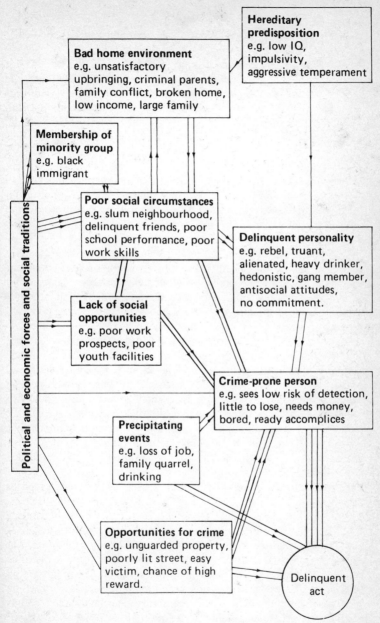

Figure 2   Diagram illustrating some of the major influences that may contribute to delinquent behaviour

personal interpretation, based more upon guesswork than science and the reader must make up his own mind about the suggestions for social policy which flow from it.

The triple arrows in the diagram represent influences that seem particularly important, the double arrows are for important influences, the single arrows represent others that seem significant but not predominant. Political and economic forces and social traditions are depicted as determining, to a greater or lesser extent, nearly all the other factors, but having a particularly direct bearing upon social adversities such as slum environments, the disadvantaged position of racial minorities and limited employment opportunities. Many delinquent acts are committed by the minority of crime-prone individuals, who are in turn the product of such influences as bad homes, poor social circumstances and 'delinquent' personality and life-style. But delinquent acts may also be committed by others, who would not ordinarily be regarded as antisocial, when they react to special circumstances or respond to particularly tempting opportunities for quick rewards.

Looking at the problem in this way it can be seen that the level of delinquency might be reduced in any number of ways by interventions at different stages of the process. Delinquency prevention might encompass grand reforms of the socio-economic structure, anti-poverty programmes, the provision of greater opportunities to young persons, the identification and preventive treatment of vulnerable groups, such as truants, school rebels and neglected children, as well as protective measures designed to make the commission of crime more difficult and punitive measures designed to discourage the offender who is caught and frighten off others who might be similarly tempted. The decision about what combination of methods to apply should ideally be made in the light of trials of effectiveness, cost and social acceptability. All too often, however, social-policy decisions are made in conformity with the prevailing political ideology, without much reference to research. At the time of writing, methods of deterrence, retribution and incapacitation appear to be in the ascendancy, while social welfare and preventive treatment are definitely out of fashion.

Problems of intervention

Disillusionment has set in since Waddington (1941) wrote a popular book suggesting that rational organization, based on sound scientific research, would solve most social ills. Today, nobody expects criminologists to produce a neat solution to crime patterns, no more than psychologists, economists and sociologists are expected to resolve the evils of poverty, famine, tyranny, religious warfare, racial strife, class conflict, over-population or global pollution. The question now being asked is whether research has anything at all of practical value to contribute to policy on the prevention, treatment and control of delinquency. The answer seems less certain than it did a generation back.

Social measures to combat delinquency are often categorized as preventive, therapeutic or punitive, but the distinctions are by no means clear cut. Some measures, such as burglar alarms, have crime prevention as a specific aim, others, such as compulsory school attendance, are introduced for different reasons but may contribute to delinquency prevention as a secondary effect. Some measures, such as financial support for the unemployed, are meant to apply to all who need them, whereas other schemes of prevention, such as special classes for difficult pupils, may be intentionally directed towards groups thought to be at special risk of delinquency. Programmes applied only to apprehended offenders, if their purpose is to help the individual to avoid further conflict with the law, are referred to as treatment. If, however, the action taken has the prime intent to administer retribution for wrong done, or to deter the individual from repeating his offence, or to deter others from imitating him, then it is classed as punishment. Sometimes what is meant to be treatment looks more like punishment, especially to the recipients. One important difference, however, is that treatments are claimed to be beneficial to offenders in other respects besides the mere avoidance of reconviction, a claim rarely made for old-fashioned corporal punishment.

Considering the multiple causes of youthful offending, no single measure can be expected to make much impression on the total incidence. As with health problems, a variety of approaches is called for, each one hopefully making some contribution, but total eradication is just not feasible. Resources have to be distributed in a balanced way between measures intended to make the commission of crime more difficult, measures to reduce pressures and temptations, and measures directed towards the reformation or rehabilitation of the established offender. The effectiveness of delinquency prevention and treatment programmes is difficult to evaluate, but many of the schemes proposed, such as social-skills training, job-creation projects and voluntary community service, have merit in themselves, regardless of their effects upon delinquency.

The maxim that 'prevention is better than cure' is a sound medical principle, although there are always limits to what is practicable. Sewers are obviously more effective and convenient than treatment after people have become infected, but compulsory screening of entire populations for the presence of venereal disease would be less readily accepted. Where social behaviour is concerned the issues are never very clear cut. Alcoholism is undoubtedly reduced more effectively by restricting the supply or raising the price of liquor than by treating individuals who have become problem drinkers, but this inevitably involves some loss of liberty and choice for everyone. Instead of concentrating upon apprehended offenders, crime might be more effectively reduced by restrictive controls, by a proliferation of bolts and bars, by branding personal possessions with ineradicable identification marks, by random police checks and body searches, by requiring schoolchildren and employees to carry cards showing their hours of work so that absentees can be picked up, by closer inspection of income and expenditure through the compulsory use of banks for all routine payments, by the use of identity cards and registration of all fingerprints, by late-night curfews, etc. The inconveniences would soon outstrip the benefits. Although experience of martial law and military occupations suggests that petty crimes can be reduced by such regimes, these are not models one would wish to emulate.

Welfare programmes, which might be expected to be less controversial than restrictive controls, also have their costs and problems. Help for unfortunate minorities, to prevent so many of them resorting to delinquency, means a political decision to divert resources from elsewhere. Conservative thinking always includes some anxiety that, by making life too easy for the poor and the unemployed, one will undermine the will to work or damage the spirit of ambition and competition on which the private-enterprise system relies. Mixed-ability classes in state schools may be better for the academically backward than being segregated in inferior groups, but it takes a lot to convince the parents of brighter pupils that their children are not being unfairly sacrificed in the process.

Social policy has always to achieve a compromise between conflicting needs and to maintain a reasonable balance between costs and benefits. Empirical research may help the decision-makers, but social values, moral considerations and acceptability to the public, in short, political considerations are the chief determinants of policy.

Programmes for the prevention and treatment of delinquency have had an unfortunate history. Ambitious schemes have been tried and found wanting. Criminological surveys have pointed with monotonous regularity to the high concentration of delinquency in the poorest areas of big cities. One might expect that a concerted attack on such neighbourhoods, aimed at eradicating overcrowding, poverty, unemployment, ill health and educational backwardness, would produce an immediate impact on the incidence of youthful crime. American experience shows that the solution is much less simple than it looks.

An early example of a community-based anti-poverty programme, the Chicago Area Project, which started in the wake of Clifford Shaw's classic survey of the delinquent zones within that city, yielded at best some ambiguous results (Kobrin, 1959). A later attempt to provide an array of new community, educational and employment opportunities for youths in the Lower East Side slum in New York, known as the Mobilisation for Youth Project, incurred massive expenditure and introduced many innovatory experiments. 'Tens of thousands of poor

. . . were reached by the agency, children were taught to read, school drop outs were given training and jobs, dilapidated apartments were renovated, families on welfare were assisted in demanding adequate allowances' (Weissman, 1969, vol. 4, p. 192). The effect on delinquency, however, was comparatively slight: an estimated reduction from 97.3 in the year 1962 to 90.6 in 1966 in the number of arrests per thousand youths aged 16–20 in the area serviced, compared with a slight increase, from 89.9 to 91.7, in those parts of the Lower East Side not helped by the project (ibid., p. 197).

The leaders of the Mobilisation for Youth schemes did not consider the relative failure of their endeavours any reflection on the assumption of a causal connection between deprivation and delinquency. It was evident that the project workers had failed to alter in any fundamental way the continuing problems of poverty that afflicted the area. They had pointed out needs, assisted many individuals and demonstrated the possibilities of guided self-help, but the eradication of the adverse social conditions underlying the high delinquency rate would have required a revolution in social policy and a political power of action that they did not possess. They were strictly limited in their ability to change policy in the state schools, or to support protest movements while they continued to depend upon funding from the authorities, or to manipulate the economy to provide permanent work instead of mere temporary training. They were obliged to watch programmes 'launched under the banner of lofty public goals', altered for reasons of political expediency and moulded 'to suit the political leadership on which the agency depends' (ibid., p. 190).

Even if stated therapeutic aims are achieved, this does not always bring about the expected reduction in delinquency, and may even have a reverse effect. In one Canadian project, random allocation of delinquents to a scheme of family-crisis intervention resulted in slightly more recidivism among the treated cases (Byles and Maurice, 1979). The singling out of individuals for treatment or prevention can produce harmful side-effects that neutralize or overwhelm any benefit that might otherwise have been derived. One can imagine that, in the brutal milieu with which many delinquents have to contend, distrustful, aggressive attitudes are necessary for survival. 'Improving' potential delinquents by training them to conform to more peaceful, middle-class norms may put them at a serious disadvantage and worsen their social problems.

The Cambridge Somerville Youth Project is frequently cited as telling evidence for the damaging consequences of misplaced effort by middle-class volunteers and social workers. A sample of 782 boys up to 12 years of age was selected from among children attending schools in a high-delinquency area of Boston. A high proportion of difficult pupils and potential delinquents was included. From this pool, 325 matched pairs were obtained. The members of each pair were similar in age and in rating of delinquency potential and also, as far as possible, similar as regards intelligence and educational attainment, health, emotional adjustment (evaluated by teachers), home background (judged by social workers) and place of residence. One member of each pair was allocated at random — by the toss of a coin — to a treatment group, the other member remaining in a control group who were left to be looked after, where necessary, by the ordinary medical and social services (Powers and Witmer, 1951). The treated group was given counsellors who were employed to befriend the boys in any way which seemed most appropriate. Some counsellors used traditional 'family casework' methods, others concentrated on practical help and persuasion. Boys were taken on trips, guided into recreational activities, introduced to various organizations and youth groups, and invited to summer camps. They were given health checks and many were referred for medical attention. There were frequent discussions with teachers about the boys' progress and backward boys received individual coaching from tutors during or after school. The help provided ranged from removing head lice to preparation for higher education. The attention lasted, on average, about five years, starting in 1939.

Ten years later the criminal records of the treated and untreated groups were compared. The numbers convicted among the treated and the controls (107 and 95) were similar, as was the total number of convictions sustained (315 and 344). There was no significant difference in the frequency of serious offences, the types of offences recorded or the incidence of recidivism (McCord et al., 1959). In a later study McCord (1978) examined the records, thirty years after the termination of the project, of the 253 men who had remained under treatment beyond 1942, together with their matched controls. Although the number of offenders in the two groups remained almost identical, there were more recidivists among the treated men. A questionnaire inquiry, based on 95 per cent of the sample who were successfully traced, revealed that in some respects the treated group appeared to have fared worse than the untreated. More of the treatment group (14 per cent against 9 per cent) had never married, there was a higher incidence of alcohol problems and mental illness among them, fewer were in white-collar jobs (29 per cent against 43 per cent) and more of them felt dissatisfied with their work. McCord suggested that the project may have fostered dependency and unrealistic expectations among those treated, leading to subsequent resentment and a feeling of deprivation. The interaction with adults from a different social milieu may have aroused conflicts contributing to illnesses in later years. My own hunch is that the findings were probably due to antecedent differences between the treated and untreated groups, which the attempt at preliminary matching, followed by random allocation, had failed to eliminate. For example, it seems there were significantly more boys of low intelligence (IQ of 80 or less) among the treated group (McCord *et al.*, 1959, pp. 202–3). Assuming that the allocation was truly random, all temptation to push the needier cases into treatment having been successfully resisted, any differences must have come about by an unlucky fluke of chance. An additional reason for the apparently damaging effect of treatment may have been a tendency on the part of the treated group, because of their past experience in ventilating personal problems, to report any current difficulties more readily than the controls. Whatever the correct interpretation, the McCord results point to the need for careful evaluation, not only to demonstrate effectiveness, but to ensure that programmes intended as helpful are not in fact causing more harm than good.

A serious criticism of the Cambridge Somerville project, from the standpoint of an evaluative exercise, and one that applies to many such endeavours, is that the nature of the treatment was diffuse and ill-defined. Whatever effect on the incidence of delinquency might have been recorded, it would have been uncertain which aspects of the treatment were responsible, for the help given included a variable mixture of practical advice, health care, extra welfare benefits, supplementary education, personal attention presumably promoting self-esteem and the experiences of a therapeutic relationship. For research purposes it is better to try one thing at a time rather than to confuse, for example, the effects of remedial education with those of family casework, unless, of course, one starts with the hypothesis that only a 'total push', utilizing as many modes of simultaneous intervention as pòssible, is likely to achieve an effect.

Claims to startling successes in some delinquency programmes are by no means lacking. Particularly impressive are the small-scale endeavours by charismatic personalities who devote their lives to the reformation of troublesome juveniles. An interesting example is the work of John Embling (1978) in Australia, who ran foul of the education authorities for his close befriending of alienated boys. These schemes point the way to highly effective therapy. Unfortunately they depend upon individualistic personal relationships between leader and led and also upon selection of cases able to respond. This makes such programmes difficult to replicate and difficult to assess in a systematic, scientific manner. Far too many intensive and expensive treatment projects, although they have every appearance of success as judged by recorded improvements in behaviour – as, for instance, in the Freudian inspired therapeutic community in Illinois described by Marohn *et al*. (1980) – lack any adequate control comparison to show that the changes associated with treatment were more than might have occurred without intervention.

Large-scale, systematic and potentially reproducible delinquency-prevention projects aimed at vulnerable individuals and yielding a measurable effect upon conviction statistics are exceptionally few and far between, especially in England, where evaluative research has never enjoyed the priority it deserves. Some apparently successful American attempts to alleviate the delinquency potential of the scholastically retarded were cited earlier (see p. 42). The Wincroft Youth Project, based on a slum area in the English city of Manchester, resembled in some ways the Cambridge Somerville enterprise, but on a much smaller scale. It appeared to have a modest, but statistically significant effect upon officially recorded delinquency (Smith *et al.*, 1972).

The ordinary youth services are apt to restrict their help to a relatively prosperous and law-abiding section of the community, or at the very least to offer it only to youngsters who are able and willing to attend an approved centre and conform to established rules and structures. The Wincroft Project followed the tradition of detached social work, reaching out into the streets and haunts where the delinquent youth of the slums normally congregate. For a period of fifteen months the project ran a café, open in the evenings, where volunteers and professional youth workers could gradually get to know the local youngsters. From among the groups they came to know, a sample of 54 boys, average age 15, was selected as a target group for treatment on the grounds that they were either already official delinquents with at least two findings of guilt, or were rated as maladjusted or pre-delinquent on a teachers' questionnaire (the Bristol Social Adjustment Guides). The café had closed, but these 54 boys were contacted again and offered intensive counselling and befriending over a period of three years. The help included practical assistance in finding jobs or claiming benefits, introduction to recreational activities and the setting up of a football team and numerous outings and leisure-time schemes, but always with an emphasis on building up the kind of trusting relationship that would facilitate intimate discussions with participants and their families, leading to a questioning of irresponsible social attitudes and behaviour.

In order to evaluate results a control group was selected from another part of the city where the environment was judged to be comparable. On most social measures (for example, population density, infant mortality, crime rate) the areas were similar or, where they were not, Wincroft usually appeared to be the worse. Matching case by case was impracticable, but the control group was selected so as to be similar to the treatment group in distribution of ages, family size, social adjustment scores (Bristol Guides) and previous court appearances. During the period of evaluation, from the beginning of treatment on 1 January 1966 to 31 January 1968, when therapeutic contacts had already terminated or were being wound up, 55.4 per cent of the controls, but only 37.0 per cent of the treated group, had appeared in court for a criminal offence (a significant difference). A year later the difference had diminished (62 per cent against 50 per cent), but was still in favour of the treated cases. At least while it lasted, the intensive preventive effort appeared to have reduced delinquency among a highly delinquent-prone group. On a measure of social adjustment, however (the Asocial Index of the Jesness Inventory), the treated and control groups showed no significant difference. Since the inventory measured attitudes rather than behaviour, the authors suggested that perhaps social attitudes in a delinquent environment may persist unchanged for some time after behaviour begins to improve (Smith *et al.*, 1972, p. 247). A similar suggestion arose from the Cambridge study findings that, at age 21, youths who had already terminated their delinquency careers were still deviant on our 'antisociality' measure, although they were no longer so three years later (see pp. 79, 81).

The results of the Wincroft Project may seem meagre, but even a small reduction in delinquency can effect considerable savings. The authors pointed out (ibid., p. 255) that during the evaluation period, 1966–9, the treated group, as a consequence of their fewer court appearances, had proportionately less than a third of the residential training ordered for the controls. The apparent saving on this, and on probation services and court costs, would probably have covered the cost of the social-work programme.

The greatest hindrance to progress is the difficulty of mounting adequate scientific evaluations of social interventions. Any new measure aimed at reducing delinquency is always in competition with a host of other influences that are difficult to control and continually changing. The effects of a new policy applied to the whole population, the intro-duction of military service, for example, are hard to distinguish from the effects of all the other changes in social conditions going on at the same time. In principle, schemes aimed at selected groups, such as samples of young unemployed, or some category of apprehended offenders, or members of lower-stream school classes, are more readily susceptible to evaluation, since a proportion of the target category can be left out of the programme in order to have a control group for com-parison. Considering the serious implications for the individuals receiving the treatment, especially if imposed compulsorily, and the importance of the outcome for society at large, treatment evaluations are highly desirable, even ethically imperative, but all too rarely carried out.

The essence of any evaluation of a treatment project is the demon-stration of a difference between treated and untreated cases which were similar before the intervention began. The neatest and most valid method of comparison is by random allocation of a large number of potential candidates between a treatment programme and an untreated control group. Unfortunately, in real-life situations this is rarely achieved.

Urgent or unforeseen considerations often prevent particular individuals being allocated according to the research plan. Ethical objections are raised on the grounds that some individuals would be unfairly deprived of the possibility of benefit, or that some would be subjected unjustly to longer-lasting restrictions than would otherwise have been the case. Administrators and practitioners engaged in operating traditional and accepted methods of dealing with delinquents often fail to share the academic researcher's sense of the urgent necessity for rigorous evaluation; they may feel they already know what to do and do not care to have outsiders trying to undermine their good work.

Methodologically satisfactory evaluations of programmes of treatment or prevention have been accomplished only rarely, so that many promising ideas have never been properly tested. The relatively few systematic evaluations of important projects that have been reported have all too often failed to demonstrate any significant decrease in the number of arrests or convictions. Extensive reviews of these preponderantly negative findings, both in the United States (Lipton *et al*., 1975; Greenberg, 1977; Romig, 1978; Wright and Dixon, 1977; Lundman and Scarpitti, 1978) and in England (Brody, 1976) have led many criminologists to a new brand of conventional wisdom, the conclusion that 'nothing works' in the realm of delinquency prevention and treatment.

Fashionable as it has become, there is a certain implausibility about this conclusion, for it seems to imply that nothing one does to delinquents, however kind or however nasty, makes the slightest difference. Actually, the conclusion that nothing works is far from certain. In view of all the difficulties with which evaluative research has to contend the findings need to be interpreted with caution whether they appear to support treatment claims or whether they point to therapeutic impotence (Elliott, 1980). For example, it often remains uncertain exactly what procedure is being evaluated, since the theoretical justification for delinquency programmes is rarely specified sufficiently or tested properly; intermediate goals, such as the defects that treatment is supposed to remedy, are not always defined or measured, and the causal connections between these goals and the reduction of delinquent behaviour is left unclear. Typically, the same mixture of ill-defined measures is given to all and sundry, regardless of individual need or suitability, with the result that benefits to some may be offset by damage to others. All too often, attempts are made to assess the impact of programmes that hardly deserve testing (Klein, 1979). Many programmes are grafted onto existing penal regimes in institutions where the limitations of outlook or tradition, or the demands of security, preclude a realistic application of treatment principles. The use of untrained and uncommitted staff, poorly motivated subjects and a half-hearted approach easily eliminates any likelihood of benefit (Quay, 1977). Financial constraints, and pressures to publish results quickly, lead to unsatisfactory reports based upon small samples and short follow-up periods which would hardly be expected to yield statistically significant results unless the reduction in reconvictions were extraordinarily pronounced.

Ideally, the outcome of a treatment programme should be compared with that of a control group receiving no attention whatsoever, but for ethical and practical reasons comparisons are most often made between slightly different kinds of treatment, which obviously reduces the expectation of a significant contrast. Individuals known to have enlisted in some special programme risk coming under closer scrutiny than usual, which may artificially inflate the records of their offences and invalidate comparisons with a control group. In practice, even when it has been agreed to in principle, random allocation between a treatment programme and a control group is difficult to achieve. The persons responsible for sentencing or classifying offenders all too often find reasons why particular individuals cannot be allocated the way research requires. Most of the published evaluations i ave been based upon *post hoc* matching techniques, comparing cases selected for treatment with others that appear similar but which have been dealt with differently. Unfortunately, it is virtually impossible for matching to take into account all the subtle and unrecorded factors which influence the selection of recruits for a treatment programme.

Regardless of the actual state of the evidence, the view is increasingly gaining ground that, since costly treatment programmes are apparently ineffectual, the only rational response to delinquency is punishment. Wait until the delinquent is proved guilty of an offence, then punish him in just proportion to the gravity of his crime. Variations of sentence to accommodate individual circumstances or hypothetical treatment needs are seen as unjust and unjustifiable. The juvenile should be dealt with as a responsible human being whose freedom, like that of the sane adult, should not be curtailed except as an appropriate punishment for a proved offence (Morris *et al.*, 1980; Taylor *et al.*, 1979).

Treatment enthusiasts, and those professionally engaged in the helping services, neither welcome nor accept these conclusions. They see no evidence nor reason to suppose that conventional penal measures are any more effective than treatment programmes. Sentencing on a strict tariff basis could result in a reversion to an impersonal, oppressive system in which belief in punishment as a means of preserving law and order over-rides any attempt to alleviate the social inadequacies from which many delinquents suffer. In the United States, where a number of legislatures have introduced statutes fixing a narrow range of mandatory punishment for each offence category, the prison population has escalated to an unprecedented peak, without any noticeable effect on crime rates. The tariff which decides the amount of punishment for each type of offence has no empirical basis and may change in response to irrational swings of public opinion. Despite all the rhetoric about soft treatment for juvenile offenders, the number of juveniles incarcerated in Prison Department establishments (borstals and detention centres) in England has increased dramatically in recent years. In 1960, when the Ingleby Committee on juvenile justice reported, 800 boys aged 14–16, representing 4 per cent of all boys of that age-group found guilty, were sentenced to Prison Department custody. By the year 1978 the figure had risen to 7297 or 12 per cent of the total found guilty (Rutherford, 1980). Nowadays, when found guilty of a serious offence, a juvenile is half as likely as an adult to receive a custodial sentence, but in 1955 he was twenty times less likely to be so sentenced (Tutt, 1981).

One has to turn to American research for an example of an objectively evaluated and successful preventive scheme in which candidates were allocated to treatment or control groups by a strictly random process (Seidman et al., 1980). The scheme sought to 'divert' juveniles, who would otherwise have been processed through the courts and experienced the usual measures of probation or institutional placement, to an active programme of prevention. The 'treatment' was carried out by student helpers trained by the research workers and assigned to clients 'on the basis of mutual interests, race and sex'. The strategies employed included 'behavioural contracting' (that is, promoting written agreements between the juvenile and his parents, or others involved, to provide specified rewards or relief from restrictions in return for specified changes in behaviour), 'relationship skills', and 'child advocacy' (that is, the mobilization, on behalf of the client, of the community resources — educational, vocational or recreational — needed to enable him to achieve legitimate goals). In two separate applications of the programme, in which treated and control groups were followed for two years, consistent and statistically significant differences emerged. The number of contacts with police, the seriousness of offences recorded by the police, and the number of referrals to the courts were all significantly less for the treated group. Curiously, however, as in the Wincroft project, no significant changes in the social attitudes of the treated group were discernible from their responses to psychological tests.

The originators of this project were at pains to point out that their system was designed for juveniles with serious delinquency problems who were at real risk of extended involvement with the penal system. Those who could ordinarily be dealt with by a caution might not benefit, or might even be harmed, by exposure to unnecessary intervention. Diversionary systems risk encouraging a 'widening of the net', through the referral of cases of a minor sort that would not ordinarily attract a penal sanction. This can nullify the prime object of such schemes, which is to provide a better alternative to conventional penal sanctions and not an extension of penal measures. In fact, something of this sort appeared to happen when the investigators turned over their temporary experimental programme to the more conservative-minded court and welfare authorities, who preferred not to use it for the more serious offenders.

Successful treatment of sentenced delinquents by means of counselling or psychotherapy, techniques dependent upon the establishment of a personal relationship, has rarely if ever been statistically validated. Experience suggests that relatively few delinquents respond to these approaches. Group methods, social-skills training and other techniques requiring the actual practice of approved styles of behaviour have more often given evidence of effectiveness. A good example was the Cascadia project, based on an institution of that name in Washington State. Male first-offenders aged 15—18, drawn from the inmate population, were allocated — 'essentially' at random — to three groups, two social-training groups (one of which employed models to act out the behaviour which the boys were required to imitate) and a control group. Each group included 64 boys comparable in intelligence and criminal history. After five years there were 31 recidivists in the control group compared with only 15 in each of the treated groups (Sarason, 1978). In another project in Florida, randomly selected delinquents given non-authoritarian guidance by student counsellors, in addition to their regular supervision on probation, committed fewer acts of misconduct subsequently than others not given this attention (Lee and McGinnes Haynés, 1980).

These occasional successes have to be viewed against a background of many reported failures, and probably many more failures never reported. There is no doubt that the pioneers of delinquency prevention and treatment were wildly over-optimistic about the magnitude of the results to be expected from their efforts. Research experience suggests that interventions are far more complex and difficult than at first envisaged, but they are not necessarily futile. Delinquent behaviour is in large part the product of social circumstances that are unlikely to change in the foreseeable future. A modest impact is all that can be expected of most well-meaning schemes for altering either the environment or individuals' reactions to their environment. The advocates of therapeutic nihilism, however, go too far and are in danger of throwing out the baby with the bath-water. At least among academic circles there has been a slight swing back towards realistically limited expectations. Ross and Gendreau (1980) have published a collection of reports of treatment evaluations that yielded positive results. Some of these seriously challenge the notion that nothing works. It is rather sad that the discipline of sociology, which has done so much to expose the pressures that provoke offending, has become associated with opposition to therapists who try to help individual offenders to modify their ineffectual and unprofitable ways of reacting. As for judges and penal administrators, who were always sceptical about claims for treatment, their disillusionment, engendered by the argument that nothing works, may last a long time.

Concluding suggestions

Although not designed to investigate the effect of social policies, the Cambridge study did provide some pointers to possible avenues for intervention. Bearing in mind all the cautionary tales in previous sections of this chapter, it will be obvious that any policy proposals must be speculative and tentative until such time as they have been tested; but since most of the current ideas about delinquency control lack empirical confirmation one need not be too concerned about adding a few more untested suggestions.

Research indicates that delinquency is the end result of complex causal paths determined by the interaction of a multiplicity of social and personal factors. This, in turn, points to the appropriateness of an eclectic social policy, deploying a variety of methods of intervention in order to interrupt, at as many different points as possible, the chain of events that leads to delinquent behaviour. There is no contradiction, therefore, in simultaneously advocating measures to improve the protection of property and the detection of offenders, measures to change the social environment in ways that may reduce pressures and temptations, and measures to help those already in trouble with the law to avoid further confrontations. Experience has shown, as theoretical considerations might have predicted, that any one method of intervention, on its own, is likely to have limited impact.

For most youngsters law-breaking is not a steady occupation, but something that happens sporadically, usually when they are not too busy with their ordinary affairs, when the time and place and company are propitious and a tempting opportunity presents. Different situations tempt different individuals. Girls may be less prone to housebreaking than boys, but, as experiment has shown, females can be as dishonest as males when presented with a chance to steal small sums covertly (Farrington and Knight, 1979). The totality of youthful crime includes occasional offences by vast numbers of different individuals and repeated offences by a small number of versatile and persistent delinquents. A rational preventive strategy, therefore, should include general provisions applicable to everyone (such as anti-theft devices, aids to detection, well-defined criminal laws and punishments and a reliable and trusted police force) as well as corrective treatment measures aimed at trying to change the chronically antisocial habits and attitudes of the small minority who create havoc out of proportion to their numbers.

Planning for the treatment of individual offenders needs to take into account the important point that most young delinquents, especially those who have been apprehended no more than once or twice, are never reconvicted again once they reach the age of 19 or 20. The study findings suggest that this is not merely the result of improved skill in avoiding detection. The behaviour of delinquents genuinely and spontaneously changes in the direction of increasing social conformity with increasing age. Furthermore, the evidence from a variety of researches indicates that processing delinquents through the juvenile justice system, especially if this involves any substantial period of detention in a penal establishment, is more likely to exacerbate than to reduce antisocial behaviour. Taken together these two sets of observations provide a strong argument for limiting referrals to the courts to the more serious cases. The fact that nowadays up to a quarter of the young male population acquire an entry in the Criminal Records Office is in itself some indication of criminal justice overkill. The juvenile courts have to deal on occasion with hardened and persistent offenders, some of whom are rightly described as a social menace, but for the most part, as this study showed, the courts are dealing with relatively trivial matters which one would have thought could have been settled in less formal ways. One of the reasons why children from middle-class neighbourhoods appear before the juvenile courts relatively infrequently is that their victims are less inclined to call in the police and their teachers and parents are more willing to handle situations themselves by appropriate disciplinary action and by paying compensation for damage.

Common experience suggests that the process of growing out of their troublesome phase is likely to be delayed if youngsters are allowed to misbehave with impunity. In warning against over-reaction to minor problems and advocating more sparing use of the justice system one is not proposing that misconduct should go unchecked — quite the contrary. As a corrective force, an impersonal, legal bureaucracy has obvious limitations. According to his age and sophistication the court is liable to appear to the offender either as a mysterious and arbitrary power over which he has no control or as an enemy to be outwitted. The niceties of justice are totally lost on the average unsophisticated offender, who finds himself caught up in a meaningless and frightening ritual of uncertain outcome (Scott, 1959). For the more hardened offender, the spectacle of the courtroom drama of confrontation between the prosecution (symbolic of outraged society) and the offender's lawyer, who has to try to extricate his client by any legal trick he can muster, does nothing to encourage realistic self-appraisal. It may teach the juvenile to be disingenuous and distrustful towards authority rather than teaching him a sense of personal responsibility. Effective training and control is far better exercised by parents and teachers, who are in daily contact with offenders. Their sanctions, though perhaps less awesome, are more immediate, understandable and flexible than a sentence of the court.

The imaginative use of supervision, to ensure that offenders undertake reparations (such as repair work by vandals or errands for old people by delinquents who have distressed an elderly occupant by house-breaking) might be more instructive than the usual doses of fines and brief detention, but these things are difficult to arrange as formal requirements by the court. Schemes that require convicted persons to make reparations to the victims they have harmed are attractive as methods of treatment, but they do not really answer the criticism that the justice system, in its concern for punishing or treating the offender, neglects the interests of victims. The victims of unidentified offenders cannot be helped by schemes of personal reparation, and many victims of known offenders — elderly persons who have been robbed, for example — might feel that further contact with their assailant was the last thing they wanted. Other than state insurance against victimization (at present limited to injury from crimes of violence), the long-term interests of potential victims are best served by efforts to reduce offences and reform offenders. Preoccupation with what to do with the offender does not necessarily imply callous neglect of the interests of victims, although criminologists are sometimes accused of harbouring such an attitude.

An attempt to convert the justice system for juveniles into an agency of the last resort, to be reserved for cases impossible to deal with by voluntary arrangements between parents, teachers and social workers, was made in England in 1969, with the passing of the Children and Young Persons Act. The intentions of the Act were clear. The minimum age for prosecution was to be raised from 10 to 14, which would have eliminated, with one stroke of the pen, all very young delinquents. Children under 14 whose behaviour was so bad as to be 'beyond control' by their parents could still be dealt with by a civil hearing, leading to parental responsibilities being taken over by the social services, but the child would not be branded with a finding of guilt or the entry of his name in criminal records. Detention centres were to be phased out and borstals reserved for offenders over 17. Instead of juvenile offenders being committed to Home Office 'approved schools', those in need of residential 'treatment' were to be placed, by means of a 'care order', in the charge of the social services, whose workers would be empowered to remove the child to a residential community home as and when they deemed it necessary.

This attempt to divert juveniles away from the courts and the penal system has failed. Due to a change of government and a reversion to a more punitive ideology, none of the provisions mentioned, save for the care-order system, has been put into effect. Even the care-order system is to be modified by introducing into it periods of mandatory custodial detention at the discretion of the court (Home Office *et al.*, 1980;

Morris and Giller, 1981). Borstals and detention centres remain, and house more juveniles than ever before. Although the police now have power to deal with juvenile offenders of any age by means of civil proceedings, on the grounds that they are in need of care, protection or control, they almost invariably choose, instead, to utilize the process of criminal prosecution.

Although the police have made considerable use of their new powers to caution juveniles officially without bringing a prosecution (Oliver, 1973; Ditchfield, 1976), and although they dealt with nearly twice as many juveniles guilty of serious offences by means of a caution in 1979 than in 1970, the number brought to the courts and sentenced has not diminished (see Home Office, *Criminal Statistics, England and Wales* (1979), tables 7.4 and 7.6). Such evidence as is available suggests that the setting up of police juvenile bureaux to administer the cautioning system has resulted in informal warnings being replaced by official cautionings, thereby widening the net and causing more rather than less juveniles to be formally labelled and processed as offenders. In police districts where cautionings have increased significantly, so has the ratio of juvenile to adult offenders (Tutt, 1978, p. 53). Farrington and Bennett (1981) showed that between 1968 and 1970, that is, before and after the setting up of juvenile bureaux in London, the Metropolitan Police statistics showed an 85 per cent increase in arrests of 10–13 year olds and a 44 per cent increase in arrests of 14–16 year olds. Such a large and abrupt increase was more likely due to police action than to a sudden change in juvenile habits, especially since arrests of older offenders had not increased anything like so much.

Diversion, in the sense of informal methods of dealing with delinquents without involving the courts, appears to be a good idea, but it has hardly had a proper trial. As pointed out by Morris *et al.* (1980, ch. 4), the police, whose training and traditions lie in the direction of bringing as many guilty persons as possible before the courts, may not be the best persons to decide when to warn, when to refer to a social agency and when to pass on to the magistrates. The officers of the police juvenile bureaux, who are given discretion to warn in place of prosecuting a juvenile if guilt is admitted and parents and victims consent, appear to base their decisions very largely upon such considerations as seriousness of the offence, history of previous arrests and the supposed need to deal similarly with all accomplices. In order to obtain effective help or guidance for those who need more than a simple warning, a close liaison between police juvenile bureaux and the local social services would be needed, but this has not developed. Social workers may be too hard pressed to take prompt action about cases notified to them, and police may decide there is no alternative to prosecution if a juvenile continues to run wild and is apprehended again in spite of having been cautioned.

For effective preventive action at an early stage, it is essential to have trust and collaboration between police and treatment agencies. The participation of offenders who have not been processed through the courts needs to be voluntary. Both these conditions were fulfilled in a California project in which the families of delinquents were befriended and counselled on such issues as the use of appropriate rewards and sanctions and ·the maintenance of a constructive dialogue with the youngster. The scheme, which was evaluated with the aid of random allocation to treatment or control groups, proved unusually successful (Binder and Newkirk, 1977).

Morris *et al*. (1980, ch. 4) would like to see instituted an independent legal check to ensure that the juvenile offences, which the police decide to prosecute formally, really warrant this serious step. A system of this kind already exists in Scotland in the shape of the Reporter, an official who sifts complaints from police and others, and decides which need to be passed on for a formal tribunal hearing, and which can be dealt with informally with the consent and co-operation of those involved, that is, the child, the parents, the schools, the local social agencies and perhaps also the victims. The proposal would be likely to be opposed by the English police, who at present enjoy unfettered discretion, but in Scotland, which already has the office of Procurator-fiscal intervening between the police and the courts for the prosecution of adults, the system seems less innovatory.

The administrative arrangements for dealing with delinquents outside the criminal justice system are less important than the development of resources to handle them. Unless schools, parents and social workers are prepared to tolerate a certain amount of disturbance, in the confident expectation that most youngsters will grow out of their troublesome phase, and unless they are prepared to tackle some of the more difficult problems themselves, instead of exporting them to an overburdened penal system, legal formulae for 'diversion' will be so much waste paper. Better utilization of existing procedures, and improved co-operation and agreement about common goals between the professional groups engaged in the work, might achieve more than further tampering with an already complicated juvenile justice system.

John Alderson (1979), Chief Constable of Devon and Cornwall, is one man who has no doubt of the benefits to be expected from improved co-operation between all the services involved, including the police. Apart from their 'hand on the collar' law-enforcement role, the police are already involved in giving advice on the protection of property, helping to settle marital and neighbourhood disputes without resort to the courts, training drivers to avoid accidents and law-breaking, directing sporting activities, and, above all, being on hand at every hour of the day or night to deal with emergencies. Alderson would like the process to go further, for police to be accepted by the communities they serve as fellow residents, so that they could partici- pate in efforts to identify the problems that generate offences and to organize volunteers from the locality to take appropriate action. The police are used to seeing crime as a situational phenomenon, preventable by social measures, whereas social workers are professionally geared to a personal approach, hoping to change the individual's attitude and life- style in ways that will lessen the likelihood of further offences. A com- bination of the two approaches, and a sharing of experience and resources between the different services, could be of benefit all round.

Engstad and Evans (1980) give illustrations of the kind of community intervention that can prove surprisingly effective. In one example, frequent calls to a particular appartment block to deal with matters of vandalism, noise and petty theft were drastically reduced when the chief cause of the trouble was traced to neglect of his duties by the tenant manager of the building. Contact with other tenants, and discussion with the manager, served to rectify the situation.

All youngsters are to a greater or lesser extent minor and temporary nuisances whose zest for excitement and need to prove their courage and independence has to be understood and on occasion restrained. Ways of avoiding trouble include a busy schedule that avoids boredom, the provision of interesting, challenging and rewarding activities at work and at play, plenty of outlets for physical energies and adventurousness, and sensible supervision by easy-going but attentive and concerned adults capable of consistent maintenance of reasonable limits of tolerance. Such elementary forms of prevention are common sense, widely accepted, and too obvious to require the support of criminological expertise.

Measures of prevention aimed at the small minority of children with a potentiality for more serious forms of antisociality require more thought and planning. Our study showed that there is no great diffi- culty in identifying large, poor, crime-prone families whose boys are at considerable risk of becoming persistent recidivists. The high concentra- tion of serious delinquents of the future among children exposed to a characteristic constellation of social deprivation points inexorably to the need to include anti-poverty measures in any coherent policy of delinquency prevention. Unfortunately, measures for alleviating poverty are matters of intense political controversy, and anti-poverty cam- paigns have not had much success in the past. Ancient disputes about whether poverty is the result of personal fecklessness or unmerited misfortune continue unabated. Strong arguments can be adduced for encouraging the socially productive and successful to reap full material rewards for their enterprise. On the other hand, egalitarian measures designed to reduce the differential of income between the struggling and the comfortable can be supported on the grounds of a probable contribution to delinquency prevention. Some mechanisms for doing this, such as rent rebates, already exist; others, such as negative taxation (that is, supplementing rather than deducting from the lowest wages) have been discussed. All such measures involve the diversion of income from one segment of the population to another.

A frequently raised objection, that money given to the ineffectual would be wasted, is something that could, in theory, be tested rather easily by presenting some to a sample of impoverished problem families and monitoring the effects. I have long thought that more might be achieved by giving money to the needy with a minimum of formality than spending money on welfare administration and complex assessments of eligibility.

Scarcity of employment aggravates the inequalities in society because it weighs most heavily upon the unskilled and upon those with an unsteady work record. Youths with poor scholastic records and no formal qualifications are the worst affected, and this is the group already prone to delinquency. Enforced idleness, shortage of money and isolation from their more successful peers can only serve to increase their liability to commit offences. Job-creation schemes and socio-economic policies aimed at improving employment prospects, together with adequate financial cover for the involuntarily unemployed are clearly in the interests of delinquency prevention; but how to achieve these goals is a matter for debate far beyond the subject of criminology. As with so many other good ideas for prevention, the effects of youth employment schemes have rarely been properly evaluated, although promising results have been reported in at least one American research (Shore and Massimo, 1979).

However generous the national provisions, some families will always run into difficulties. The group most likely to spawn delinquents are those who are both poor and managing badly, the ones who combine poverty, family disharmony and antisocial deviance. In other words, the least attractive and the least deserving are the ones who need help most. Unfortunately, as the study amply confirmed, those also tend to be the ones who are most elusive, most suspicious of authorities and social workers, and least likely to be co-operative, so that it becomes problematic how to deliver help. For example, among the samples interviewed at age 23 or 24, there were 18 men whose children were considered by the research workers to be receiving an inadequate standard of parental care, but in only 5 of these cases was there any evidence of any help having been obtained from the social services. One reason for parental reluctance to seek help may be their fear of the social workers' powers to advise upon the removal of children who are inadequately cared for or controlled. The popularity of agencies such as the Samaritans or 'walk-in' clinics, with a reputation for easy approachability and informality, suggests that a change of public image might help. In the last resort it is up to the services to demonstrate that their help is readily available and worth having.

There seems to be no certain answer to the question of what stage it is most profitable to try to intervene in the lives of children at risk. Evidence that the handling of children in their pre-school years determines to a large extent what happens later suggests that the earlier a start is made the better, and that can be very early indeed. One project for improving the attention given to 'disadvantaged' children concentrated upon two-year-old toddlers, and was able to report a significant improvement in subsequent scholastic performance (Jason *et al.*, 1978). It has never been proved, however, that interventions at later stages are valueless. There are many good reasons, practical and humanitarian, for keeping to the old adage, 'Never too late to mend'.

A vast literature on the subject of child care and training points to the importance of good parenting in moulding character and preventing antisociality. Our study did not support the idea that style of upbringing is a factor over-riding all others, but it did show that unsatisfactory upbringing was a significant feature in the histories of juvenile delinquents and persisting delinquents.

Modern developments have made the task of child-rearing more difficult. As families have decreased in size, fewer people arrive at parenthood having had the preliminary experience of looking after brothers and sisters much younger than themselves. The typical nuclear family of today lacks any additional adult to relieve the parents of some of the burden, and worse still, one-parent families have become much more prevalent. Raised material standards and expectations mean that parents are expected to provide more by way of clothing, sports gear, pocket money for record purchases and so forth, all of which puts the less able parents, and of course their children, at a disadvantage. Technological advances in communications, transport and education mean that children are exposed, from an early age, to external sources of values and interests that may conflict with their parents' ideas. The scope for conflict between the generations has enlarged.

Education of the general public in the task of child-rearing must have some bearing upon delinquency prevention. Some commentators, notably Patricia Morgan (1978), bitterly resent the emphasis placed by academic theorists upon the benefits of uncritical permissiveness, upon the notion that all you need is love, and upon the supposed dangers of old-fashioned punishments. While not endorsing Morgan's views about the dangers of 'progressive' ideas in penology, the essential 'normality' of antisocial juveniles, and the pressing need for more severe penal deterrents, one must submit that delinquency research in no way contradicts belief in the need for discipline. Recidivist delinquents rarely come from homes in which standards have been firmly maintained through diligent instruction, praise for compliance and the consistent application of appropriate, but not too extreme, sanctions for misconduct. On the other hand, ideological commitment to permissiveness is also uncharacteristic of the parents of delinquents, who are more often careless or inconsistent than calculatingly non-interventionist. Few parents of delinquents remain indifferent when their children stay out all hours, lie, truant, steal or vandalize, but a considerable number fail to train their children in the self-control that might forestall such disciplinary crises. Instead, they tend to be lax in watching over and controlling the child's activities and apt to allow behaviour to get out of hand, at which point they react with sudden, unexpected and ineffectual harshness. An attempt to exert control after disobedience has previously been unchecked is liable to meet with resentment, leading to an escalation of anger on both sides. Hence the paradox that delinquents experience too little parental control and at the same time too severe and frequent punishments.

These considerations point to the need, well recognized by a recent Select Committee on Violence in the Family (Department of Health, 1977, para. 60), for more systematic training of young people on family matters. Adequate instruction on this topic is still lacking in the educational system, in spite of persistent criticism that the later school years are filled with subjects that pupils find irrelevant to practical life. The crudely dismissive attitudes towards contraception and unwanted pregnancies expressed by some of the young men in the sample revealed their gross lack of preparation for family responsibilities (Farrell and Kellaher, 1978).

Any social policy which effectively eases the burden upon parents (the provision of child allowances, for example) might be expected to serve the interests of delinquency prevention. More nursery schools and crèches might help. If, by going out to work, mothers can relieve loneliness and frustrations and raise the family income to a comfortable level, their young children might benefit. The counter-argument that the loss of maternal attention over long periods constitutes a significant deprivation will not prevent large numbers of mothers continuing to work, so it is sensible to provide facilities for adequate substitute care in their absence.

Housing policy is clearly relevant. Ideally, the poorest and most vulnerable families should receive the largest share of the resources allocated to subsidized public housing, but sometimes it is the reverse that happens, as the poorer families find they cannot afford the rents that local authorities need to charge. Threatened evictions, and the cutting off of electricity and gas (plus further costs for later re-instatement) add to the stress upon those least capable of withstanding it. In some areas where substandard property is gradually being replaced, it tends to be the problem families who are left to the last, because their needs are the hardest to satisfy. Then again, either by accident or design, problem families may be allocated accommodation clustered into the same street, or in an unpopular high-rise block of flats, or on an estate with a bad reputation. Such artificial ghettos, in which the delinquency rates are extremely high, increase the difficulties parents experience in controlling their children and strengthen delinquent peer groups. Clearly, whatever the inconvenience, dispersion is better for delinquency prevention.

The scope for action through the schools is limitless. Our observation that secondary schools in the study area were having little influence upon the realization of their pupils' delinquency potential was both surprising and discouraging. One can only reiterate the view that more attention should be paid to the dull pupils, the absentees, and those who are unresponsive or badly behaved in the classroom. One can understand teachers feeling some relief when their more difficult charges absent themselves, but truancy is a danger signal that ought not to be ignored (Hersov and Berg, 1980). American evidence that school failures and drop-outs, who have a high rate of delinquency, improve as soon as they leave and enter the labour market, suggests that the way schools deal with these pupils aggravates their bad behaviour (Elliott and Voss, 1974).

Programmes which select particular pupils for group counselling (Meyer et al., 1965) or other special programmes have not been shown to work well. It may be preferable to try to reduce the size of the minority who fail to fit in by adjusting the school routine for all. Of course, some balance has to be preserved. Schools, like society at large, have to be run in the best interests of the majority, but more could be done to cater for the needs of the less academically able or motivated pupils, who are otherwise liable to become discouraged and alienated, to seek refuge among companions as disaffected as themselves, and ultimately to swell the ranks of the truants and delinquents. Allocation to special classes occupied exclusively by dull and difficult children may be necessary for some, but the main effort should be directed towards integration rather than segregation. Friendly competition, rewards for success, and more importantly rewards for effort, should extend beyond purely scholastic exercises into areas of behaviour (such as co-operation in the performance of common chores, or participation in adventure expeditions) in which socially deprived children may be able sometimes to excel.

Studies of racial and social-class prejudice show that children tend to follow the lead of their elders in bad things no less than in good. Being held in low esteem by a class teacher correlates with lack of popularity among classmates. Teachers bear a heavy responsibility. The nastiest pupils stand in greater need of care and attention, but it is all too easy for a teacher to respond to repellent manners and demeanour, or to lumpen unresponsiveness and lack of interest, with rejection rather than persuasion. As the responses to the study questionnaires revealed (see Appendex IV, ref. 1, p. 40), teachers differ greatly in their perception of the incidence of behavioural problems. Some are ready, after only brief contact, to consign certain new pupils to the category of potential trouble-makers and thereafter to subject them to particularly severe scrutiny, which tends to bring about the very trouble they anticipated, as the pupils concerned feel victimized and resentful and react accordingly. Teachers who are able to condemn particular offending acts, without necessarily imputing to the pupil involved a tendency to persistent troublesomeness, usually experience less disciplinary problems than the teachers who attach derogatory labels too freely (Hargreaves *et al.*, 1975, pp. 260 ff).

Teachers also vary in their willingness to interest themselves in their pupils' backgrounds and personal problems, or to make contact with parents, but this is essential when dealing with delinquent-prone individuals. The few pupils who remain recalcitrant despite their teachers' best efforts may need the attention of the school psychologist, or of the social services. If teachers are to play a greater role in the management of potential and actual delinquents, it is important for them to have easy and effective communication with these services and not to regard them as either rivals or ill-informed critics.

In a recent paper David Hargreaves (1980) indicated some of the reforms open to schools by listing a number of undesirable organizational features characteristic of schools with a high delinquency rate. These included maintenance of dubious rules concerning dress, smoking and other matters which are liable to antagonize lower-class pupils, allocation of the less committed teachers to the more difficult classes, attitudes of open distrust towards the recalcitrant, concentration of effort and praise upon an able élite, and an unofficial policy of writing off and relaxing control over the troublesome few in return for more peaceful classrooms. In an earlier survey of studies of delinquency in schools Phillipson (1971) noted two other features which are often found in high-delinquency schools. These were frequent staff changes, which tend to be linked with 'low institutional pride' and dissociation from the school by both pupils and teachers, and, secondly, the 'disjunctive articulation between the curriculum and the labour market', which promotes a belief among the less academically inclined that the school programme is irrelevant to their needs.

An improvement in school attendance might be expected to have some effect upon the level of delinquency. As noted earlier (see pp. 98–100), the particular schools attended by members of the Cambridge study appeared to exert little influence upon the incidence of either truancy or delinquency, but different policies might well produce different effects. The large overlap between truants and delinquents has been well documented in many surveys (May, 1975; Douglas *et al.*, 1968; Tennent, 1971). A majority of the 114 boys in the Cambridge study who became truants also acquired a delinquency record. Farrington (see Appendix IV, ref. 43, p. 60), in analysing the characteristics of our truants, noted: 'Many of the results quoted in relation to truancy mirror results previously published in relation to delinquency.' Background features, such as large family, low income, other delinquents in the family, unsatisfactory upbringing, disharmony between parents and early troublesomeness, were similar. As young adults both the truants and the delinquents showed a similar tendency to antisociality. To be concerned about delinquents means that one must also be concerned about truants.

Truanting often starts before officially recorded delinquency and so could be used to identify individuals 'at risk'. Robins and Ratcliffe (1980), in one of the celebrated long-term follow-up studies in St Louis, showed that, in their later years, former truants had a greatly raised incidence of problems with jobs, alcohol, marriage, crime and violence. A hint of similarly adverse long-term sequelae of truancy in Britain comes from the high incidence of former truants among prisoners (Pitts and Simon, 1954).

The National Child Development Study has produced figures for this country that point 'inexorably to the location of the overwhelming proportion of absenteeism among children of the working class' (Fogelman and Richardson, 1974). The figures also point, unsurprisingly, to a very significant association, regardless of social class, between low school performance and absenteeism. Such findings, like the findings of the delinquency studies, confirm the importance of trying to organize schools to serve the needs of the underprivileged better than they appear to do at the moment.

One obvious reason for trying to improve school attendance is that this might reduce opportunities to commit offences. Belson (1975, p. 389), in his self-report survey among London schoolboys, found that other activities were cited much more frequently than stealing when boys were asked what they did while truanting. Even so, when the boys were asked the direct question, he found 'that an appreciable amount of stealing goes on during truancy', especially amongst those who truant frequently. This would seem to lend support to the common-sense expectation that a reduction in offences might be secured by preventing truancy. Evidence for this was obtained in an interesting police project in Kilmarnock which was put into operation in response to numerous complaints of shop-lifting by juveniles. A successful campaign to reduce school absences was followed by the disappearance of juveniles from the shopping centres and a marked decrease in reported shop-lifting (Fraser, 1979). However, the benefits of enforced attendance by means of police patrols to round up truants, or by a more vigorous policy of prosecutions by education welfare officers, are likely to be short-term unless the root causes of pupil alienation are tackled simultaneously.

Turning now to the management of delinquents who have been processed through the courts and found guilty, all the good intentions of the 1969 Act and all the rhetoric about treatment needs have had little practical impact. Students of the system have observed (Priestley *et al.*, 1977) that juvenile-court decisions continue to be made on traditional penological criteria, namely the seriousness of the current offence and the number of previous court appearances. One reason for this continuance of tariff justice is that social workers' reports tend to collude with it by avoiding a too blatant confrontation with accepted practice. Recommendations, ostensibly made on social grounds, are subtly adjusted to what the magistrates are likely to accept.

The 1969 Act replaced the system whereby juvenile offenders were put under the supervision of the courts' own probation officers by a system of supervision orders, which place juvenile offenders under the surveillance of local-authority social workers. Although the declared intent has been to avoid unnecessary incarceration, the courts are making fewer supervision orders today than they used to make probation orders before 1969. Care orders, which normally result in the juvenile being removed from home, at least for a time, are often made in respect of first-offenders whose 'crimes' would never be regarded as sufficiently serious for a custodial sentence had they been committed by an adult. Within the community home system, which provides the residences for children committed to care, the amount of 'secure' accommodation for juveniles considered to require locking up has escalated remarkably (Cawson and Martell, 1979), but as a result of administrative failures rather than from any great increase in the number of otherwise uncontrollable children (Millham, 1981).

As remarked upon earlier (see p. 140), the juvenile population of borstals and detention centres has escalated even more dramatically. In spite of popular impressions to the contrary, current trends are all towards increased incarceration, and if our study sample had belonged to a younger generation it is likely that more of the delinquents would have received custodial sentences. This makes nonsense of the declared intentions of government White Papers and official reports which invariably stress the desirability of avoiding custody for young persons and the need to try to influence behaviour without removing individuals from the communities to which they have to learn to adjust. Sadly, however, the most recent White Paper on *Young Offenders* (Cmnd. 8045, October 1980) seems to have given in to the reactionary trend in the proposal to introduce powers enabling the courts, when making care orders, to direct the social services to remove the child from home for a specified period.

A policy of increased incarceration is not supported by the results of research. Reconvictions of offenders who have passed through custodial regimes are discouragingly frequent. Unfortunately, some well-meaning attempts to avoid the necessity for custody by taking preventive action at an early stage have been partly to blame for the increasingly heavy-handed sentences. For example, provisions for so-called 'intermediate treatment' (a range of placements and activities intended to help offenders or potential offenders learn to cope better in society) have been widely used for juveniles considered to be 'at risk', rather than for those who have actually begun a delinquent career. Consequently, if these youngsters do offend subsequently in such a way as to invite prosecution, the court may think that they have already exhausted the opportunities for help in the community. It is the old story of provisions intended as alternatives to incarceration being used instead to bring into the control system cases that would previously have been dealt with informally (Thorpe *et al.*, 1980).

The failure to remove nuisance cases and less serious offenders from the purview of the courts is partly responsible for the justified criticism that penal treatments are imposed unnecessarily and unfairly upon juveniles who do not need them. As our study showed, it is only the recidivist delinquent group that includes a high proportion with such severe social handicaps and seriously deviant life-style as to call for corrective intervention. Where ordinary methods of discipline would have sufficed, it is a waste of money, time, resources and professional skills, and quite possibly damaging to the juvenile concerned, to deal with him as if he were a suitable case for treatment or a candidate for residential care.

Some youngsters have to be punished, others need skilled help, others need both. The uneasy mixture of punishment and treatment ideologies which the courts have to operate has no foreseeable remedy. The punitive role will always be required to support and strengthen the powers of teachers and parents when misbehaviour threatens to get out of control, or to satisfy outraged feelings when some particularly nasty act has been committed. On the other hand, corrective treatment, rather than simple punishment by fining or detention, is called for when the current offence is but one of many symptoms of disturbance, perhaps but one example of a wide-ranging series of persistently problematic behaviours justifying the label 'antisocial personality'. Where the offenders would otherwise defy any piece of advice, or simply disappear, corrective intervention has to be compulsory. This does not mean that treatment must always be in an institution. Supervision orders rather than residential care orders should be used to secure participation in treatment whenever this is practicable.

Treatment by order of a court is effectively a punishment, and one should not pretend the contrary, for there could then be a demand for spells of punishment in addition. The youngster should be informed why he needs treatment and what goals are to be attained. Most treatments amount to social training for specifiable purposes, such as the development of a work skill, regular attendance at school, improved literacy, better use of leisure time, control of the use of intoxicants or avoidance of confrontations with parents. Voluntary treatment may last indefinitely, but treatment under compulsion should not, in the absence of further proved offences, continue so long as to constitute a disproportionate punishment. Legal appeals, statutory reviews, and statutory limitations on the length of time court orders may remain in force are all highly desirable.

All this presupposes that specialized treatments for individual offenders have a part to play. I think they have. Far from endorsing the gloomy conclusion that nothing works, or the ethically repugnant corollary that one might as well give up trying to help individuals, it is my view that the evidence points to certain types of intervention having a positive impact and suggests that certain methods of delivering help are to be preferred. For example, incarceration in authoritarian, hierarchically organized penal institutions, where obedience is inculcated through fear of reprisals, is likely to nullify treatment endeavours, and should be used as the very last resort for a tiny minority. Other things being equal, helping schemes centred upon activities in the community, and schemes of behaviour modification applied to interactions within the family are preferable to help delivered to the offender alone, especially if the help has to be given in the artificial and isolated environment of a residential establishment. After all, the aim of treatment is to help the offender cope with ordinary living, not to adjust him to an institution. Of course some deserted or seriously neglected children are better off in a residential home, and some may need time to settle down and become more amenable before placement with foster-parents, but these are extreme examples, atypical even of recidivist delinquents. Where the real reason for commitment is inadequate care, rather than the seriousness and uncontrollability of the delinquent's offences, the care order should be a matter of civil rather than criminal proceedings, so that the child is not branded unfairly with a record containing what seems like a sentence appropriate to an incorrigible offender. A recent report of the Children and Young Persons Review Group of Northern Ireland (Black, 1979) recommended that care orders should be considered separately from prosecutions and should no longer be available to the courts as a method of dealing with a juvenile found guilty of an offence.

Another principle, in accord with current thinking, is the desirability of voluntary participation whenever possible. Social aid should be a privilege sought rather than an imposition reluctantly borne. Probation officers today are showing some reluctance to accept unenthusiastic offender clients, and some psychiatrists decline to accept for psychotherapy patients who attend as a requirement of a probation order. In the case of sane adult offenders there are strong arguments in favour of removing all forms of coercion from treatment provisions. In the case of juveniles, who are already under compulsion to do many things considered by adults to be in their own interest (such as attend school and stay at home at night) the addition of some special requirement (such as attendance at an 'intermediate treatment' scheme) does not seem to much to expect. But if the end can be achieved voluntarily, even if backed up by an official police caution, the client's attitude, and hence his probable response, is likely to be better.

In advocating a more restricted use of the criminal justice system, and less resort to penal incarceration, one has to recognize that the community, educational, health and social services are all being asked to try to cope with behavioural problems which seem more severe than what they have been used to dealing with. A generation back, when there was some genuine move towards decarceration, the diversion of youths from prisons to borstals and from borstals to probation meant that these two services were obliged to cope with clients who were more difficult and less responsive than those they had previously experienced. If the trend is to be resumed and carried further, the community services will need more moral, financial and technical support to handle the job.

The development of intermediate treatment schemes in England has been slow and uneven, partly because they depend upon finance supplied by local authorities from local taxes, whereas borstals and detention centres are financed by central government. This cannot help but operate as a disincentive to the local personnel responsible for allocating juveniles to community placements. In areas where the provisions made by the local authority are meagre, the juvenile courts may feel obliged to make greater use of Prison Department institutions. A better balance between community facilities and the (usually more expensive) custodial facilities could be achieved if both were paid for out of the same budget (Morris, 1978).

In the United States, where the scale and seriousness of juvenile offending greatly exceeds our own problems, the practicability of managing delinquents in community settings has been demonstrated time and again. One successful example (Seidman *et al.*, 1980) was cited earlier (see p. 140). There have been many other examples which, if they failed to establish the superiority of community programmes for reducing recidivism, at least showed they were no worse than institutional methods. In one well-known project, the Provo Experiment (Empey and Erickson, 1972) the youths under community treatment were compared with a matched group of delinquents in a state training school. Even though the latter were supposed to be incarcerated, during brief home leaves and during times when they absconded they committed as much crime as the experimental group who were free in the community.

A particularly dramatic move away from the use of institutional training for young offenders, with its inevitable emphasis on control rather than help, came about in Massachusetts in 1971–2, with the closure of some long-established institutions and the dispersal of former inmates to hostels run by voluntary organizations, to foster homes and to a variety of community programmes (Ohlin *et al.*, 1977). Protracted political controversy surrounded this change of policy, which was bitterly resisted by powerful pressure groups, notably the older institutional staff whose job prospects, as well as their belief in the virtues of stricter control, were seriously threatened. Needless to say, resistance to change is equally strong in Britain, but much can be learned from the American experience about how to make haste slowly, allay unjustified fears, muster public support and demonstrate feasibility (Miller *et al.*, 1977).

Community-based programmes have several obvious advantages over institutional treatment. Even though they are not always any more effective than institutions in reducing recidivism they are more humanitarian, possibly cheaper, much more flexible and they avoid some of the alienation, stigmatization and contamination which the delinquent who is 'sent away' may suffer. They are in closer contact with local agencies and can mobilize a range of resources to meet particular needs. Most important of all, they can break out of the strait-jacket of exclusive attention to changing the individual client – the much criticized medical model – and enlist 'significant others', notably family members, teachers and non-delinquent peer groups, in the processes of adjustment and reconciliation. Some institutional places will always be needed for the persistently unresponsive and unruly, but hopefully less often than at present, and for limited periods of time. The successful operation of programmes which do not depend upon locking away delinquents should encourage residential institutions to develop, for their more difficult inmates, regimes that try to reconcile the needs of therapy and the needs of control (Hoghughi, 1978). It is noteworthy how often juveniles considered unmanageable in one residential setting are found to be no particular problem after transfer to another place with a different regime.

A review of the many different forms of treatment or training that have been tried with delinquents is beyond the scope of this book, but a few general comments can be made. Given the existence of effective sieves to prevent unnecessary resort to the penal system, it must be assumed that the clients who remain show serious and persistent behavioural problems. In most cases, therefore, a reduction in risk of reconviction is to be expected only if a fundamental change in style of life and attitude occurs. This may mean the acquisition of new skills, giving up old associates, coming to terms with the demands of school and family and developing some degree of confidence that reasonable social goals are within reach and worth striving for. Such changes are not easy to accomplish, and not likely to come about all at once. In order to make a realistic impression on long-standing delinquent behaviour, treatment programmes need to be determined, intensive and, as far as possible, comprehensive. For example, receptiveness to new experience with adults outside the home is unlikely to develop if nothing is done to help resolve bitter, recurring disputes with parents. New skills in reading or sports are of little help to a client unless he is in a position to use them to good effect in his own social setting outside the treatment project. If a hopeless home situation cannot be rectified, and parental neglect or incompetence can be established, the juvenile can be taken into care as in need of protection or control, with a view to placement with foster-parents. Although an extreme step, fostering is probably less damaging than a long-term stay in an institution dominated by delinquents.

Techniques of behaviour modification, such as reward tokens for good conduct or behaviour contracts subscribed to by both client and therapist, can be very helpful, but in the end the people-changing business depends upon personal relationships between therapist, clients and clients' families. Without goodwill, trust and positive motivation on the part of all concerned nothing can be expected. The commitment to change has to be greater than the pull towards old habits and loyalties. A coercive order, and, still worse, forcible detention in an institution, may be inevitable but it makes for a bad start. Formal conformity to an institutional programme merely to obtain early release is not enough. Clients have to learn to work towards a way of life compatible with continued freedom. Therapists have to accept that it is behaviour in the community that matters. A programme that ceases when the client passes out of the gate, which is the moment he most needs help, hardly deserves to be called therapeutic. All too often organizational problems, and demarcations between different services, get in the way of the continuity of attention that is wanted. Few things are more disruptive of the client's morale and commitment than being passed from one hand to another like a parcel, or observing visible conflicts between the authorities who are supposed to be guiding him.

No mention has been made of the medical role in treatment, although it was earlier pointed out that some delinquents may suffer from neurological impairments calling for specialized training to compensate for their disabilities. Others may have disturbances best controlled with drugs. If future research succeeds in extending the range of neurophysiological assessments, physical treatments might become more generally applicable. In our study, however, the delinquents passed through routine school medical examinations and other occasions of scrutiny without any relevant abnormalities being noted. Only one delinquent was admitted to a mental hospital, and that was for a condition brought about by drug abuse. A few were of very dull intelligence, but none was incapable of living in the community. Overt neurological disorder or severe psychiatric abnormality are met with only occasionally among young male delinquents. For the vast majority, treatment can be equated with guidance, social education and a variety of psychological approaches rather than with medical interventions. Traditional medical approaches to delinquency have been criticized for the use of dubious diagnostic categories, such as 'sociopathic', 'personality disorder' and 'hyperactivity'. These are dangerous labels because they seem to imply the presence of unalterable propensities unrelated to the individual's living circumstances. A 'problem profile' setting out in basic descriptive terms the main features of the youngster's behaviour and environment which are causing concern would be more helpful (Hoghughi *et al.*, 1980). If, for example, truancy is the main complaint, arising in the context of a broken home where the mother has taken to working as a prostitute, consideration of this particular cluster of problems would give a better lead to what action to take than a blanket diagnosis of behaviour disorder.

In conclusion, a few final words of caution! The Cambridge study focused on commonplace delinquents, that is, the obtrusively troublesome youngsters who make up such a large part of the Prison Department statistics, and whose activities attract the most public comment. Their criminal activities, even when persisting into adult years, remain rash, impulsive and crude. Their deviant life-styles and marginal employments suggest continued failure to integrate into mainstream society. Other forms of criminality, involving fewer offenders, are potentially more threatening, but these have not been considered. For example, there were no terrorists in the sample, no important racketeers, no fraudulent businessmen or professional persons and no organizers of bank raids, drug imports or other large-scale criminal enterprises. Maybe criminologists should pay more attention to the sophisticated, competent and socially mature offenders. They may not have been juvenile delinquents, or grown up in a lower-class, criminal milieu, but they choose a criminal way of life at some stage because they believe it pays. Their social problems, if any, begin only if they are caught. The suggestions for social reforms and the proposals for treatment schemes were not put forward with such characters in mind. Education, welfare and treatment programmes may reduce the incidence of certain kinds of commonplace crime, but they are not the solutions to every type of crime.

The suggestions made in this final chapter are hardly likely to prove popular. They run firmly counter both to the resurgent punitive ideology and to the strict non-interventionist stance. Although ultimately calculated to save much money and trouble, in the short run they would be a further burden on public money at a time when cut-backs are everywhere the order of the day. The climate for would-be reformers is unfavourable in other respects as well. Media accounts of the nuclear arms race, of appalling violence perpetrated by order of governments, of corruption in high places, of arbitrary, dishonest and brutal actions by police, of resort to strikes and terrorism by people who claim these are the only effective remedies for economic and social problems cannot but shake the confidence of young people in the message that crime does not pay and vandalism and violence are never justified.

The policies favoured in this book are far from novel. Some people might consider them wet, outworn, even reactionary. The only strong reason for believing that they could make a useful contribution is that so often in the past they have been mooted without being put into practice with sufficient determination or with adequate testing of their worth. Unless and until authorities are willing to invest and facilitate proper scientific evaluation of outcome (which by and large means random allocation to contrasting programmes), policy decisions will continue to be made on the basis of tradition, expediency and popular prejudice and the measures advocated here will have little chance of implementation.

Appendix I

List of Research Personnel

The list below contains the names of persons who have spent periods of full-time research on the Cambridge Study in Delinquent Development.

Joan Beales
John Blackmore
Joan Court
Peter Didcot
Susan Ellis
David Farrington
Janet Finney
Tony Gibson
Gwen Gundry
Ruth Hanson
Andrew Irving

Hilary King
Barry Knight
Thomas Knox
Sylvia Morrison
Martin Murphy
Stephen Osborn
Eve Road
David Scott
Donald West
Ruth Williams

Appendix II

How the Delinquents and their Convictions were Counted

Research into human affairs always involves problems of classification. However hard one tries to be precise about definitions, unexpected or anomalous cases are bound to arise. Even such an apparently cut-and-dried distinction as delinquent versus non-delinquent poses some complications. In this book tedious details of definitions and exceptions are usually omitted. They rarely make any material difference to the findings, and readers interested in such problems can consult the original research reports. However, as delinquency is the main concern, one may make an exception and explain the precise rules by which convictions were defined and counted.

Convictions (or strictly speaking 'findings of guilt' if the offender is a juvenile) were counted only when they were for offences of a kind routinely noted in the Criminal Record Office. In the case of juveniles we made an exception and included any conviction for an offence involving an element of personal aggression (for example, insult, threat or assault), but this made a negligible difference to either the number of convictions or the number of juvenile delinquents.

We obtained lists of the offences which do or do not lead to the opening of a criminal conviction file at Scotland Yard. For example, all convictions for criminal damage, under sections 1, 2 and 3 of the Criminal Damage Act 1971, are nowadays recorded, but not convictions for driving without insurance, while disqualified or 'under the influence'. The list resembles but does not exactly coincide either with offences legally classified as indictable or with the Home Office category of 'Standard List' offences. The list alters slightly from time to time following changes in the law or in recording policy. Our main problem was that once a file has been opened it not infrequently included mention of convictions for offences not on the list (offences of public drunkenness, for example) and these had to be eliminated. Inaccuracies could have occurred here because the descriptions of offences in the lists and files available to us were not always sufficiently specific, but in practice there was very rarely a doubt, the vast majority of offences being property crimes (larceny, breaking in, etc.) which are invariably recorded.

Any given court appearance ending in a finding of guilt counted as only one conviction, regardless of the number of offences involved, the number of different charges or the number of offences 'taken into consideration'. A decision was taken to count as a single occasion of conviction all findings on any one offender that were pronounced on the same day and at the same court. Convictions for breaches of probation, caused by the commission of a further offence while on licence, were not counted, because the original offence for which probation was ordered had already been counted as a conviction. Convictions under the age of 10, of which there were only three, were excluded because the age of criminal responsibility was raised from 8 to 10 in February 1964, which meant that only the older boys in the sample were at risk of such convictions over a full two years.

The accuracy of our identification of delinquents depended upon the completeness of the official records and the efficiency with which they were searched. Fortunately, the Scotland Yard recording system during the years in question was highly effective, especially in relation to London juvenile and adult courts, and it is unlikely that any of the delinquents went unrecorded. Our searches, however, unlike police searches using fingerprints, depended entirely upon names and birth dates. Occasionally a name was missed during searches through the index, an accident that can easily occur with very common names, names with alternative spellings or persons who use more than one surname. Until almost the end of the study our research officer was not permitted to look through the index herself. Even so, very few convictions can have escaped detection. Repeated searches at different times were requested for every name, and particular attention was given to cases in which the presence of a conviction was suspected from the man's own account, from newspaper reports or from other sources. Nevertheless, a few convictions were not located until a long time, even years, after the event.

At the time our record searches came to an end the youngest member of the study was 25 years 6 months. Information is believed to be complete on convictions for offences committed in England up to the twenty-fifth birthday. Offences at age 25 or older have been disregarded.

None of the boys died before the seventeenth birthday, but by that time 3 had emigrated and 3 others had spent substantial periods outside England and Wales. Inquiries were made about these 6 cases to the appropriate authorities so as to make the juvenile conviction records of all 411 boys complete. By the twenty-second birthday, the latest age at which systematic information about deaths and emigration was available, 4 had died and 10 had quit the United Kingdom, leaving 397. Sometimes, for instance when discussing adult criminal careers, it is appropriate to refer to this remaining sample of 397, but for other purposes, as for instance when discussing juvenile delinquency, reference is made to the total sample of 411.

The time elapsing between the commission of an offence and the final court decision, especially in adult crime, was sometimes several months and occasionally over a year. Substantial delays were usually due to time awaiting trial rather than time taken for detection and apprehension. Instead of counting the age when finally convicted, most of our calculations have been based upon the age the latest offence was committed, which was nearly always recorded. As an example of the kind of difference this made, 2 cases counted as 'juvenile' delinquents were not in fact first convicted until after their seventeenth birthday, although their offences had been committed earlier. When the sample was interviewed at age 18, 11 delinquents were found to have committed offences before the interview for which they were not convicted until later.

Appendix III

Can our Self-Reports be Trusted?

One common source of error, non-response bias (that is, the effect of failing to include the less willing or more elusive clients, who are often the most delinquent), was avoided in the Cambridge study. Virtually every member of the sample was questioned on one or more occasions.

Although given no reason to suppose that the interviewers had access to their police records, boys who had been convicted nearly always admitted the fact and also admitted to the corresponding offences on the self-report schedule. When they did not, this was more often due to confusion about the definition of the offence than to wilful denial (see Appendix IV, refs. 21 and 29). Only 2 non-delinquents made what were almost certainly false claims to non-existent convictions. The boys' descriptions of incidents already known from police reports were surprisingly frank, but where discrepancies occurred they were usually in the direction of minimizing rather than exaggerating involvement in delinquent activity (Appendix IV, ref. 3, p. 24). On the whole, the extent of the bias in self-reports appeared less than might have been expected, and for this the interviewers deserve some credit. They made good contact with the subjects and succeeded in assuring them that no harm would come from their admissions. Such bias as occurred was predominantly in the direction of underestimating delinquency, which was the impression gained by most previous investigators (Clark and Tifft, 1966). Belson (1975, p. 13), who also suggested that underclaiming was a greater danger than over-claiming, was particularly impressed by the increase in the frequency of admissions that occurred when refinements were introduced into the technique of questioning, showing that the boys' initial tendency had been to under-report.

Whatever bias may have been caused by forgetfulness, deliberate concealment or boastful exaggeration was insufficient to prevent the self-report scores from being significantly predictive of future convictions. Moreover, individuals were consistent, in that they tended to preserve roughly similar rankings on self-report on the different occasions when they were tested. This was so not only when assessments based on the same questionnaire at ages 14 and 16 were compared (see Appendix IV, ref. 27), but also on comparing assessments at 18, derived from much fewer questions directed to specific criminal acts, with assessments from the questions at 14 and 16 (Appendix IV, ref. 3, p. 30).

When the sample was re-interviewed at age 18 the men were asked about their own delinquency more directly than before. They were first questioned about any experiences of prosecution that they may have had. Later they were asked about each of seven specific criminal acts, being required to say if they had committed such an act at any time in the past three years, and if so how many times and under what circumstances. The items included: 'Driving a car, van, motor bike, scooter, etc. that has been taken without the owner's consent', and 'Breaking and entering and stealing'.

At age 21, when as many of the delinquents as possible, together with a quota sample of non-delinquents, were re-interviewed, the men were asked once again about eight specific criminal acts, six of which were the same as had been asked about at age 18. They were required to say if they had committed each act at any time in the past two years.

Although, by the age of 21, the incidence of delinquent acts had diminished considerably, and the men may also have become less candid in their admissions, the limited number of items asked about at this stage still sufficed to discriminate between officially convicted delinquents and others. At 21, as at 18, the self-report scoring system took into account the frequency with which the admitted offences were said to have occurred. Among the 389 men interviewed at 18, the 97 who gave high self-reported delinquency scores included 57 (58.6 per cent) who, at the time they were interviewed, had an official conviction record, whereas the remainder of the interviewed sample included only 44 (15.0 per cent) who were official delinquents (see Appendix IV, ref. 3, p. 30). At age 21, out of 218 men interviewed (half of them delinquents), the 46 highest scorers included 41 (89.1 per cent) who had by then acquired a criminal record, whereas the remainder of the interviewed sample included proportionately only a half that number of officially convicted delinquents — 73 (42.4 per cent).

In addition to the continued close relationship between self-reported delinquency and official conviction records, there was also a significant

consistency in the rank positions of individuals on self-reported delinquency at ages 18 and 21. Of the 200 men seen at both ages, the 44
high scorers at 21 included 21 (47.7 per cent) who had been high scorers
at 18. In contrast, of the 156 who were not high scorers at 21, only 26
(16.7 per cent) had been among the high scorers at 18 ($\chi^2 = 16.7$,
$P < 0.001$). This consistency was equally evident among men without
an official conviction record, so it could not have been produced solely
by the admissions of those who had actually been caught.

The self-report responses displayed impressive internal consistency.
For example, the schedule administered at ages 14 and 16 contained 38
separate items. If a boy said 'yes' to any one of these he was more
likely to say 'yes' to other items also (see Appendix IV, ref. 25). As in
other studies (Shapland, 1978; Belson, 1975), factorial analysis of the
correlations between responses to the different items revealed an important component of generalized misbehaviour that was reflected in
the total scores. Apart from providing evidence that the subjects were
not just answering haphazardly, the result showed that some boys had
a tendency to commit a wide variety of misbehaviours that included,
but were by no means limited to, the specialized forms of misconduct
— notably stealing and breaking in — that lead to the likelihood of being
convicted. The finding that delinquents had so often been reportedly
troublesome in a variety of ways in their school classes also pointed to
The same conclusion (see pp. 31–3). The validity of the self-report
scores was further confirmed by the significant correlations with these
troublesomeness ratings by independent observers. Thus, among the
boys assessed as 'troublesome', 34 per cent were self-reported delinquents, compared with only 15 per cent among the rest of the sample.

Our conclusion that individuals defined as delinquents by their own
self-reports shared, to a large extent, the high incidence of adverse
characteristics typical of officially ascertained delinquents conflicts
with the conclusions of some other investigators. For example, in a
number of surveys (Hirschi, 1969; Kelly and Pink, 1975; Williams and
Gold, 1972) self-reported delinquents have been found to be no more
prevalent among the lower socio-economic groups than among the
more affluent classes. The reasons for such conflicting findings merit
some consideration.

We used family income in preference to father's occupation as a
measure of socio-economic status and found a significant excess of
self-reported delinquents among the poorest group. Virtually every
member of the sample was tested, whereas in many surveys based upon
schools truants and drop-outs, who may contribute heavily to the
link between low status and delinquency, are lost to the investigators.
Income seemed a better measure of social class than occupation. In our
working-class sample the poorest quarter on income ratings were
probably more truly representative of the significantly deprived minority
that produces many delinquents than the much larger segment of the

total population who have low-status occupations. In restricting the category of self-reported delinquents to the worst fifth of the sample, we effectively eliminated many minor and occasional offenders who might otherwise have diluted the results. Finally, the administration of the self-report questions in the course of individual interviews, where subsequent discussion was possible, may have increased the conscientiousness and accuracy of the responses.

We found that a significantly high proportion, about a third, of both the self-reported and the official delinquents had a history of separation from a parent before reaching the age of 10, for reasons other than death or hospitalization. (Of the 90 'separated' boys 27 were among the 80 self-reported delinquents, and 29 were among the 84 official juvenile delinquents.) In contrast, in the survey by Belson (1975, p. 309) there was no more than a slight and doubtful association between reported stealing and separations. Similarly, Belson (ibid., p. 319) found no link between stealing and a broken home during the first thirteen years of life, whereas we found a distinctly raised incidence of homes broken for reasons other than death among self-reported delinquents (20.0 per cent) compared with the incidence among the remainder of the sample (9.7 per cent).

We counted as a broken home one in which either natural parent went permanently missing at some stage before the boy was 15 as a result of desertion, divorce or any reason other than death. Belson counted breaks whatever the reason, but discounted those in which the missing parent was replaced by a stable substitute. It is apparent, however, from the details given in Belson's published report, that the differences between our findings are not accounted for by such minor variations in definitions. The general trend of Belson's findings, like that of a number of self-report surveys, casts doubt upon the existence of any causal link between self-reported delinquency and unsatisfactory home backgrounds. For example, his comparison of boys who reported many rows between their parents with an equated control sample of boys who reported less rows yielded only a slight tendency for the former group to report more thieving (Belson, 1975, pp. 264–70).

Among many possible reasons for the differences between Belson's findings and those of the present study two appear especially obvious. All his information about home backgrounds came from the boys themselves, ours from home visits and interviews with parents, supplemented by social records. Young boys are probably not the best judges of their own home situations. In the matter of early separations, for example, they may well not remember or not have been told of all that happened to them in earlier years. Their own emotional involvement may hinder objective reporting, especially on such matters as what to count as a family 'row'. The relative insensitivity of youthful reports about their home circumstances may have masked the true level of family disturbance among the self-reported thieves.

A second and possibly more important reason for the different findings is the difference in the degree of misbehaviour that counts as a high self-report score. In the present study the self-reported delinquents were the worst 20 per cent of a working-class sample from a fairly delinquent neighbourhood. Belson's sample, drawn from a wider area, seems to have had fewer delinquents, but most of his analyses were based on the quarter with the most reported thefts. This group must have included many boys who would not have been sufficiently badly behaved to be counted as self-reported delinquents in the present study. In our sample the individuals whose scores were only just sufficient to qualify for inclusion in the self-reported delinquent group tended to be relatively non-deviant in background. Belson's inclusion of many lesser degrees of misconduct in the category of 'thieves' may have concealed the strength of the association which exists between deviant backgrounds and persisting delinquency. A third reason for our different results might be that the combination of self-report responses from two occasions of testing counteracted some of the response bias attributable to temporary variations in the subject's mood and thus helped to make the self-report scores in our study a more effective reflection of real-life behaviour.

The findings from the present self-report inquiry, while revealing self-reported delinquents as somewhat less deprived and deviant than official delinquents (see Appendix IV, ref. 41), tend to refute the fashionable contention that the link between delinquency and deprivation is merely an artificial product of selective prosecution. The validity of the findings is therefore of some practical importance.

Appendix IV

Bibliography of books and articles reporting the findings of the Cambridge Study in Delinquent Development

Books

(1) West, D. J. (1969), *Present Conduct and Future Delinquency*. London: Heinemann Educational Books.
(2) West, D. J. and Farrington, D. P. (1973), *Who Becomes Delinquent?* London: Heinemann Educational Books.
(3) West, D. J. and Farrington, D. P. (1977), *The Delinquent Way of Life*. London: Heinemann Educational Books.

Articles

(4) Gibson, H. B. (1963), 'A slang vocabulary test as an indicator of delinquent association'. *British Journal of Social and Clinical Psychology*, **2**, 50–5.

(5) Gibson, H. B. (1964), 'A lie scale for the Junior Maudsley Personality Inventory', *British Journal of Educational Psychology*, **34**, 120–4.

(6) Gibson, H. B. (1964), 'The Spiral Maze. A psychomotor test with implications for the study of delinquency', *British Journal of Psychology*, **55**, 219–25.

(7) Gibson, H. B. and West, D. J. (1964), 'Family patterns and juvenile delinquency', paper given at 1st National Conference on Research and Teaching in Criminology, Cambridge.

(8) Gibson, H. B. (1965), 'A new personality test for boys', *British Journal of Educational Psychology*, **35**, 244–8.

(9) Gibson, H. B. (1966), 'The validation of a technique for measuring delinquent association by means of vocabulary', *British Journal of Social and Clinical Psychology*, **3**, 190–5.

(10) Gibson, H. B. (1967), 'Self-reported delinquency among schoolboys, and their attitudes to the police', *British Journal of Social and Clinical Psychology*, **6**, 168–73.

(11) Gibson, H. B. (1967), 'Teachers' ratings of schoolboys' behaviour related to patterns of scores on the new Junior Maudsley Inventory', *British Journal of Educational Psychology*, **37**, 347–55.

(12) Gibson, H. B., Hanson, Ruth and West, D. J. (1967), 'A questionnaire measure of neuroticism using a shortened scale derived from the Cornell Medical Index', *British Journal of Social and Clinical Psychology*, **6**, 129–36.

(13) Gibson, H. B. and West, D. J. (1968), 'Some concomitants of early delinquency', paper given at 3rd National Conference on Research and Teaching in Criminology, Cambridge.

(14) Gibson, H. B. (1968), 'Self-reported delinquency: Preliminary results of an on-going study', paper given at 3rd National Conference on Research and Teaching in Criminology, Cambridge.

(15) Gibson, H. B. (1968), 'The measurement of parental attitudes and their relation to boys' behaviour', *British Journal of Educational Psychology*, **38**, 233–9.

(16) Gibson, H. B. and Hanson, Ruth (1969), 'Peer ratings as predictors of school behaviour and delinquency', *British Journal of Social and Clinical Psychology*, **8**, 313–22.

(17) Gibson, H. B. (1969), 'The Tapping Test: a novel form with implications for personality research', *Journal of Clinical Psychology*, **25**, 403–5.

(18) Gibson, H. B. (1969), 'The Gibson Spiral Maze Test: retest data in relation to behavioural disturbance, personality and physical

measures', *British Journal of Psychology,* **60**, 523–8.

(19) Gibson, H. B. (1969), 'Early delinquency in relation to broken homes', *Journal of Child Psychology and Psychiatry,* **10**, 195–204.

(20) Gibson, H. B. (1969), 'The significance of "lie responses" in the prediction of early delinquency', *British Journal of Educational Psychology,* **39**, 284–90.

(21) Gibson, H. B., Morrison, Sylvia and West, D. J. (1970), 'The confession of known offences in response to a self-reported delinquency schedule', *British Journal of Criminology,* **10**, 277–80.

(22) Gibson, H. B. and West, D. J. (1970), 'Social and intellectual handicaps as precursors of early delinquency', *British Journal of Criminology,* **10**, 21–32.

(23) Farrington, D. P. and West, D. J. (1970), 'Research into early signs of violent attitudes and behaviour: seven measures of aggressive attitude and behaviour among adolescent boys', paper given at 4th National Conference on Research and Teaching in Criminology, Cambridge.

(24) Farrington, D. P. and West, D. J. (1971), 'A comparison between early delinquents and young aggressives', *British Journal of Criminology,* **11**, 341–58.

(25) Gibson, H. B. (1971), 'The factorial structure of juvenile delinquency: a study of self-reported acts', *British Journal of Social and Clinical Psychology,* **10**, 1–9.

(26) Farrington, D. P. (1972), 'Delinquency begins at home', *New Society,* **21**, 495–7.

(27) Farrington, D. P. (1973), 'Self-reports of deviant behaviour: predictive and stable?' *Journal of Criminal Law and Criminology,* **64**, 99–110.

(28) West, D. J. (1973), 'Are delinquents different?' *New Society,* **26**, 456–8.

(29) Blackmore, J. (1974), 'The relationship between self-reported delinquency and official convictions among adolescent boys', *British Journal of Criminology,* **14**, 172–6.

(30) Farrington, D. P., Gundry, Gwen and West, D. J. (1975), 'The familial transmission of criminality', *Medicine, Science and the Law,* **15**, 177–86.

(31) Knight, B. J. and West, D. J. (1975), 'Temporary and continuing delinquency', *British Journal of Criminology,* **15**, 43–50.

(32) Farrington, D. P. (1976), 'Statistical prediction methods in criminology', paper given at NATO Advanced Study Institute, Cambridge.

(33) Farrington, D. P. (1977), 'The effects of public labelling', *British Journal of Criminology,* **17**, 112–25.

(34) Farrington, D. P. (1977), 'Young adult delinquents are socially deviant', *Justice of the Peace,* **141**, 92–5.

(35) Knight, B. J. and West, D. J. (1977), 'Criminality and welfare dependency in two generations', *Medicine, Science and the Law,* **17**, 64–7.

(36) Knight, B. J., Osborn, S. G. and West, D. J. (1977), 'Early marriage and criminal tendency in males', *British Journal of Criminology,* **17**, 348–60.

(37) Farrington, D. P. (1978), 'The family backgrounds of aggressive youths', in Hersov, L. *et al.* (eds.), *Aggressive and Antisocial Behaviour in Childhood and Adolescence.* Oxford: Pergamon.

(38) Farrington, D. P., Osborn, S. G. and West, D. J. (1978), 'The persistence of labelling effects', *British Journal of Criminology,* **18**, 277–84.

(39) Osborn, S. G. and West, D. J. (1978), 'The effectiveness of various predictors of criminal careers', *Journal of Adolescence,* **1**, 101–17.

(40) Osborn, S. G. and West, D. J. (1979), 'Conviction records of fathers and sons compared', *British Journal of Criminology,* **19**, 120–33.

(41) Farrington, D. P. (1979), 'Environmental stress, delinquent behaviour and convictions', in Sarason, I. G. and Spielberger, C. D. (eds.), *Stress and Anxiety,* vol. 6. Washington: Hemisphere.

(42) Osborn, S. G. and West, D. J. (1979), 'Marriage and delinquency: a postscript', *British Journal of Criminology,* **19**, 254–6.

(43) Farrington, D. P. (1980), 'Truancy, delinquency, the home and the school', in Berg, I. and Hersov, L. (eds.), *Out of School: Modern perspectives in truancy and school refusal.* Chichester: Wiley.

(44) Osborn, S. G. (1980), 'Moving home, leaving London and delinquent trends', *British Journal of Criminology,* **20**, 54–61.

(45) Osborn, S. G. and West, D. J. (1980), 'Do delinquents really reform?' *Journal of Adolescence,* **3**, 99–114.

(46) Farrington, D. P., Biron, L. and LeBlanc, M. (1981), 'Personality and delinquency in London and Montreal', in Gunn, J. C. and Farrington, D. P. (eds.), *Abnormal Offenders, Delinquency and the Criminal Justice System.* Chichester: Wiley.

(47) Farrington, D. P. and West, D. J. (1981), 'The Cambridge Study in Delinquent Development', in Mednick, S. A. and Baert, A. E. (eds.), *Prospective Longitudinal Research.* London: Oxford University Press.

(48) Farrington, D. P., Berkowitz, L. and West, D. J. (1982), 'Differences between individual and group fights', *British Journal of Social Psychology,* **21**, at press.

References

Alderson, J. (1979), *Policing Freedom*. Plymouth: MacDonald & Evans.

Baldwin, J. (1979), 'Ecological and areal studies in Great Britain and the United States', in Morris, N. and Tonry, M. (eds.), *Crime and Justice: An Annual Review of Research*, vol. 1. Chicago: University of Chicago Press.

Bell, D. S. and Champion, R. A. (1979), 'Deviancy, delinquency and drug use', *British Journal of Psychiatry*, **134**, 268–76.

Belson, W. A. (1975), *Juvenile Theft: The Causal Factors*. London: Harper & Row.

Belson, W. A. (1978), *Television Violence and the Adolescent Boy*. Farnborough: Saxon House.

Bennett, I. (1960), *Delinquent and Neurotic Children: A Comparative Study*. London: Tavistock.

Berg, I., Consterdine, M., Hallen, R., McGuire, R. and Tyrer, S. (1978), 'The effect of two randomly allocated court procedures on truancy', *British Journal of Criminology*, **18**, 232–44.

Binder, A. and Newkirk, M. (1977), 'A program to extend police service capability', *Crime Prevention Review*, **4**, 26–32.

Black, H. (1979), *Report of The Children and Young Persons Review Group*. Belfast: HMSO.

Bonnell, M. L. (1980), *Child at Risk: A Report of the Standing Senate Committee on Health, Welfare and Science*. Ottawa: Canadian Government Publishing Centre.

Bowlby, J. (1951), *Maternal Care and Mental Health*. Geneva: World Health Organization.

Bowlby, J. (1973), *Separation: Anxiety and Anger*. London: Hogarth Press.

Bowman, P. H. (1959), 'Effects of a revised school program on potential delinquents,' *Annals of the American Academy of Political and Social Sciences*, **322**, 53–61.

Brody, S. J. (1976), *The Effectiveness of Sentencing*. Home Office Research Unit Study No. 35. London: HMSO.

Brown, W. K. and Gable, R. J. (1979), 'Social adaptation of former delinquents', *International Journal of Offender Therapy and Comparative Criminology*, **23**, 117–28.

Buikhuisen, W. and Hoekstra, H. A. (1974), 'Factors related to recidivism', *British Journal of Criminology*, **14**, 63–9.

Burgess, R. L. and Couter, R. D. (1978), 'Family reactions in abusive, neglectful and normal families', *Child Development,* **49**, 1163–73.

Byles, J. A. and Maurice, A. (1979), 'The juvenile services project: an experiment in delinquency control', *Canadian Journal of Criminology,* **21**, 155–65.

Casler, L. (1961), *Maternal Deprivation: A Critical Review of the Literature.* Lafayette, Indiana: Society for Research in Child Development.

Cawson, P. and Martell, M. (1979), *Children referred to closed units.* DHSS Statistical Research Division Research Report No. 5. London: HMSO.

Christensen, R. (1967), 'Projected percentage of US population with criminal arrest and conviction records', *President's Commission on Law Enforcement and the Administration of Criminal Justice.* Taskforce Report: Science and Technology. Washington, DC: US Government Printing Office.

Christiansen, K. O. (1977), 'A preliminary study of criminality among twins', in Mednick, S. and Christiansen, K. O. (eds.), *Biosocial Bases of Criminal Behavior.* New York: Gardner Press.

Clark, J. P. and Tifft, L. L. (1966), 'Polygraph and interview validation of self-reported deviant behaviour', *American Sociological Review,* **31**, 516–23.

Clarke, R. V. G. (1977), 'Psychology and crime', *Bulletin of the British Psychological Society,* **30**, 280–3.

Clarke, R. V. G. (1978), *Tackling Vandalism.* Home Office Research Study 47. London: HMSO.

Clarke, R. V. G. (1980), ' "Situational" crime prevention: theory and practice', *British Journal of Criminology,* **20**, 136–47.

Clarke, R. V. G. and Softley, P. (1975), 'The male : female ratio among the siblings of delinquents', *British Journal of Psychiatry,* **126**, 249–51.

Cline, H. F. (1980), 'Criminal behavior over the life span', in Brim, O. G. and Kagan, J. (eds.), *Constancy and Change in Human Development.* Cambridge, Mass.: Harvard University Press.

Conger, J. J. and Miller, W. C. (1966), *Personality, Social Class and Delinquency.* New York: Wiley.

Conklin, J. E. (1971), 'Criminal environment and support for the law', *Law and Society Review,* **6**, 247–59.

Corrigan, P. (1979), *Schooling the Smash Street Kids.* London: Macmillan.

Cortes, J. B. and Gatti, F. M. (1972), *Delinquency and Crime: A Biopsychosocial Approach.* New York: Seminar Press.

Council of Europe (1979), *Social Change and Juvenile Delinquency.* Report of the European Committee on Crime Problems. Strasbourg: Council of Europe.

Delfini, L. F., Bernal, M. E. and Rosen, P. M. (1976), 'Comparison of deviant and normal boys in home settings', in Mash, E. J. *et al.* (eds.), *Behavior Modification and Families.* New York: Brunner/Mazel.

Department of Health and Social Security (1977), *First Report from the Select Committee on Violence in the Family.* London: HMSO.

Dinitz, S. and Conrad, J. P. (1980), 'The dangerous two per cent', in Shichor, D. and Kelly, D. H. (eds.), *Critical Issues in Juvenile Delinquency*. Lexington, Mass.: D. C. Heath.

Ditchfield, J. (1976), *Police Cautioning in England and Wales*. London: HMSO.

Douglas, J. W. B. (1964), *The Home and the School*. London: Mac-Gibbon & Kee.

Douglas, J. W. B., Ross, J. M. and Simpson, H. R. (1968), *All Our Future*. London: Peter Davies.

Elliott, D. S. (1980), 'Recurring issues in the evaluation of delinquency prevention and treatment programme', in Schichor, D. and Kelly, D. H. (eds.), *Critical Issues in Juvenile Delinquency*. Lexington, Mass.: D. C. Heath.

Elliott, D. S. and Ageton, S. S. (1980), 'Reconciling race and class differences in self-reported and official estimates of delinquency', *American Sociological Review*, 45, 95–110.

Elliott, D. S. and Voss, H. L. (1974), *Delinquency and Dropout*. Toronto: Lexington Books.

Embling, J. (1978), *Tom: A Child's Life Regained*. Harmondsworth: Penguin Books.

Empey, L. T. and Erickson, M. L. (1972), *The Provo Experiment: Evaluating Community Control of Delinquency*. Lexington, Mass.: D. C. Heath.

Engstad, P. and Evans, J. P. (1980), 'Responsibility, competence and police effectiveness in crime control', in Clarke, R. V. G. and Hough, J. M. (eds.), *The Effectiveness of Policing*. Farnborough, Hants: Gower.

Erickson, M. L. (1972), 'The changing relationship between official and self-reported measures of juvenile delinquency', *Journal of Criminal Law, Criminology and Police Science*, 63, 388–95.

Eysenck, H. J. (1977), *Crime and Personality* (3rd edn). London: Routledge & Kegan Paul.

Farrell, C. and Kellaher, L. (1978), *My Mother Said: The Way Young People Learn about Sex and Birth Control*. London: Routledge & Kegan Paul.

Farrington, D. P. (1978), 'The effectiveness of sentences', *Justice of the Peace*, 142, 68–71.

Farrington, D. P. (1979), 'Longitudinal research on crime and delinquen-cy', in Morris, N. and Tonry, M. (eds.), *Crime and Justice: An Annual Review of Research*, vol. 1. Chicago: University of Chicago Press.

Farrington, D. P. (1981), 'The prevalence of convictions', *British Journal of Criminology*, 21, 173–5.

Farrington, D. P. and Bennett, T. (1981), 'Police cautioning of juveniles in London', *British Journal of Criminology*, 21, 123–35.

Farrington, D. P. and Knight, B. J. (1979), 'Two non-reactive field experiments on stealing from a "lost" letter', *British Journal of Social and Clinical Psychology*, 18, 277–84.

Farrington, D. P. and Nuttall, C. P. (1980), 'Prison size, overcrowding, prison violence, and recidivism', *Journal of Criminal Justice*, 8, 221–31.

Fogelman, K. and Richardson, K. (1974), 'School attendance: some results from The National Child Development Study', in Turner, B. (ed.), *Truancy*. London: Ward Lock.

Fraser, R. (1979), 'Operation shoplift', *Police Review* (20 July), 1138.

Frease, D. E. (1973), 'Delinquency, social class and the schools', *Sociology and Social Research*, 57, 443–59.

Friday, P. (1980), 'International review of youth crime and delinquency', in Newman, G. (ed.), *Deviance and Crime: International Perspectives*. New York: Sage.

Friedlander, K. (1947), *Psycho-analytic approach to Juvenile Delinquency*. London: Routledge & Kegan Paul.

Fromm-Auch, D., Yeudall, L. T., Davies, P. and Fedora, O. (1980), 'Assessment of juvenile delinquents: neuropsychological, psychophysiological, neurological, EEG, and reading test findings', (personal communication from Department of Neuropsychology, Alberta Hospital, Edmonton, Canada).

Gath, D., Cooper, B., Gattoni, F. and Rockett, D. (1977), *Child Guidance and Delinquency in a London Borough*. Maudsley Monographs 24. London: OUP.

Gibbens, T. C. N. (1963), *Psychiatric Studies of Borstal Lads*. London: OUP.

Gibbons, D. C. (1970), *Delinquent Behavior*. Englewood Cliffs, NJ: Prentice-Hall.

Gibbons, D. (1980), 'Explaining juvenile delinquency: changing theoretical perspectives', in Shichor, D. and Kelly, D. H. (eds.), *Critical Issues in Juvenile Delinquency*. Lexington, Mass.: D. C. Heath.

Glaser, D. (1975), *Strategic Criminal Justice Planning*. Rockville Md: National Institute of Mental Health, Center for Studies of Crime and Delinquency.

Glueck, S. and Glueck, Eleanor T. (1950), *Unravelling Juvenile Delinquency*. Cambridge, Mass.: Harvard University Press.

Glueck, S. and Glueck, E. (1956), *Physique and Delinquency*. New York: Harper & Row.

Glueck, S. and Glueck, E. T. (1968), *Delinquents and Non-delinquents in Perspective*. Cambridge, Mass.: Harvard University Press.

Gold, M. (1969), *Delinquent Behaviour in an American City*. Belmont, California: Brooks/Cole.

Gold, M. and Williams, J. R. (1969), 'National Study of the Aftermath of Apprehension', *Prospectus*, 3, 3–12.

Gove, W. R., Hughes, M. and Gale, O. R. (1979), 'Overcrowding in the home: an empirical investigation of its possible pathological consequences', *American Sociological Review*, 44, 59–80.

Greenberg, D. F. (1977), 'The correctional effects of corrections: a survey of evaluations', in Greenberg, D. F. (ed.), *Corrections and Punishment*. Beverly Hills, Ca.: Sage.

Hackler, J. C. and Hagan, J. L. (1975), 'Work and teaching machines as delinquency prevention tools: a 4 year follow up study', *Social Science Review*, 49, 92–106.

Hamparian, D. M., Schuster, R., Dinitz, S. and Conrad, J. P. (1978), *The Violent Few*. Lexington, Mass.: D. C. Heath.

Hardt, R. H. and Hardt, S. Peterson (1977), 'On determining the quality of the delinquency self-report method', *Journal of Research in Crime and Delinquency*, 14, 247—61.

Hargreaves, D. H. (1967), *Social Relations in a Secondary School.* London: Routledge & Kegan Paul.

Hargreaves, D. H. (1980), 'Classrooms, schools and juvenile delinquency', *Educational Analysis*, 2, 75—87.

Hargreaves, D. H., Hester, S. K. and Mellor, F. J. (1975), *Deviance in Classrooms.* London: Routledge & Kegan Paul.

Hersov, L. and Berg, I. (eds.) (1980), *Out of School.* Chichester: Wiley.

Hindelang, M. J. (1971), 'Age, sex and versatility of delinquent involvements', *Social Problems*, 18, 522—35.

Hindelang, M. J. (1974), 'Moral evaluations and illegal behaviors, *Social Problems*, 21, 370—85.

Hirschi, T. (1969), *Causes of Delinquency.* Berkeley: University of California Press.

Hirschi, T. and Hindelang, M. J. (1977), 'Intelligence and delinquency: a revisionist view', *American Sociological Review*, 42, 571—87.

Hoghughi, M. S. (1978), *Troubled and Troublesome: Coping with severely disordered children.* London: Burnett Books (Andre Deutsch).

Hoghughi, M. *et al.* (1980), *Assessing Problem Children.* London: Burnett Books.

Home Office (1970), *The Sentence of the Court.* London: HMSO.

Home Office *et al.* (1980), *Young Offenders* (Cmnd 8045). London: HMSO.

Hood, R. and Sparks, R. (1970), *Key Issues in Criminology.* London: Weidenfeld & Nicolson.

Hutchings, B. and Mednick, S. A. (1977), 'Criminality in adoptees and their adoptive and biological parents', in Christiansen, K. O. and Mednick, S. O. (eds.), *Biosocial Bases of Criminal Behavior.* New York: Gardner Press.

Janson, C. G. (1978), *The Longitudinal Approach: Problems and Possibilities in the Social Sciences.* Project Metropolitan. Report No. 9. University of Stockholm Department of Sociology.

Jason, L. A., De Amicis, L. and Carter, B. (1978), 'Preventative intervention programs for disadvantaged children', *Community Mental Health Journal*, 14, 272—8.

Jessor, R. and Jessor, S. L. (1977), *Problem Behaviour and Psychological Development: A longitudinal study.* New York: Academic Press.

Johnson, R. E. (1979) *Juvenile Delinquency and its Origins: an integrated theoretical approach.* Cambridge: CUP.

Johnstone, J. W. C. (1980), 'Delinquency and the changing American family', in Shichor, D. and Kelly, D. H. (eds.), *Critical Issues in Juvenile Delinquency.* Lexington, Mass.: D. C. Heath.

Jones, M. B., Offord, D. R. and Abrams, N. (1980), 'Brothers, sisters and antisocial behaviour', *British Journal of Psychiatry*, 136, 139—45.

Kelly, D. H. (1980), 'The educational experience and evolving delinquent careers', in Schichor, D. and Kelly, D. H. (eds.), *Critical Issues in Juvenile Delinquency.* Lexington, Mass.: D. C. Heath.

Kelly, D. H. and Pink, W. T. (1975), 'Status origins, youth rebellion and delinquency: a re-examination of the class issue', *Journal of Youth and Adolescence*, 4, 339–47.

Klein, M. W. (1974), 'Labelling, deterrence and recidivism: a study of police disposition of juvenile offenders', *Social Problems*, 22, 292–303.

Klein, M. W. (1979), 'Deinstitutionalisation and diversion of juvenile offenders: a litany of impediments', in Morris, N. and Tonry, M. (eds.), *Crime and Justice: An annual review of research*, Vol. 1. Chicago: University of Chicago Press.

Kobrin, S. (1959), 'The Chicago Area Project: A twenty five year assessment', *Annals of the American Academy of Political and Social Science*, 322, 19–29.

Kornhauser, R. R. (1978), *Social Sources of Delinquency: An appraisal of analytic models*. Chicago: University of Chicago Press.

Kraus, J. (1977), 'Causes of delinquency as perceived by juveniles', *International Journal of Offender Therapy and Comparative Criminology*, 21 (1), 79–86.

Kvaraceus, W. C. (1960), 'Forecasting delinquency: a three year experiment', *Exceptional Children*, 27, 429–35.

Landau, S. F. (1981), 'Juveniles and the police', *British Journal of Criminology*, 21, 27–46.

Lee, R. and McGinnes Haynes, N. (1980), 'Project CREST and the dual treatment approach to delinquency', in Ross, R. R. and Gendreau, P. (eds.), *Effective Correctional Treatment*. Toronto: Butterworths.

Lefkowitz, M. M., Eron, L. D., Walder, L. O. and Rowell Huesmann, L. (1977), *Growing Up to be Violent: A longitudinal study*. New York: Pergamon.

Lewis, D. O. and Shanok, S. S. (1977), 'Medical histories of delinquent and non-delinquent children: an epidemiological study', *American Journal of Psychiatry*, 134, 1020–5.

Lickona, T. (1976) (ed.), *Moral Development and Behavior*. New York: Holt, Rinehart & Winston.

Lie, N. (1981), 'Young law breakers: a prospective longitudinal study', *Acta Paediatrica Scandinavica*, supplement 288.

Lipton, D., Martinson, R. and Wilks, J. (1975), *The Effectiveness of Correctional Treatment: A survey of treatment evaluation studies*. New York: Praeger.

Loeb, L. and Mednick, S. A. (1977), 'A social behaviour and electrodermal response patterns', in Christiansen, K. O. and Mednick, S. A. (eds.), *Biosocial Bases of Criminal Behaviour*. New York: Gardner.

Lundman, R. J. and Scarpitti, F. R. (1978), 'Delinquency prevention: recommendations for future projects', *Crime and Delinquency*, 24, 207–20.

McCord, W., McCord, J. and Zola, I. K. (1959), *Origins of Crime*. New York: Columbia University Press.

McCord, J. (1978), 'A thirty year follow up of treatment effects', *American Psychologist*, 33, 284–9.

Marohn, R. C. *et al.*, (1980), *Juvenile Delinquents: Psychodynamic Assessment and Hospital Treatment*. New York: Brunner/Mazel.

May, D. (1975), 'Truancy, school absenteeism and delinquency', *Scottish Educational Studies*, 17, 97–107.

Mayers, M. O. (1980), *The Hard-Core Delinquent*. Farnborough: Saxon House.

Mayhew, P., Clarke, R. V. G., Stuman, A. and Hough, J. M. (1976), *Crime as Opportunity*. Home Office Research Study No. 34. London: HMSO.

Mednick, S. O. and Christiansen, K. O. (eds.) (1977), *Biosocial Bases of Criminal Behaviour*. New York: Gardner Press.

Meyer, H. J., Borgatta, E. F. and Jones, W. C. (1965), *Girls at Vocational High*. New York: Sage.

Miller, A. D., Ohlin, L. E. and Coates, R. B. (1977), *A Theory of Social Reform*. Cambridge, Mass.: Ballinger.

Millham, S. (1981), 'The therapeutic implications of locking up children', *Journal of Adolescence*, **4**, 13–26.

Mills, J. (1958), 'Changes in moral attitudes following temptation', *Journal of Personality*, **26**, 517–31.

Morgan, P. (1978), *Delinquent Fantasies*. London: Temple Smith.

Morris, A. and Giller, H. (1981), 'Young offenders: law, order and the child care system', *Howard Journal*, **20**, 81–9.

Morris, A., Giller, H., Szwed, E. and Geach, H. (1980), *Justice for Children*. London: Macmillan.

Morris, C. R. (1978), 'The Children and Young Persons Act: Creating more institutionalisation', *Howard Journal*, **16**, 154–8.

Murray, C. A. (1976), *The link between learning difficulties and juvenile delinquency*. Washington: National Institute of Juvenile Justice and Delinquency Prevention, US Department of Justice.

Offord, D. (1981), 'Family backgrounds of male and female delinquents', in Gunn, J. C. and Farrington, D. P. (eds.), *Abnormal Offenders, Delinquency and the Criminal Justice System*. Chichester: Wiley.

Offord, D. R., Poushinsky, M. F. and Sullivan, K. (1978), 'School performance, IQ and delinquency', *British Journal of Criminology*, **18**, 110–27.

Ohlin, L. E., Miller, A. D. and Coates, R. B. (1977), *Juvenile Correctional Reform in Massachusetts*. Washington, DC: National Institute of Juvenile Justice and Delinquency Prevention, US Department of Justice.

Oliver, I. T. (1973), 'The Metropolitan Police juvenile bureau scheme', *Criminal Law Review*, August, 499–506.

Olweus, D. (1979), 'Stability of aggressive reaction patterns in males: a review', *Psychological Bulletin*, **86**, 852–75.

Parker, H. and Giller, H. (1981), 'More and less the same: British delinquency research since the sixties', *British Journal of Criminology*, **21**, 230–45.

Patterson, G. R. (1981), *Coercive Family Processes*. Eugene, Oregon: Castalia.

Peterson, M. A., Braiker, H. B. and Polich, S. M. (1980), *Doing Crime: A Survey of California Prison Inmates*. Santa Monica, Ca.: Rand Corporation.

Phillipson, C. M. (1971), 'Juvenile delinquency and the school', in Carson, W. G. and Wiles, P. N. P. *Crime and Delinquency in Britain*. London: Martin Robertson.

Phillpotts, G. J. and Lancucki, L. B. (1979), *Previous Convictions, Sentence and Reconviction*. London: HMSO.

Pitts, R. and Simon, A. (1954), 'A psychological and educational study of a group of male prisoners', *British Journal of Educational Psychology*, **25**, 106–21.

Polk, K. (1969), 'Class, strain and rebellion among adolescents', *Social Problems*, **17**, 214–24.

Polk, K. and Schafer, W. E. (1972), *Schools and Delinquency*. Englewood Cliffs, NJ: Prentice-Hall.

Power, M. J., Benn, R. T. and Morris, J. N. (1972), 'Neighbourhood, school and delinquents before the courts', *British Journal of Criminology*, **12**, 111–32.

Power, M. J. *et al.*, (1974), 'Delinquency and the family', *British Journal of Social Work*, **4**, 13–38.

Powers, E. and Witmer, H. (1951), *An Experiment in the Prevention of Delinquency*. New York: Columbia University Press.

Prentice, N. M. and Kelly, F. J. (1963), 'Intelligence and delinquency: a reconsideration', *Journal of Social Psychology*, **60**, 327–37.

Priestley, P., Fears, D. and Fuller, R. (1977), *Justice for Juveniles*. London: Routledge & Kegan Paul.

Pringle, M. K. (1974), *The Needs of Children*. London: Hutchinson.

Quay, H. C. (1977), 'The three faces of evaluation', *Criminal Justice and Behavior*, **4**, 341–54.

Radzinowicz, L. (1966), *Ideology and Crime*. London: Heinemann Educational Books.

Reid, J. B. (ed.) (1978), *A Social Learning Approach to Family Intervention*, Vol. 2 *Observation in Home Settings*. Eugene, Oregon: Castalia.

Reynolds, D., Jones, D. and St Leger, S. (1976), 'Schools do make a difference', *New Society*, **37**, 223–5.

Robins, L. (1966), *Deviant Children Grown Up*. Baltimore, Md: Williams & Wilkins.

Robins, L. (1978), 'Sturdy childhood predictors of adult antisocial behaviour: replications from longitudinal studies', *Psychological Medicine*, **8**, 611–22.

Robins, L. and Ratcliffe, K. (1980), 'The long-term outcome of truancy', Hersov, T. L. and Berg, I. (eds.), *Out of School*. Chichester: Wiley.

Roff, M., Sells, S. B. and Golden, M. M. (1972), *Social Adjustment and Personality Development in Children*. Minneapolis: University of Minnesota Press.

Romig, D. A. (1978), *Justice for our Children*. Lexington, Mass.: D. C. Heath.

Ross, R. R. and Gendreau, P. (1980), *Effective Correctional Treatment*. Toronto: Butterworths.

Rossi, P., Waite, E., Bose, C. and Berk, R. E. (1974), 'The seriousness of crimes: normative structure and individual differences', *American Sociological Review*, **39**, 224–37.

Rutherford, A. (1980), 'Why should courts make non-custodial orders?' in *Juvenile Offenders: Care, Control or Custody*. London: Howard League Day Conference Report.

Rutter, M. L. (1972), *Maternal Deprivation Reassessed*. Harmondsworth: Penguin Books.

Rutter, M. L. (ed.) (1972), *The Child, His Family and the Community*. New York: Wiley.

Rutter, M. (1980), 'Raised lead levels and impaired cognitive/behavioural functioning: a review of the evidence', *Developmental Medicine and Child Neurology*, 22, (1), supplement 42.

Rutter, M. and Madge, N. (1976), *Cycles of Disadvantage*. London: Heinemann Educational Books.

Rutter, M., Maughan, B., Mortimore, P. and Ouston, J. (1979), *Fifteen Thousand Hours: Secondary Schools and their effects on Children*. London: Open Books.

Sandberg, S. T., Wieselberg, M. and Shaffer, D. (1980), 'Hyperkinetic and problem conduct children in a primary school population', *Journal of Child Psychology and Psychiatry*, 21, 293–311.

Sarason, I. G. (1978), 'A cognitive social learning approach to juvenile delinquency', in Hare, R. D. and Schalling, D. (eds.), *Psychopathic Behaviour: Approaches to Research*. New York: Wiley.

Scott, P. D. (1959), 'Juvenile courts: the juvenile's point of view', *British Journal of Delinquency*, 9, 200–11.

Seidman, E., Rappaport, F. and Davidson, W. S. (1980), 'Adolescents in legal jeopardy: initial success and replication of an alternative to the criminal justice system', in Ross, R. R. and Gendreaux, P. (eds.), *Effective Correctional Treatment*. Toronto: Butterworths.

Sellin, T. (1958), 'Recidivism and maturation', *National Probation and Parole Association Journal*, 4, 241–50.

Shapland, J. (1978), 'Self-reported delinquency in boys aged 11 to 14', *British Journal of Criminology*, 18, 255–66.

Shore, M. F. and Massimo, J. L. (1979), 'Fifteen years after treatment: a follow up of comprehensive vocationally-oriented psychotherapy', *American Journal of Orthopsychiatry*, 49, 240–5.

Slavin, S. (1978), 'Information processing defects in delinquents', in Hippchen, L. J. (ed.), *Ecologic–Biochemical Approaches to Treatment of Delinquents and Criminals*. New York: Van Nostrand Reinhold.

Smith, C. S., Farrant, M. R. and Marchant, H. J. (1972), *The Wincroft Youth Project: A social-work programme in a slum area*. London: Tavistock.

Stewart, M. A., Cummings, C. and Singer, S. (1981), 'The overlap between hyperactive and unsocialised aggressive children', *Journal of Child Psychology and Psychiatry*, 22, 35–46.

Stott, D. H. (1962), 'Evidence for a congenital factor in delinquency and maladjustment', *American Journal of Psychology*, 118, 781–94.

Taylor, L., Lacey, R. and Bracken, D. (1979), *In Whose Best Interests?* London: The Cobden Trust and MIND.

Tennent, T. G. (1971), 'School non-attendance and delinquency', *Educational Research*, 13, 185–90.

Thorpe, D. H., Smith, D., Green, C. J. and Paley, J. G. (1980), *Out of Care: the community support of young offenders*. London: George Allen & Unwin.

Trasler, G. B. (1962), *The Explanation of Criminality*. London: Routledge & Kegan Paul.

Tutt, N. (ed.) (1978), *Alternative Strategies for Coping with Crime*. London: Martin Robertson.

Tutt, N. (1981), 'A decade of policy', *British Journal of Criminology*, **21**, 246–56.

Van den Haag, E. (1975), *Punishing Criminals*. New York: Basic Books.

Waddington, C. H. (1941), *The Scientific Attitude*. Harmondsworth: Penguin Books.

Wadsworth, M. (1979), *Roots of Delinquency*. Oxford: Martin Robertson.

Waldrop, M. F., Bell, R. Q., McLaughlin, B. and Halverson, C. F. (1978), 'Newborn minor physical anomalies predict short attention span, peer aggression, and impulsivity at age 3', *Science*, **199**, 563–5.

Walker, N. D. (1977), *Behaviour and Misbehaviour: Explanations and non-explanations*. Oxford: Blackwell.

Walker, N. D., Hammond, W. and Steer, D. (1967), 'Repeated violence', *Criminal Law Review*, 465–72.

Wechsler, D. (1958), *The Measurement of Adult Intelligence*. Baltimore, Md: Williams & Wilkins.

Weissman, H. H. (ed.) (1969), *Individual and Group Services; Community Development; Employment and Educational Services; Justice and the Law – in the Mobilisation for Youth Experience* (4 vols.). New York: Association Press.

West, D. J. (1969), *Present Conduct and Future Delinquency*. London: Heinemann Educational Books.

West, D. J. and Farrington, D. P. (1973), *Who Becomes Delinquent?* London: Heinemann Educational Books.

West, D. J. and Farrington, D. P. (1977), *The Delinquent Way of Life*. London: Heinemann Educational Books.

Williams, J. R. and Gold, M. (1972), 'From delinquent behavior to official delinquency', *Social Problems*, **20**, 209–29.

Williamson, H. (1978), 'Choosing to be a delinquent', *New Society*, **46**, 333–5.

Wilson, E. C. (1975), *Sociobiology: The New Synthesis*. Cambridge, Mass.: Harvard University Press.

Wilson, H. (1974), 'Parenting in poverty', *British Journal of Social Work*, **4**, 241–54.

Wilson, H. (1980), 'Parental supervision: a neglected aspect of delinquency', *British Journal of Criminology*, **20**, 203–35.

Wilson, J. Q. (1975), *Thinking about Crime*. New York: Basic Books.

Wolfgang, M. E. (1974), 'Crime in a birth cohort', in Hood, R. (ed.), *Crime, Criminology and Public Policy*. London: Heinemann Educational Books.

Wolfgang, M. E., Figlio, R. M. and Sellin, T. (1972), *Delinquency in a Birth Cohort*. Chicago: University of Chicago Press.

Woodward, M. (1955), 'The role of low intelligence in delinquency', *British Journal of Delinquency*, **5**, 281–303.

Wright, W. E. and Dixon, M. C. (1977), 'Community prevention and treatment of juvenile delinquency', *Journal of Research in Crime and Delinquency*, **14**, 35–67.

Yeudall, L. T. and Wardell, D. (1978), 'Neurophysiological correlates of criminal psychopathy', in Beliveau, L., Canepa, G. and Szabo, D. (eds.), *Human Aggression and Dangerousness*. Montreal: Pinel Institute.

Index of Names

Subject Index